More praise for *Terror and Liberalism*

"This book is a symphony. I didn't think that anybody understood Islamic militancy, Islamic activism, in the twentieth century more than I did. . . . I couldn't have written it better. He had the advantage of drawing parallels and analogies to make the Muslims part of history, to make our region part of the globe, because that is what it is, that is what it should be, and that is what will continue." —Saad Eddin Ibrahim,
former political prisoner and leading democracy advocate,
Ibn Khaldun Center, Egypt, speech to Social Democrats, USA

"We need to challenge the bigoted hostility of certain fringe radical movements within fringe elements of Islam. We need to challenge them. I believe that anyone who wants to know more about this should read Berman's book." —Richard Holbrooke,
former ambassador to the United Nations,
appearing on *The Charlie Rose Show*

"Mr. Berman's most important argument—and one that helps make this compact, focused book one of the most challenging acc[illegible]nts of the post-9/11 world—is that the war on terror doesn't ju[illegible] the war on totalitarianism, it is *literally* a continuation [illegible]-tual and political roots of Islamic terror, he su[illegible]
—Edwar[illegible]

"Berman's book is an elegantly wri[illegible] philosophical bedrock of those who woul[illegible] of God."
[illegible]ow, *Boston Globe*

"This is the best book I have read on Muslim fundamentalism and what to do about it. . . . If the West is to defend itself, and democratic progress in the Middle East is to be more than a pipe dream, socialists, trade unions and intellectuals must take a principled stand against Muslim radicalism, as some did against Communism in the Cold

War. Reading this book, with its echoes of Koestler and Camus—both truth-tellers about totalitarian terror—would be a good beginning."

—George Walden, *Sunday Telegraph* (London)

"Paul Berman has written an accomplished intellectual history of fanatical Islamism and shed light on the ideas and prejudices that currently predominate in the Western Left. Although he addresses the liberal and leftist reader, his book has insights for everyone across the political spectrum who seeks a better understanding of the present danger. In this sense *Terror and Liberalism* is a book in the tradition of Camus, Orwell, and Koestler. Like these anti-totalitarian giants, who also emerged from the political Left, Berman is helping to illuminate the mechanisms and expose the threat of the totalitarian idea."

—Adrian Karatnycky, *National Review*

"The left is about fighting against fascism irrespective of cultural or national boundaries, or it has forgotten its own core principles. Those who doubt this—especially those who opposed the second Gulf War—should urgently read *Terror and Liberalism*."

—Johann Hari, *Independent on Sunday* (London)

"Wonderfully rich and illuminating."

—Bret Stephens, *Wall Street Journal*

"Berman successfully has honed a beautiful style. . . . *Terror and Liberalism*, a bold, creative investigation of Islamic fascism's roots in European totalitarian movements, demonstrates his cross-cultural fluency."

—Carlin Romano, *Philadelphia Inquirer*

"*Terror and Liberalism* is an important entry in the debate over the meaning of 9/11 and after, not least beause it is clearly written from a left-of-center perspective." —Ellen Willis, *Salon.com*

"A new and important book by a leading American intellectual, Paul

Berman, may lead to a deeper rethink on the American left. . . . Berman's latest book, *Terror and Liberalism*, is a minor masterpiece of moral seriousness and scholarly research."

—Andrew Sullivan, *Sunday Times* (London)

"*Terror and Liberalism* breaks its bounds. . . . It is an intellectual horror story, taken seriously, plumbed to its depths, a story in which Al Qaeda's terror war has both deep roots and a future to be made."

—Greil Marcus, *Bookforum*

"[*Terror and Liberalism*] is a coolly reasoned but blisteringly written book. . . . A shimmering polemic." —Paul Gray, *The New Leader*

"An engaging, delusion-busting history primer."

—Howard Hampton, *Village Voice*

"[*Terror and Liberalism*] is clear and accessible, presenting a powerful but controversial analysis and prescription. It is wide-ranging, drawing on a great variety of literatures and touching on the major cultural and political movements of the last 200 years. . . . Highly recommended."

—*Choice*

"[Berman's] thesis is developed with elegance, learning and historical insight . . . a marvelously urbane, beautifully written volume."

—*Spectator* (London)

"*Terror and Liberalism* [is] brilliant, stirring."

—Tom Sime, *Dallas Morning News*

"Berman's intellectual history is a perfectly timed must-read."

—*Booklist*

"Original . . . a new analysis of today's world."

—*Publishers Weekly*, starred review

"Berman's book is an accurate philosophical-political map of the new world in which we live." —*Die Zeit* (Hamburg)

"Paul Berman is one of the best-known liberal intellectuals in the USA and one of the most important representatives of the American anti-communist left." —*Die Tageszeitung* (Berlin)

"Paul Berman's *Terror and Liberalism* is the most important political book this year." —*Die Welt* (Berlin)

"Fascinating . . . a convincing case." —*Daily Yomiuri* (Tokyo)

"Written by one of the best American essayists. . . . He puts his finger on the difficulty that democracies have in understanding totalitarian thought." —*Le Devoir* (Québec)

"Paul Berman, the most polemical North American intellectual of the moment, thinks that Islamic fundamentalism draws inspiration from Nazism and fascism, and that the anti-war movement should take that into account, in order to avoid old errors."

—*La Nación* (Buenos Aires)

"Author of the recently published *Terror and Liberalism*, Paul Berman is one of the liberal thinkers with the greatest impact in the urgent battle of ideas." —*Letras Libres* (Mexico City)

TERROR

AND

LIBERALISM

Paul Berman

W. W. Norton & Company

NEW YORK

LONDON

Printed in the United States of America
First published as a Norton paperback 2004

Manufacturing by Victor Graphics, Inc.
Production manager: Julia Druskin

Library of Congress Cataloging-in-Publication Data
Berman, Paul.
Terror and liberalism / Paul Berman.
p. cm.
Includes bibliographical references.
ISBN 0-393-05775-5 (hc)
1. Terrorism. 2. Liberalism. I. Title.

HV6431 .B4794 2003
303.6'25—dc21 2002156445

ISBN-13: 978-0-393-32555-3 PBK.
ISBN-10: 0-393-32555-5 pbk.

W. W. Norton & Company, Inc.
500 Fifth Avenue, New York, N.Y. 10110
www.wwnorton.com

W. W. Norton & Company Ltd.
Castle House, 75/76 Wells Street, London W1T 3QT

3 4 5 6 7 8 9 0

Contents

Here, suicide and murder are two sides of the same system.

—ALBERT CAMUS

Death comes to all, but for him there is martyrdom. He will proceed to the Garden, while his conquerors go to the Fire.

—SAYYID QUTB

Preface to the Norton Paperback Edition

THE HARDCOVER EDITION of *Terror and Liberalism* came out in the early spring of 2003, and a good many readers responded by asking two very pointed questions. They wanted to know, "So, what do you think, *now*—given the many astounding and terrible events that are lately taking place?" And the readers asked, "This book of yours—where does it fit on the political spectrum, on the left or the right?"

These two questions came at me from everywhere at once—from the audiences at bookstore readings and lectures, from inquisitive talk-show hosts, from magazines and newspapers in America and abroad, and from far corners of the Internet. Old friends stopped me on the sidewalk, their kindly faces wrinkled into puzzled expressions. And so, I had better reply, and here is the place to do it, on the front stoop of the new edition, before anyone rushes up the steps to the first chapter and starts to read.

The book was written, most of it, in the summer and fall of 2002. Those were frightening times. Nearly everyone was still reeling from the terrorist attacks of 2001, and cringing at the prospect of new attacks at any moment. The invasion of Afghanistan had already taken place, and the occupation was proving to be difficult. But the invasion of Iraq was in those days merely an ominous light glimmering over the Mesopotamian horizon—something that might take place in the months to come, and seemed likely to, but, then again, might not, depending on backroom machinations at the United Nations, or military contingencies, or the pressure of anti-war demonstrations.

I wrote these pages, then, with no way to predict, none whatsoever, what was going to happen in Iraq, or anywhere else, for that matter.

The new invasion duly took place. Events turned out to be grimmer even than in Afghanistan. Each day's news came swathed in black. And so, with my freshly published book in hand, people did want to know how things seemed to me, looking back. Was something missing from my analysis, some crucial point? People wanted to know if I felt deceived or manipulated by high government officials. Had I constructed my views and judgments on a pile of false or misleading information, concocted by crafty politicians at the White House and seconded by their counterparts in London?

I can answer this last question easily enough. My faith in crafty politicians has always been wanting. In the last chapter of the book, I went so far as to paste the label "dishonest" over some of the White House arguments about Iraq, which might have seemed a shrill and partisan thing to do in the days before the war. But then, once the invasion was under way and the dike of Saddam's dictatorship was forever broken, torrents of news and information began to pour out of Iraq, for the first time in more than thirty years. The torrents did not sustain some of those White House arguments. My complaints about governmental dishonesty began to look fairly sober and even cautious, in retrospect. My book holds up reasonably well, on that one small point. But I want to emphasize something else. For the torrents of news and information kept on pouring, and every new fact seemed to flow in the same direction, until, amid the rising waves, something enormous hove into view, which has seemed to me bigger and more significant than the many shady maneuvers of Washington and London in those long-ago days of 2002 and 2003.

My book proposes an interpretation of modern history, and I will mention a few elements of that interpretation here. In the last couple of centuries, a new kind of society has come into being—a society that tries to encourage individual freedom, and tries to keep religion and government in separate corners, and to encourage open debate, and in those several ways to inculcate a public habit of rational decision making. This is the kind of society that I describe as "liberal"—meaning liberal in the philosophical sense, based on liberty. Liberal societies and liberal ideas have prospered during these last centuries, and have spread to ever-larger portions of the globe, and have produced a few successes, here and there. These successes have filled many people with hope for a better world. But liberal society and habits of mind have also aroused, among other people and sometimes among the same people, feelings of violent revulsion. In the twentieth century, those feelings combusted into a series of political rebellions, which set out to overthrow liberal society and demolish the liberal ideas.

The anti-liberal rebellions were, in the beginning, strictly European. They were movements of the extreme right and extreme left—Fascists, Phalangists, Nazis, and Communists—each movement with its own set of paranoid conspiracy theories, its own apocalyptic fantasies, and its own fashion of celebrating death: totalitarian movements, each and all. The movements wrecked Europe. Yet they spoke to powerful feelings about modern life, and their inspiration spread outward to the world, and this did not exclude the regions nearest at hand, namely, the Muslim countries. A new kind of totalitarianism, drawing on the European model, grew quite strong, after a while, in portions of the Muslim world—a totalitarianism that flourished in several, sometimes contradictory, versions. Islamism the radical political movement (not to be confused with Islam the ancient religion) was one of those versions, and came in several variations of its own. The Baath movement of Iraq and of Syria was another, and the peculiar movement led by Muammar el-Qaddafi, still another.

These were rebellions in the twentieth-century mode, and just as bloody. Some of the totalitarian factions never did come to power—yet, even so, launched frantic campaigns of random murder. Some of the factions did come to power. During the months when I was writing *Terror and Liberalism*, reports came flooding out of occupied Afghanistan, and I pointed to those reports to show what totalitarianism's triumph was like—the ease with which entire societies could be decimated, cultures destroyed, populations reduced. But that was before the second, more difficult invasion—before people had begun to ask me, what do you think, *now*?

So, then: I think the events in Iraq brought the picture I have drawn into a sharper and more tragic focus than before. Before the invasion, some people had imagined that Iraq under the Baath was merely a gangster state, ruled by a Mafia chieftain named Saddam. The revelations post-invasion did reveal a gangster state—but also something more. Sizable numbers of Iraqis in at least one region of the country plainly subscribed to the Baath's paranoid conspiracy theories and its cult of cruelty and death. The leader's followers chanted, "With our souls, our blood, we sacrifice ourselves for you, Saddam!" and went on chanting even after his arrest—a chilling scene of fanaticism, and doubly so to anyone with a sense of European history.

The news pouring out of Iraq told us that three hundred thousand Iraqis were estimated to be missing, and possibly hundreds of thousands more, murdered by the Baath. We learned about hundreds of mass graves. We read one hair-raising story after another about nephews killed, brothers killed, athletes tortured, students raped, villages destroyed. And we saw something strange and unnerving. In the first months after the invasion, a portion of the Iraqi people appeared to be in a stupor—the stupor of people who had spent thirty-five years with a boot stamping on their face, in Orwell's phrase, and who, in their grogginess, hardly knew how to react, once the boot was removed. We saw looting, assassinations, suicide bombings, and massacres—as if the face beneath the boot had become, over the years, covered with sores.

We saw nobler things. We saw the august medieval universities, the mosques new and old, the new police forces and the ancient merchant neighborhoods. And we saw that, in a great many of those institutions and places, some people were rousing themselves to put up a fight against the old order—sometimes only a few people, sometimes a large number. Their struggles seemed to be, from afar, confused and murky—disheartening struggles, often. Those were recognizable struggles, even so. They were struggles to create a normal political society in Iraq—the sort of struggles that have engaged vast portions of the world during most of the last century, struggles against the totalitarian movements not on the grand scale, but on the local scale, where life is lived.

We saw admirable people. And we saw the kind of support and solidarity those people received from elsewhere in the world—saw how miserly was that support, how cautious, how self-interested and sometimes how deluded. And this, too, the spectacle of people around the world failing to rally to the anti-totalitarians in their moment of crisis, conformed to a main pattern of modern history. For liberal-minded people have always had a good deal of trouble understanding the totalitarian rebellions against liberal society, therefore a lot of trouble in putting up a resistance. That was a big problem during the times of Hitler and Stalin. Forward-thinking and well-educated people with the most generous of ideals sometimes found it hard in those days to believe that Nazis and Stalinists were as bad as they seemed. And this phenomenon of the past, a deep-grained naïveté of liberal society, turned out to be a phenomenon of the present. We saw a few signs of it even among people who prided themselves on their sophistication, and even on the brutality of their sophistication—the kind of people who would rather have died than commit the soft-headed errors of mere idealists.

Yet what else but a soft-headed naïveté can explain the many curious American blunders that accompanied the invasion of Iraq? The commanders and strategists back in Washington seem to have planned for every possible thing, except an enemy who was driven by fanatical zeal. These were the same strategists who, after all, had never imagined that anyone would be so crazy as to fly a plane into the Pentagon. And so, the strategists threw America's soldiers and the rest of the coalition into battle with nothing even remotely approaching adequate preparation, and the strategists had trouble recognizing their own errors, and the cost was terrible.

But then, what did everyone else do, good-hearted people all over the world, during those moments of American bungling? The invasion revealed that ordinary Iraqis were desperately in need of more help than the coalition armies could provide; and, around the world, some of the richest and most powerful of nations, pursuing their national interests, lifted not one finger in aid. The coalition soldiers likewise needed help; and still no aid. It became clear that Washington, in its underestimation of the enemy, was spending not nearly enough money; and the cry went up in the United States Congress that Washington was spending too much. The wars in Iraq and Afghanistan were new flare-ups of an old war, which has been going on for most of a century—the war between liberal society and the anti-liberal rebellions—this time in a series of Muslim landscapes. But the meaning of these Afghan and Iraqi battles remained invisible to entire populations all over the world, and a great many people went on gazing at those faraway battles in a spirit of detachment or even schadenfreude, faintly satisfied to see the United States floundering.

So the struggles in Afghanistan and Iraq had to go forward despite the feckless naïveté and irresponsibility of the strategists and commanders back in Washington, and despite the indifference and even the opposition of masses of liberal-minded people around the world. The American and British soldiers, the Spanish, Poles, Italians, and other partners in the coalition, the local administrators, together with the anti-totalitarian Afghans and Iraqis, whose sufferings were endless—these people, all of them, had to improvise as best they could. And they did improvise. The world is not without heroes. And what were the final consequences?

Scenes of tragedy and nobility flit before our eyes, darkest shadow and brightest light, blurring our focus. We see, and don't see. Fifty years will pass before we know the final consequences. Still, a few provisional consequences seem detectable even now. We can see that, in Afghanistan and Iraq, two of the worst political movements in the modern world have been driven from state power—though both of those movements, in their strength, have gone on fighting as guerrilla insurgencies. We can see that some 45 million people in those two countries have climbed up from a pit of eternal damnation to a still-miserable place in which a better future and a free society have become, at least, imaginable—a better society that has already loomed into sight, here and there within both of those countries. We can see that totalitarian impulses in the larger Muslim world have been dealt two very serious blows, and liberal impulses in the Muslim world have been given two very shaky, but also very unprecedented, boosts. And we are still in the middle of events, and things might go either way.

That is what I think, now.

BUT—my readers insist on asking—should these views of mine be regarded as left-wing or right-wing? The question dismays me. I mean, what difference should it make? A more serious question would ask, do analyses like mine help illuminate the present reality, or not?—the only question that ought to matter. But, okay, I understand the question about left and right. In this modern age, a great many people do divide the world into Column A and Column B, the left and the right, and they deploy those two columns to think about political and social questions and even sexual questions. To be honest, I am one of those people myself. Whenever some new and complicated public issue arises, the ancient traditions of the political left rush unbidden to my brain, and I arrive at my opinions partly on the basis of everything I know from the left-wing past. I don't recommend this particular habit of mind as a universal formula for perfect wisdom, yet this does happen to be my habit of mind.

My picture of a long worldwide struggle between liberalism and its enemies is not in itself either left-wing or right-wing—not in any modern sense of those terms. Still, ideas do have provenances, and the kind of analysis that I have offered traces back into the 1930s and '40s, to a past that happened to be, in its own habits, decidedly left-wing. A number of writers in those years, people who hated fascism with all their hearts, wanted to take their insights into fascism and extend them into a larger view of world affairs. And a larger view did emerge, in time. It was a philosophy of anti-totalitarianism. Some of those writers came out of the revolutionary left, and some of them out of the reformist left, but, either way, the stamp on their thinking was plainly marked. Those writers formed a kind of dissident and liberal left—a left whose reigning spirit descended from the anti-fascism of the Spanish Civil War and the Second World War, a left whose spirit was one of active solidarity across borders and against tyrants of every sort, right-wing or left-wing. That kind of spirit has always seemed to me the grandest tradition of the left—not always the most popular spirit on the left, but the deepest and largest, morally speaking. My whole purpose in writing *Terror and Liberalism* was to try to revive something of that spirit and apply it to our modern predicament.

Then again, I have to acknowledge that these left-wing and liberal instincts of mine, in their antique and dissident style, do seem to have put me at odds with a lot of other people who picture themselves as the embodiment of the modern left. A few weeks after I had turned in the manuscript to the publisher, but before the book had gone to press, a gigantic movement arose in many countries to forestall the impending invasion of Iraq. The movement called for street demonstrations in the early months of 2003, and these demonstrations turned out to be, in one country after another, absolutely enormous, the largest mass demonstrations in the history of the world—an epochal event. To be sure, the demonstrators did not subscribe to any one set of ideas.

Some people demonstrated because they wanted to express procedural and legal objections to the planned invasion—objections to the lack of United Nations approval and to the flouting of international law. Other people demonstrated because they doubted the White House argument about Saddam's weapons and conspiracies, and because they could not imagine any other reasons for war—could not picture the existence of a larger Muslim totalitarianism, nor the danger that totalitarian movements posed to the rest of the world, and therefore could not imagine any reason to roll that larger movement back.

Other people understood perfectly well that Saddam's regime was a classic totalitarian regime, but figured that every country ought to stage its own revolutions. Some people recognized that fascists were fascists, but figured that anyone who tries to overthrow fascists from abroad is likewise a fascist. Some people ardently wished to see Saddam's regime overthrown, but hoped that hundreds of thousands of American troops could achieve this goal by hovering around the borders of Iraq until the regime expired of old age, perhaps in a few decades. Some people felt that invading Iraq was going to weaken the United States in the Muslim world, instead of strengthening it, and therefore the invasion should be avoided. Other people felt that, on the contrary, invading Iraq was going to strengthen the United States in the Muslim world, and do so unduly, and would amount to an act of imperialism.

Some people listened to the White House closely enough to know that weapons and conspiracies were not the only reasons for war, and humanitarian and anti-totalitarian concerns did exist, at least in occasional phrases issuing from the top officials. But these demonstrators looked on the high-minded talk as so much cant, intended to cover up a mysterious other goal, something hidden—perhaps an ever-greater control of Middle Eastern oil, perhaps power for power's sake, perhaps a goal of fighting wars out of a love for war. Some people detected the aroma of dishonesty emanating from the White House, and, without theorizing about hidden agendas, feared for democracy in America itself. Some people worried about civil liberties, about the sufferings of Muslim immigrants in America, about the proper way to treat prisoners of war. Some people considered that, for all the millions of deaths brought about by the sundry wings of Muslim totalitarianism, the United States posed a still greater danger to the world, and ought to be restrained. Some people observed that, back in the 1980s, the United States had lent support to Saddam, and the whole relation between America and the Baath movement was too murky for words, and war represented a sinister twist in the policies of elites who felt no loyalty to ordinary people and their interests.

Some people honestly believed that most Iraqis preferred life under Baath dictatorship to liberation by foreign armies, and these demonstrators therefore opposed the war in the name of Iraq itself. Some people considered that we in the Western world had no business judging political arrangements in a different society, and human rights are not universal, and only an imperialistic racist could suppose otherwise. Some people looked on Saddam as a more-or-less progressive force against imperialism. There were not many such people, and yet, even so, placards in praise of Saddam did get carried through the streets of Paris during the gigantic anti-war demonstrations there. In the United States, the supporters of Saddam were minuscule in number—yet, oddly enough, a group of those people, organized into a pro–North Korea Marxist sect, happened to be, in secret, among the principal organizers of the largest of the anti-war demonstrations in Washington, D.C.

Some people demonstrated against the invasion because they were supporters of radical Islamism, and looked on the proposed invasion of Iraq as a danger to their own cause; these people were among the principal organizers of the mass demonstrations in London. Some people blamed Israel. Some people hated McDonald's. Some people recoiled at George W. Bush's smirk. Some people took no view on any of these matters, but merely assumed that any military action at all was likely to plunge America and its allies into a sea of Vietnam-style calamities. In the United States, some people marched in the anti-war demonstrations because they were capital-D Democrats, and would never have marched to protest a similar war led by a Democratic president. Some people regarded the war as a plot to advance the electoral prospects of the Republican Party.

And so, there were a thousand reasons to demonstrate against the invasion, and some of those reasons were quite respectable, in my eyes; and some of them, not. Yet all of those reasonings, in their splendid variety, led to the same spectacular fact. The largest mass demonstrations in the history of the world were aimed at preventing the overthrow of one of the worst tyrannies in the modern age. And this, in the judgment of many people, was the proper role for anyone who boasted of left-wing credentials—this, somehow, the correct stance for every true friend of the downtrodden. Hence the curiosity about the ideological leanings of *Terror and Liberalism*. The hardcover edition arrived in the bookstores, and people assailed me with the question: Could analyses like mine, so sharply at odds with those marchers in the street, have surged from a genuinely left-wing soul? To which I can only reply by saying—

But, wait. I see that the readers, impatient, are already climbing the stoop toward the first chapter. And just as well. The book is my reply.

Brooklyn
January 2004

TERROR

AND

LIBERALISM

I
Against Nixon

DURING THE BUILDUP to the Persian Gulf War of 1991, Richard Nixon wrote an op-ed for *The New York Times*, endorsing the coming war and explaining its goals. "It will not be a war about democracy," he said. He wanted to keep the American public from sailing away on clouds of idealistic expectation. The war was going to be, instead, about "vital economic interests." Saddam Hussein had conquered Kuwait and the oil beneath its sandy soil, and he was nicely poised to grab hold of still other parts of the Arab world, including Saudi Arabia and still more oil.

Control over the Persian Gulf and the Arabian peninsula was going to allow him to dictate terms to Europe and Japan, because of their dependence on oil from the Gulf. And so, in Nixon's eyes, the United States had good reason to push Saddam and his army out of Kuwait, and quickly, too, before any of the benefits of conquest came his way. Nixon fretted over something else, as well. He wanted to maintain America's "credibility," meaning the ability to frighten people out of their wits. He wanted to ensure that, during any future quarrel around the world, if America's president pounded the table and muttered threats, the object of those threats would cringe and tremble. Such were Nixon's concerns. In the jargon of foreign policy writers, those were "realist" arguments.

His op-ed appeared in the first week of January 1991. In those tense days the editors at the *Times* invited all kinds of people to contribute op-eds, from as many stations of life and ideological predispositions as possible; and one of those invitations came to me. I duly wrote my 750 words. It was my rebuttal to Nixon. My rebuttal did not dispute his every point. To endorse the coming war filled me with unspeakable horror and fear (and, I must say, to endorse any sort of war still fills me with horror and fear). Even so, I did think a war against Saddam represented the better part of wisdom. My reasoning wasn't Nixon's, though. In my analysis, there were wars and wars. Idealistic wars, and cynical wars. Pragmatic wars, and wars that are hopelessly wrong-headed. And Nixon's war and mine were not the same.

I didn't give a damn about the politics of oil, per se, nor about "vital interests"—though I'm sure it was naive of me not to take those things a little more seriously. I didn't spend my days fretting over America's ability to scare its enemies. The very word "credibility" gave me the willies. In the years when he was president, Nixon used to defend his Indochina bellicosity by hammering away on that single word, until "credibility" came to seem like insanity itself—an argument in favor of fighting wars in order to prove that we could fight wars. "Credibility" in Nixon's day brought nothing but calamity to America and Indochina alike.

Still, I did worry about Saddam Hussein. I thought that, in Saddam and his government, we were facing a totalitarian menace—something akin to fascism. Saddam's regime was aggressive, dynamic, irrational, paranoid, murderous, grandiose, and demagogic. He belonged to a political party called the Baath Socialists, and he and the Baathi seemed to have persuaded huge numbers of people throughout the Arab Middle East and in other countries, too, that little groups of evil imperialists and conspiratorial Zionists were to blame for the misery and sufferings of tens of millions. Saddam had whipped up a lot of hatred in that fashion. Scapegoating was his special genius. He had already fought a horrendous war with Iran, which featured poison gas attacks by his own army. In northern Iraq, he and his soldiers went on a rampage, and entire towns and villages were razed and the people were hideously gassed. Saddam was terrifying. Here was credibility. He and his government were bound to go on with their crimes and murders, too—bound to do so for ideological reasons, in order to unite the Arab world against the Satanic American and Zionist foe; and bound to go on for practical reasons, as well. Maniacal dictatorships do not prosper in times of peace and plenty, when the citizens have sufficient tranquility to go out in the sunlight and look around; but war and hysteria keep everyone down in the basement.

I did worry that Saddam and his fanatics were going to end up with Arabia and the other Gulf states in their hands; and, in one respect, I worried about oil, too. I could see that Saddam's control of oil, already vast, was going to swell into something gargantuan, and gushers of wealth were going to coat him with a superpower's sheen, which was going to multiply his power yet again. It seemed obvious that, left unchecked, his scientists were going to make their laboratory breakthroughs someday. And, with his new wealth and his new province and his weapons growing more ominous by the minute, Saddam was going to loom everywhere in the Middle East as the single person capable of standing up to the American superpower, the one hero powerful enough to fend off the insidious oppressors and redeem the Arab masses. He radiated a weird hatred of Zionism, which was frightening to see. Iraq's border lies hundreds of miles from Israel. Even so, in the months before his invasion of Kuwait, Saddam addressed his soldiers and said, "We will make the fire eat up half of Israel if it tries to do anything against Iraq." The *Times* published a tiny report of that statement, and the tiny report put me in mind of the Kurdish villages. He announced that he was going to march to Jerusalem.

The entire situation had the look of Europe in 1939, updated to the post–Cold War Middle East. Everything about Saddam and his conquest of Kuwait pointed toward a general disaster. There didn't seem to be much of a spirit of compromise about the man. He was unlikely in the extreme to respond to the pressures of an economic boycott. Besides, how could anyone enforce a boycott of a regime whose oil so many people desperately wanted to buy, in almost every part of the world? The Middle East experts, not all of them but quite a few, took the line that, sooner or later, we were going to have to stand up to Saddam, and the sooner the better, for us and for everyone else around the world, and especially for the poor and oppressed people whose misfortune was to find themselves living under the shadow of Saddam Hussein. That argument made sense to me. And so, in my own op-ed, I proposed a policy that was not diplomatic or pacifist, and not Nixonian, either. I proposed an anti-totalitarian war. I called it, in the musty language of the old-fashioned political left, an "anti-fascist" war—a war with "progressive" goals.

But what could those words possibly mean in the world of the early 1990s? My op-ed gestured a little forlornly in the direction of political reform in Kuwait, as a tiny indication of the possible goals that America ought to keep in mind. I did think that, in the Persian Gulf, an American war ought to be "a war about democracy." If hundreds of thousands of American soldiers were going to decamp halfway across the world to preserve the independence of a tyrannical emirate in the Persian Gulf, I didn't see how we could allow the emir to persist in his tyrannical ways. Shouldn't the Arab Middle East be as forward-thinking as other parts of the world? Are Western freedoms only for Westerners? (No one thinks that Middle Eastern oil is only for Middle Easterners.) Those were my instinctive questions. But once I had drawn my comparison to the fascists of Europe long ago, and had unveiled my phrase about a "progressive" war, there seemed to be no point in spelling out my argument in full.

That was because, in the many months of crisis and then of war, almost everyone who supported the first President Bush and his Iraqi policy rested the case on grounds like Nixon's. "Vital economic interests," "credibility"—those were the arguments. There were a handful of neoconservatives on the right, veterans of the Reagan years, who never did approve of Bush the Elder and who resisted his businessman's approach to the war. The neoconservatives, though, had an odd way of mixing their foreign policy opinions with their larger outrage at the cultural and political reforms of the 1960s, which made no sense to me. I couldn't understand those people; and I think the feeling was returned. The neoconservatives had a visceral revulsion to drippy, left-wing words like "progressive" and the rest of my anti-fascist vocabulary. As for the people who did appreciate that kind of language, my stouthearted comrades of the democratic left and some of the liberals—those people tended to oppose the war altogether. Opposition was instinctive for them. They worried about America's imperial motives, about the greed of big corporations and their influence on White House policy; and could not get beyond their worries. War, to them, was always the Vietnam War, a debacle in the making. They figured that, whatever might be the problems and miseries of the Middle East, America bore much of the blame, and more Americans in the Middle East could only mean more blame, and there was nothing to be gained.

Besides, most people on the left and a good many of the liberals recoiled almost physically from any sort of military operations, at least by the United States. Such was the landscape of opinion—a moonscape of Vietnam fears, anti-corporate resentments, and pacifist instincts. And over that landscape hovered the Democratic politicians, trying to calculate the political advantages; and the politicians, having made their calculations, retired to their tents. Sulking led to silence, except in the case of Al Gore, who was a senator in those days, and Joseph Lieberman and a few other hard-liners on the foreign policy conservative wing of the Democratic Party, who did speak up for the war. But those people, the Democratic hawks, tended to sound like the White House and the Republicans. They had no message or voice of their own.

In the entire country, maybe fifteen or twenty persons seemed to uphold positions like mine, pro-war and left-wing—and most of those fifteen or twenty appeared to be the readers, writers, and editors of

Dissent magazine, whose circulation was minuscule. That was my impression. Even at *Dissent,* not everyone supported the war. (There was dissent at *Dissent.*) Rumor brought me the news that, somewhere in America, an ex-Trotskyist Arab-American likewise favored the war, on properly left-wing grounds. One of the liberal editors of the *American Prospect* adopted a view like mine. Such was the party of the left-wing hawks. Our ranks were less than imposing. My op-ed about Middle Eastern fascism and a progressive war was destined, then, to influence hardly anyone at all. I took a fatalistic view of the whole affair. The *Times* did publish the piece. It came out three weeks after Nixon's. Operation Desert Storm had already begun. And afterward, having had my say, I didn't bother spelling out the further implications of my argument—the larger difference between Nixon's "realism" and my sort of liberalism or leftism, between Nixonian war and anti-totalitarian war.

But now, when I look back, I think it might have been a good idea to spell out those differences.

FOREIGN POLICY "realism," by my lights, is a specific doctrine, which is why I put it in quotation marks. It is a doctrine from the nineteenth century. It is a kind of materialism, even if most of its adherents would swear otherwise. Karl Marx, the king of materialists in the field of politics, figured that world history was driven by a single tangible force, namely, the system of economic production. Hippolyte Taine, the king of materialists in the field of literary criticism, figured that world literature was driven by three tangible forces, which he identified as race, time, and geography. In that same vein, the "realists" of today—in my caricature—figure that world politics is likewise driven by three tangible forces. These are wealth, power, and geography. All of the nineteenth-century materialist doctrines give off a confident air of hard-bitten sophistication, and that is true of foreign policy "realism" as well. A "realist," like a Marxist, is someone who, no matter what bizarre events may take place around the world, will profess not to be surprised. This is "realism"'s weakness, though. Wisdom consists of the ability to be shocked.

In the "realist" picture of the world, wars break out because some nation's desire for wealth, power, and geography brushes up against some other nation's equally tangible desire for the same. Nation number two summons its allies; and everyone draws his gun. That was how Nixon and his school of "realists" tended to see the Persian Gulf crisis of 1990–91. Saddam pursued his tangible interest in wealth and power, which meant oil. Six hundred thousand people fled in terror across the desert. Kuwait, the neighbor, summoned its allies, who pursued their own equally tangible interest in oil. Everyone fell to squabbling over geography. And voilà.

Every war naturally leads to new controversies and demands, which are no less tangible; and so it was in 1991. The allies chased Saddam's army back into Iraq, and, in the flush of victory, stipulated a few additional demands: that Saddam abandon his search for weapons; that he keep his air force out of the north, and out of the south; that he offer restitution to the Kuwaitis, who had suffered horribly; that he liberate his prisoners of war; and so on—a discrete series of well-defined new issues, bearing on material facts. The main point was always the original point, though. Get out of Kuwait, or be killed. Those oil wells are not your oil wells. That was the meaning of the 1991 war, in the "realist" interpretation.

It's true that, during the buildup to the fighting, President Bush the Elder compared Saddam to Hitler, and the comparison did raise a somewhat different question, which had to do with Saddam's larger ambitions and outlook—a question of ideas, instincts, and even basic sanity, something intangible. Bush wasn't serious, though. The line about Hitler was mostly an insult, and it went hurtling in Saddam's direction, and, falling a little short, plunged into the Persian Gulf, never to be seen again. That was probably just as well, from a practical point of view. Bush the Elder's first impulse, after Saddam conquered Kuwait, was to put together a gigantic, worldwide coalition to back a military response. Giant coalitions are considered the acme of political principle, in the realm of international politics. But giant coalitions do not like to speak about ideas and ideals, apart from legal technicalities.

Bush the Elder labored earnestly at assembling his coalition, and did so with enormous skill, too, until, by the time he had finished, his alliance stretched all the way, ideologically speaking, to the Baathist dictatorship in Syria, which was not much different from the Baathist dictatorship in Iraq. The medieval despots of Saudi Arabia took their place in the grand coalition. The alliance turned out to be a pirate crew of terrorists, dictators, kings, anti-Zionists, oil moguls, and one-eyed gangsters. It was terrifying to behold. It was the United Nations General Assembly. What would some of those sinister coalition partners have thought, if the American president had gone on speaking about Hitler and waving an anti-fascist flag? The coalition partners would have shifted in their seats, fingering their daggers. Bush had no intention of making anyone uncomfortable, though. His thing was not the "vision thing." He got his start in politics as something of a Nixon protégé, and hard-nosed, business-oriented "realism" was his natural instinct.

But that was then, and now we are in the throes of the new crisis, and we might ask ourselves, what were "realism"'s results in that earlier conflict, the 1991 war? American soldiers were killed, and mysterious diseases afflicted many thousands of the soldiers afterward, a frightening matter. And yet, except for those individuals, the war was, on our side, terrifically successful. Bush the Elder kept his giant coalition together long enough to complete the military operations, which was a solid achievement, and long enough even to put some pressure on

Saddam afterward. The American military showed that every war is not, in fact, the Vietnam War. America's weapons and strategies were revealed to be forceful and efficient (except when they weren't). The British fought bravely, and so did the French, though the Americans like to complain about the French. Saddam's power shriveled. No one could imagine any longer, once the war had ended, that Saddam was going to march across the sands and liberate Jerusalem from the Jews and resurrect the Caliphate of yore, as he had wanted to do. Saudi Arabia was plainly going to survive.

On the other hand, once the war had ended, the Kurds in the Iraqi north made the fatal error of listening to American advice, and rebelled, and some 20,000 were slaughtered. Eventually a million Kurds fled for their lives to Turkey—and only then did the American and British military move into the northern region and set up a zone of protection. In the Iraqi south, the Shia and Marsh Arabs, as they are called, likewise heeded America's advice, and rebelled, and between 30,000 and 60,000 were slaughtered, until the allies again provided a measure of protection. Meanwhile Saddam proclaimed that, in the Gulf War, victory was his. His proclamation seemed lunatic. Years went by, and no one overthrew him, though.

Control of the White House passed into newer hands, and pinprick American attacks never entirely came to a halt, and Saddam yielded not at all. Bush the Elder, as ex-president, visited Kuwait in 1993, and Saddam's forces plotted to assassinate him. American missiles flew into Baghdad (and hit the wrong people). Saddam showed no fear. The United States did begin to show fear, however, and with good reason. Saddam's weapons production was discovered, after the war, to have been greater than previously imagined; and production, postwar, never came to a halt. Inspectors inspected, and Saddam, in his debilitated state, allowed them to proceed. But he grew stronger, and he threw the inspectors out.

The United States complained from the sidelines. And each new complaint revealed America's ever-increasing anxiety. France and Russia pursued their business interests, which led them to agitate for fewer, not greater, restrictions on Saddam. His role in the Israeli-Palestinian conflict, having diminished for a while, resumed. Even after the 9/11 attacks on the United States, he jacked up his own oil prices, and explained it as a blow against Zionism. And, all the while, he kept up the political culture of his dictatorship, his cult of war, his barrage of threats, his spiritual celebration of death, and his loathing of Israel—a sulfurous hatred, full of conspiracy theories about Jewish plots against the entire world. He showed that, in spite of having endured the brunt of an attack by half a million American troops and their allies from around the world, a mad enough tyrant could survive and prosper and rebuild and instill mortal fear in the Americans. He breathed vigor into the idea of suicide terrorism by paying Palestinians to blow themselves up at the rate of $25,000 a martyr, which was a lot of money for the impoverished Palestinians. Those were the consequences of the Gulf War of 1991—or, at any rate (given that causes and results are hard to prove), those were the after-waves, which very much looked like consequences.

And further waves: The most violent and fanatical of the anti-American and anti-Zionist groups all over the Middle East did seem to notice that American power, for all its vastness, had limits. Saddam had fought against the United States and had survived, and other people seemed to conclude that, with sufficient heroism and willingness to suffer on their own part, they, too, might be able to keep up their attacks on the United States, or perhaps even launch stronger attacks, and survive and even prosper. The war had gone as planned, and yet, even so, America seemed to have established not one whit of the credibility that so preoccupied Richard Nixon.

Kuwait was the main beneficiary of the American war effort, but

Saudi Arabia benefited, too, and in a big way. The Saudis had every reason to look on the United States with warmth and gratitude—not only for having rescued them from Saddam, but for having worked wonders at constructing the worldwide industrial system whose reliance on oil had made the Saudis rich. And yet, warmth and gratitude seemed to play, over the next few years, a surprisingly modest role in Saudi policies. On the contrary, over the course of the 1990s, the Saudi elite went on subsidizing all kinds of medieval-style Islamic academies around the world, where the students were instructed to despise the United States, not just passively. The United States pressured Israel and the Palestinians to sign the Oslo Accords and make a peace; and the Saudis offered no support at all. Far from it—the Saudis, too, according to their own government Web site, paid for Palestinian suicides, though at the more frugal rate of $5,000 per martyr.

The multi-millionaire scion of Saudi Arabia's bin Laden family organized his suicide army, and a good many people in Saudi Arabia evidently lent him their support. And Osama bin Laden's army, together with Saudi Arabian Hezbollah and a series of other underground groups, launched their war on American sites and people—the attack on the U.S. Marines in Mogadishu in 1993; a truck bombing in Riyadh, the Saudi capital, in 1995; the bombing of the Khobar Towers in Dhahran, Saudi Arabia, in 1996; the bombing of the American embassies in East Africa in 1998; the attack on the USS *Cole* in 2000—plus a few other attacks that failed to come off or were foiled at the last minute by quick-thinking police officers or customs agents. The United States in its bovine stupidity failed to recognize those fleabites as war. Yet the fleas kept biting, and Saudi Arabia's role was dark and ambiguous.

The Saudi princes exiled bin Laden; and Saudi money went on pouring in his direction. The princes said friendly things about the United States in public statements; and declined to participate in

American investigations. Now and then somebody in Washington would stand up and explain that, in spite of their image, the Saudi princes were good fellows, after all, owing to backroom cooperations that would never see the light of day. But how could anyone know? Saudi Arabian society was secretive, closed, obscurantist, feudal, and oppressive. Journalists penetrated almost never. From time to time excerpts from the Saudi press appeared in English translation, expressing sentiments and superstitions so bizarre and medieval as barely to seem possible. The beheadings, the veils, the oppression of women, the intolerance, the Satanic conspiracy theories about Jews—this was, in Saudi Arabia, the visible aspect.

It was striking, too, that, in the aftermath of 9/11, the Saudi government rushed to protect bin Laden by spiriting his relatives out of the United States, which prevented any of them from revealing his whereabouts. And it was striking that, when the United States launched its air attack on Al Qaeda and the Taliban in Afghanistan, Saudi Arabia declined to permit full use of the American air bases. The Saudis declined even to allow American investigators to interrogate Qaeda prisoners in Saudi Arabia. Such was the princely response exactly ten years after America fought a war partly on the princes' behalf. Theirs was a mix of amity and enmity—the visible and the invisible.

And so, "realism" triumphed in the Persian Gulf War of 1990–91, and triumph proved to be a tragedy on every count. Back in January 1991, Nixon brought his op-ed to a stirring conclusion by saying, in favor of the first Gulf War, "It will be a war about peace—not just peace in our time, but peace for our children and grandchildren in the years ahead." He sounded like Woodrow Wilson talking about the war to end all wars, except without Wilson's noble demeanor. And, sure enough, the 1991 war, which resembled the Vietnam War not at all, resembled the First World War quite a lot. A seeming victory that turned out to be a defeat. A victory that required a second round, graver and more dangerous than the first.

BUT WHY bother speaking about an anti-fascist or anti-totalitarian alternative? Those words—"anti-fascist," "anti-totalitarian"—are fifty or sixty years old, and even older, which makes them positively ancient; and vocabularies from ancient times do tend to droop and sag when anyone tries to revive them in the present. I would never expect a language from long ago to fit the present moment to a tee. Still, I did think the old-fashioned vocabulary served a useful purpose back in 1991, and I think so even now, with a few caveats. But the clearest way to show the useful purpose, given everything that has lately happened, is to turn away from the fiascoes of 1991 and glance instead at our current predicament.

In 1993 Samuel P. Huntington, the Harvard professor, wrote his famous essay about a "clash of civilizations" (though the phrase was Bernard Lewis's), and everyone has lately had to acknowledge a virtue in his analysis. Huntington pointed out that, all along the borders of the Muslim world, in the Philippines, Kashmir, Chechnya, Kosovo, Bosnia, the Sudan, Nigeria, and other places, not to mention Palestine—in every place where Muslim populations border on non-Muslim populations—some kind of war, large or small, had broken out in recent years, Muslims against non-Muslims. "Islam," he wrote, "has bloody borders." And though on each of those borders the wars might have seemed isolate and particular, each conflict its own tragedy, without connection to any of the others, Huntington pointed out their common aspect, and he was very astute in doing so. He tried to alert the United States to large dangers. He was on to something there. America has lately ballooned into the world's single hyperpower, as the French say, which means that America's own borders, in their swollen state, nestle up against every country around the world, including the Muslim countries. From Huntington's standpoint, those many wars were bound to catch up with the United States sooner or later, and, in fact, had done so long ago, without anyone bothering to notice. That was a shrewd observation, and it had the further merit of echoing what was said, on the other side of Huntington's civilizational "clash," by the militants of Islam and their followers, sympathizers and apologists, who are legion.

Still, it is worth asking in what degree America's policies and actions over the last few decades bear out the idea of clashing civilizations. What is, for instance, the tally of America's military interventions in recent years? There have been quite a few interventions—this is a bellicose epoch in American history—and, oddly enough, most of those actions have been undertaken in defense of Muslim populations. There was the Gulf War itself, fought in defense of the Kuwaitis, the Saudis, and nearly everyone else in the Middle East; the air defense of Iraq's northern Kurds and southern Shia; the intervention in Somalia to rescue people from famine; and the defense of Bosnians and then Kosovars, who were getting slaughtered by crazed Serbs in the name of ancient Christian hatreds.

A thousand commentators have pointed out, in retrospect, that Ronald Reagan's policy in Afghanistan back in the 1980s did lead to difficulties in later years, which is indisputable. In Afghanistan, just as in Saudi Arabia, America's beneficiaries turned out to be America's worst enemies. The world is full of back-stabbing sons-of-bitches: such is the lesson of modern history. (It is not a new lesson.) Reagan aided the *mujahadeen* in their war against the Soviet occupation, and Bush the Elder continued the aid, and even Bill Clinton continued the aid, for a while, and the *mujahadeen* turned against us. Still, American policy in Afghanistan during those many years does offer one more example of America's willingness to support the world's far-flung Muslims in their struggles. A foolish policy, maybe, in the Afghan instance, but pro-Muslim, even so—and we might as well claim the credit, given that we have had to endure the consequences.

And why does everyone forget how much time and effort and personal prestige America's presidents have invested in trying to establish an independent state for the Palestinians? As long ago as 1978 Jimmy Carter talked the Israelis into giving back the Sinai Peninsula to Egypt, and Israel's acquiescence established the principle of giving up conquered land in exchange for peace—not such a bad principle. After the Gulf War, Bush the Elder inaugurated the grueling effort to bring Israelis and Palestinians together in direct negotiations, with the obvious end goal of creating a Palestinian state. Clinton took his predecessors' efforts and multiplied them by a thousand. Shlomo Ben-Ami, the principal Israeli negotiator at Camp David in 2000, has said, "No European country, no international forum, has done as much for the Palestinian cause as Clinton did."

The United States against Islam? In all of recent history, no country on earth has fought so hard and consistently as the United States on behalf of Muslim populations—a strange thing to say, given what passes for conventional wisdom. But how is this claim false? To be sure, American policies have also weighed *against* one or another group of Muslims—against Saddam and the Baath, to begin with. The entire Arab region seethes over America's support for Israel—even if America has also given the Palestinians a lot of support. The intervention in Somalia, which was intended to feed the Muslim masses, was also intended to crush the Muslim few who stood in the way. Still, the worst that can be said about the United States vis-à-vis the Muslim world is that American policy has tilted every which way. As might be expected. None of this indicates a clash of civilizations.

Somebody might reply by remarking that, even so, bin Laden's grandly named World Islamic Front Against Jews and Crusaders does cast the United States in the role of the Crusader capital, or else in the role of Zionist puppet, which is just as bad. And if the members of the World Islamic Front Against Jews and Crusaders insist on seeing a clash of civilizations, shouldn't we take their views seriously? We should. Still, in the matter of clashing civilizations, a few complicating details pop up even from the ranks of bin Laden's Islamic Front and his suicide army. The modern era is an age of multiple identities—an era in which vast numbers of people are doomed by circumstances to display one personality on Monday, and a different personality on Tuesday, and are doomed on Wednesday to cope with their own complexities. And among those vast numbers can be found Osama bin Laden himself and his troop of warriors.

For who is bin Laden (or who was he, since I am writing in a time when his fate remains a mystery)? He is a man from the Saudi plutocracy, instructed by some of the most brilliant and radical of the anti-Western Islamist radicals—yet, at the same time, a man whose relatives have studied in universities all over the Western world, and have donated to some of the best of those universities: Harvard, Tufts, and Oxford. He is a man whose family has functioned for many years within the elite of the Western world. The family has even gone into business with Bush the Elder in an enterprise called the Carlyle Group (a shocking fact in regard to Bush the Elder's sense of judgment—but let it pass). And who are bin Laden's foot soldiers? The 9/11 terrorists, most of them, likewise turn out to have been people with claims on both the Arab past and the Western present.

The suicide warriors may have passed their young years in Saudi Arabia, Egypt, and other places in the Arab world. But they moved along to an adult life in Belgium and Germany, not to mention their years of preparation in Florida, Southern California, and New Jersey. Those people enrolled in schools, they paid their rent. They were flecks of foam on the giant wave of immigrants to the modern West. And, like everyone else in the immigrant population, the suicide warriors ended up, we can assume, spending years of their lives inhabiting two universes at the same time—the here-and-now of their Western and modern reality, and the faraway cosmos of their remembered homelands.

Exactly how the 9/11 suicide warriors coped with their double existence, what thoughts they arrived at, what dreams of Koranic glory flitted through their minds as they made their way along the sidewalks of modern life—all of this will forever remain a mystery. Still, we can speculate. Salman Rushdie has been writing for many years about people who endure that kind of split existence—people who dwell by day in the modern West, and, in their imaginations, recede to their own homelands and to the world of Muslim religious fantasy. The whole purpose of Rushdie's *The Satanic Verses*, which got him in trouble with Ayatollah Khomeini, was to evoke that kind of double existence.

A lot of people, not just the ayatollah, figured that Rushdie's novel was horribly disrespectful to Islam, and was meant to be disrespectful, and Rushdie was a nasty provocateur. But look at *The Satanic Verses* today. Rushdie describes the allure of ultra-radical, even lunatic political protest, in the immigrant neighborhoods of London. He describes the allure of the most delirious of Islamic ravings, and he even conjures up religious ravings that, in their agonized confusion, distort and desecrate the Muslim faith. Rushdie has a lot of fun with those themes—too much fun, someone might say (though what is too much fun in a novel?). But Rushdie did not invent these themes. Critics like to call him a "magic realist." But in *The Satanic Verses* Rushdie is, on the contrary, a social realist, faithfully reporting on the reality before his eyes.

For what was the world of the 9/11 terrorists, during their years of workaday life in the Western countries? It must have resembled the phantasmagoric landscape of *The Satanic Verses*, vivid with wild dreams and desecratory urges and lunatic political ideas. If bin Laden's suicide warriors differed in some important fashion from Rushdie's characters or from millions of more typical real-life immigrants, it was only because, owing to Saudi Arabia's wealth and the prosperous success of some of their own families, the suicide warriors tended to be men of privilege. These were not the huddled masses. The suicide warriors were professionally educated people with enviable futures—young men who strutted about the world with more advantages in life than many of their European and American neighbors, not to mention most of their fellow immigrants.

Is there something picayune or perverse in emphasizing the other side of these people's hyphenated identity—their Western half? Let us glance at some of bin Laden's other troops—or, at least, at people who, in the murk of the moment, have been accused, falsely or accurately, of being his troops. A group of young men from Yemeni backgrounds were arrested in Lackawanna, New York, a run-down suburb of Buffalo, in September 2002 (and still another man from Lackawanna was arrested in Bahrain), and were accused of forming a Qaeda cell—or, at minimum, of having visited one of bin Laden's training camps in Afghanistan. The Qaeda cell, if that is what it was, turns out to be a product of Lackawanna High School. The soldiers of jihad are Lackawanna High's soccer team—boys from upstate New York who enjoyed one too many adventures in revolutionary tourism. An old story.

José Padilla, accused of plotting to construct a "dirty bomb" on behalf of Al Qaeda, began life as a Christian—in his case, a Puerto Rican tough guy from the streets of Brooklyn and Chicago. Richard Reid, the shoe bomber, was likewise born a Christian in England. These men took up bin Laden's murderous version of Islam of their own volition—no one brought them up to do it. More than twenty Canadians have been accused of maintaining some sort of Qaeda affiliation in the last few years; one of those Canadians is said to have killed an American medic in Afghanistan. And let us look at some of the people who have served as bin Laden's brothers-in-arms in other organizations.

John Walker Lindh, the bearded Taliban, began life as an ordinary Christian from the wealthy zones of Northern California. Yesar Esam Hamdi, who is accused of fighting with the Taliban, grew up in Saudi Arabia—but was born in Louisiana. There is the curious case of Ahmed Omar Sheikh, who helped organize the kidnapping and murder in Pakistan of Daniel Pearl, the *Wall Street Journal* reporter. Omar is himself of Pakistani origin. But he is British-born. He studied at the London School of Economics—George Soros's alma mater, the school where many a young Trotskyist and Maoist and ultra of the New Left trod the corridors, not too long ago, and then ascended into the British elite. The doors of British success were open to Ahmed Omar Sheikh. Yet he is a man who, nonetheless, seems to strike the fundamentalist warriors of Pakistan as not at all foreign or exotic—someone they can recognize and acclaim as their own. In homage to this one particular British student from the LSE, a scattering of Islamist terrorist groups in Pakistan joined together in late 2001 and took the name "Omar's Army." And Omar's Army dutifully went about its business, which was to commit massacres.

I don't mean to deny or ignore for one minute the authentically Muslim and local roots of bin Laden's enterprise and of the many other Arab and Islamic terrorist organizations of recent times. Still, an amazing number of the Arab and Muslim terrorists do turn out to have second and even primary identities as Westerners. It's good to glance eastward, and at the history of the Arab and Muslim world from hundreds of years ago. But in trying to make sense of these people's very strange behavior, we ought to glance westward, too—not just at Western politics and policies, but at literature and philosophy, at the deepest of Western ideas, not just now but in the past, and in the long-ago past. In the West we do have our own customs and traditions, some of which are perfectly horrible. The world is full of exotic things; but not every exotic thing is a foreign thing.

II

Armageddon in Its Modern Versions

IN THE YEARS around 1950, writers from several parts of the world set out to produce a new literature of political analysis, different from any political literature of the past, with the goal of describing and analyzing the totalitarian political passions of the twentieth century—the topic of the hour. There were a lot of those writers—Hannah Arendt, George Orwell, Albert Camus, Sidney Hook, C. L. R. James, Alejo Carpentier, Czeslaw Milosz, David Rousset, Arthur Koestler, Arthur M. Schlesinger, Jr., Richard Wright and the other contributors to Richard Crossman's anthology *The God That Failed*, and many others. Their new literature came packaged in every shape—philosophical inquiry, science fiction, historical fiction, literary criticism, journalism, historical research, and autobiographical confession. The writers disagreed with one another. These people were not a faction. Still, their tracts and essays and novels did share one very noticeable quality. It was a tone of voice. And the tone expressed a shared emotion, which was this: astonishment.

Every one of those writers had started out as an enemy of fascism and the extreme right in the 1930s and '40s; and every one of them, glancing over his shoulder, had begun to notice after a while that communism in the age of Stalin was pretty scary, too. And each of those writers made one additional observation, which was positively alarming. Fascism and communism were violent enemies of each other—bitter opposites. But, caught in a certain light, the bitter opposites looked oddly similar. And visible similarity led to an anxious worry. Was it possible that fascism and communism were somehow related? Mightn't both of those movements have evolved out of some other, deeper, primordial inspiration? Mightn't fascism and communism be tentacles of a single, larger monster from the deep—some new and horrible creature of modern civilization, which had never been seen and never been named but was, even so, capable of sending up further ghastly tentacles from the sinister depths?

In Europe, and not just there, a new kind of politics did seem to be stirring, which sometimes called itself left-wing and sometimes right-wing—a demagogic politics, irrational, authoritarian, and insanely murderous, a politics of mass mobilization for unachievable ends. Mussolini had embraced the word "totalitarian" to describe his own movement; and "totalitarian" in its stuttery sharp syllables seemed to fit the new kind of politics in each of its versions, right-wing and left-wing alike. The implications did seem fairly obvious. During the whole of the nineteenth century and the first years of the twentieth, a great many enlightened and progressive thinkers had supposed that a main danger, perhaps the principal danger, to modern civilization came from a single political tendency, which was the extreme right, and mostly from a single country, which was Germany, the sworn foe of the French Revolution. But that sort of outlook seemed hopelessly antique by 1950. In the new era, no one doubted that political movements on the extreme right could still make you worry. No one felt much confidence in Germany and its political traditions.

But the midcentury writers saw all too plainly that a danger to civilization had meanwhile cropped up in Russia and among the hard-bitten Stalinists, and among other people, too. The writers worried about the many mush-headed liberals and fellow travelers all over the world who, without being Stalinists themselves, managed to admire the Stalinist enterprise. The writers worried about totalitarian advances even in regions where the Red Army was unlikely to send in its tanks. They worried that hidden flaws had cracked open across the whole of civilization, and the danger was universal.

But this fear raised and still raises a question, which the writers of half a century ago tended to evade. It is the same question that Huntington has posed in his theory about clashing civilizations—and, along with Huntington, many other people as well. There is, to cite a notable example, Tariq Ramadan, a philosopher of contemporary Islamism, who has written a book called *Islam, the West and the Challenges of Modernity*, which the Islamic Foundation brought out in English translation in 2001. Ramadan poses the question with considerable nuance. What do we mean when we use the word "civilization," he wants to know. Is there such a thing as universal civilization? His eye runs along the bookshelf of fifty years ago, and he picks out one writer for critical interrogation on this point. It is Albert Camus, whose book on totalitarianism, *The Rebel*, came out in 1951. Camus wanted to identify the precise traits in modern civilization that had led to totalitarianism and its horrors. He looked for those traits in ancient mythology and in modern literature. He found them, too—the cultural traits, anyway.

But Ramadan observes that, in looking for the roots of totalitarianism in mythology and literature, Camus confined himself to the myths and literary classics of the West. Civilization, to Camus, meant Western culture, and did not mean Islam. But then, if Camus was right about the roots of totalitarianism, which ran through the unique and flawed culture of the West, how can anyone say that totalitarianism poses a universal danger? The West is not the universe and Western traditions have nothing to do with the Muslim world.

Ramadan thinks that, if we wish to understand the special problems and promise of the Muslim world, we should not, in fact, glance westward, nor at Albert Camus and books like *The Rebel*. Ramadan says, "We are indeed dealing with two different universes of reference, two civilizations and two cultures." The profoundest mentality and emotions of the Muslim world, the cultural memories, the intellectual instincts—these are not only different from those of the West, they are nearly incomprehensible to the Western mind. And the implication of this analysis is plain enough. Anyone who agrees with Tariq Ramadan would have to conclude that, in looking for a general cause of the dangers facing modern civilization, Camus and the writers of half a century ago wandered down the wrong road entirely. Modern civilization does not exist—only civilizations, in the plural. A general cause of modern problems, operative around the world, will never be found. That is a plausible argument, and widely shared, too.

Still, I would like to make an observation. It is the same observation that I have made about the suicide army of bin Laden and his comrades—a biographical observation, applicable to any number of people in our present age. Tariq Ramadan is a prestigious figure among Islamist intellectuals today. He explains in *Islam, the West and the Challenges of Modernity* that he is the son of a persecuted militant of the Muslim Brotherhood of Egypt—which is to say, Ramadan's prominence in the Islamist movement comes to him by birthright, as well as through his own achievements. He doesn't even mention that he is, to boot, the grandson of Hassan al-Banna, the founder of the Muslim Brotherhood, a martyr to the cause, assassinated in Egypt—one of the most influential figures in the history of modern Islam, all over the world.

Even so, the promotional copy on the back cover of Ramadan's book does mention, by way of affirming his authority, that he teaches philosophy and Islamic Studies at the University of Fribourg, in Switzerland—an excellent credential, which any publisher would invoke. But let us pause over that credential. Why shouldn't we regard Tariq Ramadan, the Islamist philosopher, as, at bottom, a Swiss professor? He has written a book which takes issue with Albert Camus. Nothing could be more natural—a Swiss professor who quarrels with a Parisian philosopher. Allow me, then, to raise a skeptical eyebrow over the purity of Tariq Ramadan's cultural identity. And having done so, I would like to raise my other eyebrow over Camus and the purity of his own reflections on civilization and its Western roots. Who was

Albert Camus, after all? An Algerian. He left Algeria and made his home in Paris. Yet even in *The Rebel* Camus paused for a moment to bathe himself in Algerian nostalgias, reminiscing about the beaches of his youth and the girls on the beaches—his Mediterranean soul, radiating African sunbeams long after he had moved to the chilly North.

So Ramadan disputes Camus. Fine. It is a quarrel between a Swiss and a Parisian, which, seen from another vantage point, is a quarrel between two North Africans. In the modern world, we are all hyphenated personalities. "Nobody is anything," said C. L. R. James. And the distinction between Western civilization and non-Western civilization looks blurrier and blurrier the more you try to get it into focus.

I agree with Ramadan on one issue, though. We hyphenated moderns have good reason to dwell closely on Camus and *The Rebel*. Something about that book does cry out for attention, in these troubled days. Among the many commentators from half a century ago, the philosopher from Algeria was the single one who intuitively recognized a crucial reality. He recognized that, at a deep level, totalitarianism and terrorism are one and the same. He recognized that, if only we could discover the roots of totalitarianism, we would have discovered the roots of terror as well, and vice versa.

WHAT were those roots, then? Camus pointed to a specific human impulse, ancient and august, which is the impulse to rebel—the impulse that got its start as an impulse to rebel against God. And he pointed to the peculiar ways in which the ancient and august impulse has evolved.

Now, in Ramadan's view, this particular impulse, the urge to rebel, marks the exact place where Western civilization and Islam diverge. In Western religious tradition, there is a place for skepticism and doubt. These two attitudes, skepticism and doubt, are elements of faith—the elements that prove the authenticity of belief in God. The God of the Old Testament instructs Abraham to sacrifice his son, Isaac, and Abraham doubts the instruction and struggles to resist it, for a little while—and Abraham's doubt and his struggle testify to the sincerity of his belief. In Ramadan's opinion, the impulse to rebel in Western culture follows directly from the esteem that is accorded to skepticism and doubt. You begin with skepticism and doubt, and you push those attitudes one step further, and you arrive at full-scale rebellion. And those particular traits—skepticism, doubt, rebellion—have, in the end, produced a lot of misery in the Western countries today.

Muslim tradition does not have those traits. In Islam, Ramadan tells us, there is no impulse to rebel. The Koran recounts the same story about Abraham and Isaac, but the Koran puts no emphasis on Abraham's skepticism and resistance. In the Koran's version, Abraham hears God's instructions, and readies himself to comply. There is no struggle, no temptation to rebel. In Islam, submission is all. Submission to God allows Islam to create a unified, moral, and satisfying society—at least potentially, even if the flesh-and-blood Muslims in any given era have forgotten their religious obligations. Submission is the road to social justice, to a contented soul, and to harmony with the world.

Those were not the attitudes of Albert Camus. The author of *The Rebel* was himself a rebel. He contributed articles to *Révolution Prolétarienne*, the anarcho-syndicalist journal in France—the journal of the freethinking, anti-authoritarian left. Rebellion, in his eyes, was the best thing that has ever happened. Camus invoked the myth of Prometheus the titan, who goes further than Abraham and, in a spirit of radical action, takes that final step into full-scale rebellion. Prometheus steals Zeus' fire and gives it to man. He is punished horribly for his transgression—and yet, the titan's transgression is man's benefit. Camus applauded. He shook his fist in solidarity. He looked on Promethean rebellion as the basis of human progress, and of human freedom, too, and, in his enthusiasm, he plucked the word "libertarian" out of the old-time anarchist vocabulary and laid it at Prometheus' feet.

Still, Camus was a man of the middle twentieth century, and he gazed at the ruins of Europe, and, in a somber mood, he had to agree that, over the centuries, the Promethean impulse to rebel had taken an odd turn, not entirely for the good. The impulse to rebel, in its modern version, was still a libertarian urge, he thought. And it was still a source of progress, at least potentially. But the impulse had acquired a new and slightly contradictory element—a complication that had never existed before. The impulse, in its new version, was a dance step which began by gazing upward into human freedom and progress—and then, with the quickest and most graceful of dips, leaned downward into death. The libertarian and the sinister had somehow blended together, and the love of freedom and progress had become weirdly inseparable from a morbid obsession with murder and suicide.

This sort of thing got underway, he thought, during the French Revolution—and not just because of people like Saint-Just, the leader of the revolutionary Terror, whose zeal had its peculiarities. The marquis de Sade was hard at work composing his literary texts in those years, and Camus detected some of that same morbid rebelliousness there. The rebellious, the sinister, and the sexual were mixed together from the start. Saint-Just and Sade were mostly precursors, though. In Camus's estimation, the fully mutant impulse to rebel came into flower in the middle years of the nineteenth century, in the elegant form of a new élan or attitude in French poetry. Camus figured that Victor Hugo, the greatest of the Romantic poets in French, was too cheerful and positive-thinking, too much the national poet of France, to give vent to this mutant new impulse—the joining together of rebellion and crime. But Camus missed something here. Among the Romantic writers in France, it was Hugo, more than anyone else, who celebrated the urge to rebel. And it was Hugo who consummated his celebration with morbid rites of murder and suicide, in a version for the theatre.

He did this in a verse play called *Hernani*, which no one puts on anymore—a creaky antique of a play, lost among the forgotten writings of an author whose more successful works, his cathedral hunchback and his Parisian sewers and (for French readers) his epic and lyrical poems, have never been forgotten even for a moment. *Hernani* was a giant success in its own day, though, and, in one fateful respect, it was all too modern. The play told the story of a Romantic hero who conspires to kill the king in a rebellious act of vengeance—and ends up participating in a triple suicide, if only to consummate his rebellion by dominating the circumstances of his own death. Murder as rebellion, suicide as honor, murder and suicide as the joint emblem of human freedom—those were Hugo's themes. His play rebelled against authority even in the texture of its dialogue. The first actor to speak a line enjambs one alexandrine into another, thereby breaking a fundamental rule of traditional French verse, which might not seem like much of a rebellion today. But at the play's opening night—this was in 1830—Hugo's infraction of the rules of prosody set off hoots and catcalls in the audience. A riot at the theatre. And so, here was a play about rebellion which was itself an act of rebellion—a play in which the hero aimed at freedom, and arrived at murder and suicide.

That was Camus's theme, almost entirely. Victor Hugo led the way. And then, exactly as Camus described, the impulse went a little further, and a new writer came along, and took a further step into still darker zones. This new writer was Charles Baudelaire, from the generation younger than Hugo's—Baudelaire, who wanted to escape the tiresome encumbrances of traditional morality, wanted to get out from under Christianity's thumb, and wanted to flee from Christianity's secular legacies as well, its moral and liberal heritage. The civic virtue of solid citizens like Victor Hugo struck Charles Baudelaire as too much to endure. And, with those several resentments and desires pushing him forward, Baudelaire, in a haughty spirit of impudence and provocation, rebelled against God Himself and declared for Satan. Baudelaire composed his *Flowers of Evil* and presented one of the editions to the public by saying,

> If you haven't studied rhetorical
> method with Satan, the cunning master,
> Throw this book away! You'll understand
> nothing, or will think me hysterical.

And what was Satan's rhetorical method? It was rebellion in the name of absolute freedom: the freedom to do what is absolutely forbidden. It was a plunge into the experience that is more than fleeting or partial: the experience of total annihilation. It was, therefore, murder—and suicide. It was murder and suicide not as acts of a virtuous and responsible rebellion, as in *Hernani*, but as acts of Satanic transgression. Murder and suicide for their own sake—for the sake of crime. It was nihilism: the rebellion against all moral values.

Camus quoted Baudelaire: "The true saint is the person who whips and kills the people for the good of the people." Citizen Hugo would never have said such a thing. Baudelaire looked on both sides of revolutionary violence—on killing, and on being killed—as equally attractive. "Not only would I be happy to be a victim," he wrote, "I wouldn't hate being the executioner, in order to *feel* the revolution in both ways." To be sure, Baudelaire was a literary man, and crime was poetry, for him. Camus called him a "dandy"—someone who strikes poses in order to strike poses. His rebellion was, in Camus's word, "metaphysical." Still, there was something new and genuine and thrilling in these attitudes. And Baudelaire was not the only one to give them voice.

Camus pointed to Dostoevsky, or rather, to Dostoevsky's character

Ivan, who says, "Everything is permitted." Meaning: moral values do not exist, and nihilism is the only truth. Nor is this the cry of a person driven to desperate extremes by hopeless conditions. Ivan turns to nihilism because he wants to. Despair is his desire. And Ivan, too, in his nihilism, gropes his way to murder. Camus pointed to the surrealists in France. The surrealist movement, he tells us, "was rash enough to say—and this is the phrase that André Breton must have regretted ever since 1933—that the simplest of surrealist acts consisted in going down to the street, revolver in hand, and shooting randomly into the crowd." Camus concluded, "The theory of the gratuitous act is the culmination of the demand for absolute liberty."

That was the twisted new impulse in Europe—the rebellion that begins with freedom and ends with crime. The rebellion that is indistinguishable from murder and suicide—the rebellion that makes perfect sense at the start, and quickly produces deaths that make no sense at all. Nor was any of this merely "metaphysical." The young idealists in Dostoevsky's *The Devils* loathe the restraints of ordinary morality, and put their loathing into action; and people like that were a reality in the Russia of Dostoevsky's time. A young man named Nechaev organized a conspiracy called the Society of the Ax in 1866, whose purpose was to overthrow the tsar and make a social revolution—a libertarian purpose, with human progress as the goal. But the Society of the Ax required its members to swear total obedience to secret leaders, known to no one, whose principles were to break every principle. Nechaev murdered one of his followers and ended up in jail, and his conspiracy evaporated. But the taboo had been broken, and the real-life murders and suicides were already underway.

In 1878 a young woman named Vera Zassulich shot the governor of St. Petersburg—and, as Camus carefully recorded, launched a kind of fad for political assassination. It was mostly a Russian fad. Someone tried to kill the tsar in 1879, and two years later a little circle of revolutionaries did kill him—a sensational event. Minor officials were killed right and left. But the fad became more than Russian. There were attempts on the emperor of Germany and the king of Spain. The empress of Austria was murdered in 1898. The king of Italy was killed by an anarchist from New Jersey. In 1901, President McKinley was murdered in Buffalo, New York. And the assassinations and *attentats*, as they were called, rolled on, until Archduke Franz Ferdinand was killed at Sarajevo, which sparked the First World War—and still the *attentats* kept rolling on, in the United States, Spain, Argentina, and around the world.

Camus judged those assassinations and the assassins in a careful and discriminating spirit. He appreciated the lofty intentions of the early Russian terrorists, who went about their work with a solemn purpose and a sense of the moral meaning of their own deeds. He recalled the plot to assassinate Grand Duke Sergei by the revolutionary Kaliayev, who belonged to the Organization for Combat of the Russian populist movement, the Socialist Revolutionary Party, in the era of the tsars. Kaliayev was known as "the Poet"—just in case anyone had forgotten the literary origins of these terrorist inspirations. "The Poet" was devoted to his own honor and moral rectitude. The first time that Kaliayev set out to kill Grand Duke Sergei, he held back, because when the grand duke's carriage came into view, children were at the grand duke's side, and the children were innocent of any crime.

Camus pointed to Boris Savinkov, the leader of the Organization for Combat. Savinkov argued against trying to kill a tsarist admiral on the Petersburg-Moscow Railroad: "With the slightest carelessness, the explosion could take place in the car and kill strangers." Savinkov, invoking what he called his "terrorist conscience," indignantly denied having made a sixteen-year-old child take part in an *attentat*. Those Russian terrorists from tsarist times felt justified in trying to kill the tsar and his aristocrats, yet they knew that murder, no matter its justification, remains a crime. The terrorists recognized their own culpability, and insisted on atoning with their lives. They brought together,

Camus wrote, "respect for human life in general and contempt for their own lives which went as far as yearning for the supreme sacrifice." They were morally fastidious. "Delicate," in his word. At least, they meant to be.

Camus pointed to Dora Brilliant, who took no interest in the political goals. Terrorist action, in her eyes, "was primarily embellished by the sacrifice it demanded of the terrorist." Camus quoted Savinkov, who observed that Kaliayev, "the Poet," was ready to sacrifice his life at any moment. And more: "Better yet, he passionately desired this sacrifice." While drawing up a plan to assassinate one of the tsar's ministers, Kaliayev announced his intention to throw himself under the horses' hooves. Camus pointed to Voinarovsky, another terrorist. "With Voinarovsky, too, the desire for sacrifice comes together with the attraction of death. After his arrest he writes to his parents: 'How many times during my adolescence the idea came to me to kill myself! . . .' "

Those people, every one of them, were Hernanis from Hugo's play; and, in the years around 1905, the Hernanis were everywhere at hand, and the spectacle of their assassinations and deaths was heart-rending. So many sensitive young people, so many hopes for social justice and liberty, so much sacrifice and death! There was grandeur in those people. Let us not tut-tut, from our homes in the land of the free. Dora Brilliant apart, those people were dreaming of something better than life under a tsar and a feudal system—dreaming not even for themselves but for other people. And yet—this, too, is undeniable—there was something strange about the Russian zeal for bringing assassination together with suicide. Hugo wrote about murder and suicide, but that was in a play for the stage. The heroes of the Socialist Revolutionary Party were not putting on plays.

Then came the unavoidable next step in the twisted new idea of rebellion. I will cite a couple of American examples from those same years to illustrate it—the easy glide from the fastidious to the less fastidious. There was the case of Alexander Berkman, an anarchist from Russia with solid roots in the Socialist Revolutionary Party, who immigrated to the United States. In 1892 Henry Clay Frick, the robber baron, hired a group of Pinkerton guards to suppress a steelworkers' strike in Homestead, Pennsylvania, and the Pinkertons killed a number of striking workers. Berkman concluded that Frick was a despot worthy of death. He forced himself into Frick's office in Pittsburgh and got off a few shots from his pistol—though Frick survived.

It was an ugly and inappropriate deed on Berkman's part. Even in the age of the robber barons, Pennsylvania was not a tsarist province, and the Homestead workers had better recourses than a lonely act of violent revenge. Still, Berkman conceived his *attentat* in the old-fashioned Russian spirit. His attack on Frick was pretty well guaranteed not to injure anyone else—yet was also guaranteed to result in Berkman's arrest or even his death. It was the deed of an immigrant Hernani. It was the act of a man who regarded himself as free, in the manner of the Russian terrorists—free, therefore doomed.

Then the fastidious yielded to the not fastidious. A quarter century after Berkman's *attentat*, another immigrant anarchist in the United States, Luigi Galleani—a cultured man, an eloquent writer in Italian—led his followers into a violent campaign based on indiscriminate killings. Galleani, too, expressed a lofty spirit. He boiled with indignation at the injustices of capitalism and exploitation. He pictured a better life, based on a principle of uncoerced solidarity—the principle of anarchism or what he called, citing Fichte, "the Ideal." His idea was a life of absolute individual freedom, of free will, governed only by the freely accepted moral code of workers and artisans and by the aesthetic sensibility of the finest art.

This was a libertarian idea, pushed to the maximum. Galleani wanted his followers to preach those principles to the world. But, most of all, he wanted his followers to live by those principles in the workaday environment of the present—to form a counterculture of the libertarian Ideal even within the capitalist world of poverty and oppression. In his tract *The End of Anarchism?* Galleani wrote, "We must be ourselves, according to the strict character of our faith and our convictions." But what did the strict character of their faith require? It required individual acts of rebellion, intended to "kindle the torch of the victorious revolution."

Galleani knew that acts of rebellion entailed risking many bitter blows—the "sacrifice of our freedom, our well-being, even our loved ones for many long years, sometimes forever." But sacrifice was, in its fashion, the Ideal itself. Sacrifice was a perfect act of selfless solidarity, adopted freely and without coercion—the very model of the yearned-for revolutionary new society. He explained, "the Ideal, a solitary aspiration of poets and philosophers, is embodied in the martyrdom of its first heralds and sustained by the blood of its believers."

Martyrdom was magnificent, seen in that light. And so, Galleani's followers, dreaming of liberty, set out to commit their acts of rebellion. Paul Avrich, the historian of anarchism, tells us that some of Galleani's militants mailed letter bombs to prominent people, though with no effect at all, except for the murder of a senator's secretary. One of Galleani's followers tried to poison the archbishop of Chicago and some two hundred guests at a banquet in the archbishop's honor. The arsenic caused the banqueters to vomit up the poison instead of digesting it, and no one was killed.

But in 1920, somebody from Galleani's group planted a bomb on Wall Street, in order to avenge the arrest of a couple of members of the group, Sacco and Vanzetti. The bomb killed a random crowd of thirty-three people. The Wall Street bomb remained for many years the bloodiest terrorist act that America had ever seen—until Timothy McVeigh's bombing of the Federal Building in Oklahoma City in 1995, which killed approximately five times as many people. And what was the logic of the Galleani group's deed in 1920? Why detonate an explosive on Wall Street? For symbolic reasons, of course. And why kill those thirty-three people in particular? For no reason. Because they happened to be walking by.

Galleani and his followers had arrived at the very reasoning that would govern the attacks on Manhattan's center of finance more than seventy years later—not just the World Trade Center attack of 1993, but the suicide-hijack attacks of 2001, which once again took the previous record of terrorist killings (in this case, McVeigh's) and multiplied the dead, this time, by a factor of about fifteen. Galleani's idea was to commit an aesthetic act of terror—"aesthetic" was his own word—in which the beauty or artistic quality consisted in murdering anonymously. Here the nihilism was unlimited, and the transgression, total.

Violence of that sort attracted a lot of attention in the later nineteenth century and the early twentieth. And yet, in those decades, most people seem to have stayed more or less calm. Society as a whole seems to have remained convinced that, no matter how many terrorist bombs went off, the tiny bomb-throwing groups with their ever more casual and "aesthetic" views on death were never going to be anything but tiny, and massive crowds were never going to march through the streets chanting slogans in praise of murder and suicide, and the Luigi Galleanis of this world were never going to rise to power, and the lure of death was resistible.

Some of the greatest of novelists felt drawn to the terrorist theme—not just Dostoevsky but Henry James in his *Princess Casamassima*, and Conrad in *The Secret Agent*, not to mention Chesterton and a few others. The novelists were definitely alarmed. And yet each of those writers, when he bent over his manuscript to conjure the terrorists and their personalities, ended by creating characters who appeared to be at least mildly ridiculous—marginal screwballs animated by preposterous ideas, losers through and through, the doomed and the super-doomed. Now and then a talented writer gazed on the terrorists with more sympathetic eyes. There was Frank Harris, who wrote *The Bomb*, which described the anarchists of Chicago in a respectful spirit, admiring of their ideals (which were, in fact, lofty). But, in the novels as in life, the terrorists and their bombs and guns seemed, to most people in those years, a marginal affair—a problem in crime prevention, a philosophical problem, a mystery, but nothing larger. And this attitude among the public, the confident self-assurance, is easy to understand.

The whole experience of Europe and North America during an entire century, from the end of the Napoleonic Wars to the First World War, had tended to be, after all, one of visible progress; and progress makes strength. The ancient evils of suffering, poverty, and exploitation continued being ancient evils. And yet, during those hundred years, the Western countries seemed to have discovered the secret of human advancement—seemed to be making forward strides in the here and now, seemed to have discovered the principle that, if allowed to function, would continue to generate progress indefinitely into the future. Science, rational thought, and general education seemed to be steadily moving forward. Superstition, ignorance, and illiteracy seemed to be in retreat. Technology and industry advanced, wealth increased, human rights spread somewhat, democracy and self-government grew stronger—at least, in some countries. And what was the secret behind those many areas of progress, the all-powerful, all-conquering principle?

It was the recognition that all of life is not governed by a single, all-knowing and all-powerful authority—by a divine force. It was the tolerant idea that every sphere of human activity—science, technology, politics, religion, and private life—should operate independently of the others, without trying to yoke everything together under a single guiding hand. It was a belief in the many, instead of the one. It was an insistence on freedom of thought and freedom of action—not on absolute freedom, but on something truer, stronger, and more reliable than absolute freedom, which is relative freedom: a freedom that recognizes the existence of other freedoms, too. Freedom consciously arrived at. Freedom that is chosen, and not just bestowed by God on high. This idea was, in the broadest sense, liberalism—liberalism not as a rigid doctrine but as a state of mind, a way of thinking about life and reality.

In the nineteenth century, each new philosopher and political movement proposed a new and different way of organizing society around those liberal principles, and a different way of picturing the expected progress. There were "whig" ideas of steady, gradual progress, and "positivist" ideas of scientifically led progress. There were left-wing theories of progress achieved through lurches and upheavals, and capitalist theories of benign market equilibriums. Libertarian theories, technocratic management theories—dozens, scores of theories, each of them resting, in the nineteenth-century style, on two or three tangible factors: economics, geography, and so forth. Most of those theories, maybe all of them, had their inconsistencies. Liberal ideas were yoked together with principles that could only lead in illiberal directions—and the inconsistencies turned out to be, in times to come, a serious problem for everyone who tried to put those theories into practice. But, in the meanwhile, the many theories conveyed the same general idea. It was an idea of progress toward ever more freedom, ever more rationality, and ever more wealth. And each of those theories pictured human progress as a universal event, not just confined to Western Europe and North America.

Even in tsarist Russia, where the terrorists were relatively strong, a great many people imagined that, sooner or later, despite the terrorists, or because of them—because of terrorism's revolutionary effectiveness—Russia was going to follow Western Europe's example, or even surpass it and go vaulting into the future. Latin Americans resolutely set out on the path of progress in its French version, or else in its United States version—in either case, a proven path of liberal advancement. The European empires went on spreading into Asia and

Africa, and the United States expanded its own borders and even began to construct a halfhearted empire of its own, with footholds in the Caribbean and the far Pacific—and each of those several empires, European and American, likewise postulated human progress as its goal. A good many people among the colonized populations approved of those imperial goals, too. They harbored the keen and touching hope that history held out a promise for more than the favored few, and that Europe and North America's progress into freedom, wealth, science, and stability differed from everyone else's only by being a few steps ahead, and everyone else was going to catch up, in time. For liberal civilization belonged to all mankind, and people around the world looked on liberal ideas as their proper heritage, and tried to claim what was theirs. And, around the world, hearts pounded with excited anticipation at the achievements to come.

Those attitudes were not entirely foolish. And yet Camus, in his study of rebellion and its peculiar evolution, took note of a few anomalies in world progress, which did complicate the picture. The anomalies consisted of imperialist crimes. Camus's references to these events (he mentioned the cases of India, Algeria, and South Africa) were thoroughly inadequate, and I'm not going to make up for his inadequacy here. Still, it is worth recalling what sort of thing he had in mind.

There was the astonishing case of King Leopold's campaign in the Congo—the Belgian campaign of destruction against Congolese that Conrad recorded in the annals of literature, and Adam Hochschild more recently in the annals of history. What was the logic behind the slaughter of Congolese by Belgians? The Belgians would have given various explanations. But ultimately there was no logic. The Belgians took up murder for murder's sake. The colonial slaughter was an insanity, not so different from the terrorist insanity that Conrad recorded in his other novel, the one about the nihilist radicals of London. There was the case of the Germans in their own colony in

Southwest Africa. In 1904, the Germans set up extermination camps in order to wipe out a troublesome ethnic group, the Herero tribe. Such was the white man's burden.

Those massacres showed that, even in the days when liberal rationality and human progress seemed to be making their greatest strides, an irrationalist cult of death and murder was already springing up—not among Africans but among Europeans, and not just among crazed Russian terrorists or revolutionary millenarians. The cult of death was springing up among Western Europeans in positions of responsibility and power, the captains of civilization, who had the ability to bring about the death of millions. The death of millions duly came about—and hardly anyone, apart from the victims, sounded a protest. A few noble individuals, no one else. Then one murder more, that of the archduke at Sarajevo, and something unpredictable took place. War broke out in Europe, and seemed to be following a traditional, even rational path, at least a comprehensible path—the path of previous wars in Europe.

France pursued its ancient rivalry with Germany; the Germans expressed their traditional anxiety about the combined weight of the French and the Russians; each little nation fretted about its neighbors. And so, the First World War got underway in the logical manner of a pinball machine, with war bouncing from one corner to another. Only, something was new. The tides of European irrationality and mass murder, which had been surging up and down Africa, now went pouring across the European continent itself. Soldiers from the most advanced and civilized of countries slaughtered one another on a factory basis, until 9 million people had been killed, and another 21 million wounded—industrial statistics that seemed to bear no connection at all to the narrow and rational concerns that everyone had invoked at the start of the war. It was, in the phrase of Lieutenant Charles de Gaulle, "a war of extermination." And why did such things take place?

How did Europe's war get so badly out of control—what was the logic behind the frenzy? There was no logic.

A hundred years of rationality and progress had led to that. Every last thing that people in the nineteenth century had believed about human advancement, the conviction that progress was inevitable, the satisfied belief that Western Europe and North America had discovered the royal road to wealth and freedom and that everyone else was bound to follow sooner or later, the grand optimism, the feeling of certainty on behalf of all the world—every brick in that magnificent edifice came tumbling down. It was shocking to see. It was unpredicted. Worse, it was unpredictable, at least from the perspective of those many nineteenth-century theories of human behavior. None of those theories could begin to explain an outbreak of mass slaughter. And, as a result, everybody, absolutely everyone, even the most sophisticated and brilliant of observers, was left staring at the disaster with jaws agape. The elderly Henry James, who had so clearly observed the terrorists in *Princess Casamassima* years before and had so confidently sneered at them, wrote to one of his equally elderly correspondents in August 1914 to express his reaction.

He said, "You and I, the ornaments of our generation, should have been spared this wreck of our belief that through the long years we had seen civilization grow and the worst become impossible. The tide that bore us along was then all the while moving to *this* as its grand Niagara—yet what a blessing we didn't know it. It seems to me to *undo* everything, everything that was ours, in the most horrible retroactive way—but I avert my face from the monstrous scene."

AND NOW the deepest disaster of all got underway. The old Romantic literary fashion for murder and suicide, the dandy's fondness for the irrational and the irresponsible, the little nihilist groups of left-wing desperadoes with their dreams of poetic death—those several tendencies and impulses of the nineteenth century came together with a few additional tendencies that Camus had never bothered to discuss: the dark philosophies of the extreme right in Germany and other countries, with their violent loathing of progress and liberalism; the anti-Semites of Vienna with their mad proposal to cleanse Vienna of its most brilliant aspects; the demented scientists of racial theory. All this, which had once been small and marginal, began to metastasize and spread. The cult of death and irrationality now took hold of entire mass movements. The mass movements were transformed into something new and different, never previously seen—movements "of a new type," in Lenin's phrase (from *What Is to Be Done?*, in 1902). And the movements of a "new type" devoted themselves to a single, all-consuming obsession, which was a hatred of liberal civilization.

The movements of a "new type" did not avert their faces from the monstrous scene. Despair was their desire; and they despaired. They gazed across the landscape of liberal civilization, across the many achievements of democratic freedom, social justice, and scientific rationality. And everywhere they saw a gigantic lie. Liberal civilization seemed to them a horror. Liberal civilization was exploitation and murder—a civilization that ought to be destroyed as quickly and violently as possible. And so, the newly mutated mass movements set out on a path of radical destruction—the path that Lenin liked to describe, with a comradely nod at Saint-Just and the guillotine, as "terror."

Lenin's was the first of those new anti-liberal movements. He created it by joining together two of the currents of the past, the social democracy of Europe and the militarized terror of Russia's Socialist Revolutionaries from the years around 1905—and the combination gave to his own movement, the Bolsheviks, a noble program (that of Social Democracy) and an air of fastidious moral severity (that of the Socialist Revolutionaries). But fastidiousness in Lenin's movement gave way instantly to the cult of the indiscriminate. The old-fashioned insistence on distinguishing between the guilty and the innocent, the earnest recognition that even the most justified of violent acts may be morally culpable, the scrupulous custom of examining one's own motives—all of that, the mental habits of the world around Kaliayev "the Poet," was dismissed as the sentimental legacy of a hypocritical past. Man was guilty, in Lenin's eyes; but History with a capitol H was innocent. When Lenin acted, he acted in History's name. He ordered killings en masse; and everything he did was, by definition, as innocent as the lamb.

"Shoot more professors," was one of Lenin's secret orders. Not even Saint-Just had ever given such an order. And, very quickly, Lenin's movement, having seized power in St. Petersburg in 1917, spread all over Europe and around the world. Everywhere the new movement displayed a weirdly frenetic dynamism, beyond anything that could have been seen in the nineteenth century. It was an emotional forcefulness that derived, ultimately, from the movement's cheerful willingness to put Bolshevism's enemies to death, and an equally cheerful willingness to put to death random crowds whose views on Bolshevism were utterly unknown, and a further willingness to put to death the Bolsheviks themselves (no one has ever murdered more Communists than the Communist Party of the Soviet Union), and a willingness to accept one's own death, too—all for the best of reasons. The idea was, in Baudelaire's phrase, to whip and kill the people for the good of the people. And the whipping and killing got underway.

But that was, as I say, only the beginning. In 1922, Mussolini's Fascists marched on Rome. Were the Fascists in Italy anything like the Bolsheviks in Russia? They appeared to be different in every respect. Bolsheviks dreamed of liberating all mankind, and Fascists dreamed of liberating only part of mankind, at the expense of everyone else. Bolsheviks claimed to be the champions of rationalism and science (though their rationalism and science were mystical dogma, by and large), and Fascists claimed to be the champions of irrationalism (and were right in claiming to be). Bolsheviks were internationalists, and organized their parties in every country as branches of a single agency, centralized, uniform, employing a single rhetoric, reading the same mandated texts and chanting the same slogans everywhere. (Communist internationalism: the original Golden Arches.) Mussolini's Fascists, by contrast, were nationalists, proud and vainglorious of national tradition, as defined by themselves.

And yet, for all those differences, Mussolini's Fascists set off tremors of excitement and envy around the world that were not unlike the Bolshevik tremors set off by Lenin and the October Revolution. Mussolini was a giant in Lenin's mold—a man of ferocious will, powerful enough to transform chaos into order, capable of taking the iron rods of history into his own hands and bending them to his desire. Left-wing, right-wing—these were, from a certain point of view, petty distinctions. Mussolini himself had begun on the extreme left (from the anarchist zone of Italian leftism that had produced Luigi Galleani), and he felt no compunction about moving over to the extreme right. And, just as Bolshevism spread at once around the world, fascism, too, as a movement of the ultra-right with little admixtures from the ultra-left, began to spread with fantastic speed. Naturally, fascism's spread followed a different pattern from Bolshevism's—a pattern of national differences, instead of international uniformities.

Mussolini's movement was noisily Italian, whereas Franco's Spanish Phalange, by contrast, was noisily Spanish—strictly right-wing and ultra-Catholic, seething with hatred for the French Revolution. The extreme rightism of the French, then again, proved to be noisily French, yearning for the French monarchy of yore and seething with even greater hatred for the French Revolution. And thus it was in every country of Europe—everywhere a new and fervent movement of nationalist die-hards, everywhere claiming to embody a deep, true, and authentic local tradition of the national blood and the local soil, everywhere affirming its own inimitable particularities.

And yet, each of those deep, true, and authentic fascist variations turned out to be recognizably like the others. Hitler's National Socialism was the most extreme—the only movement on the European right that, in its love for Nietzsche, actively railed against Christianity instead of claiming to be its champion. The Nazis were wild, and fascists from other parts of the world, in their Christian piety, had to wonder about those Norse gods and the pagan revival. Still, those other fascists gazed in Hitler's direction and saw in him a friend, comrade, and leader, someone to endorse and cheer, the greatest and strongest hero of the national idea anywhere on earth—the most willful of the willful. And this was not wrong. On the topic of death, the Nazis were the purest of the pure, the most aesthetic, the boldest, the greatest of executioners, and yet the greatest and most sublime of death's victims, too—people who, in Baudelaire's phrase, knew how to *feel* the revolution in both ways. Suicide was, after all, the final gesture of the Nazi elite in Berlin. Death, in their eyes, was not just for others, and at the final catastrophe in 1945 the Nazi leaders dutifully converted their safehouses into mini-Auschwitzes of their own.

The left-wing and right-wing movements of the "new type" loathed one another, and their mutual loathing fueled most of the political and even military battles in all of Europe from the 1920s until the end of the Second World War, and even after. In Latin America, the mutual loathings of Bolsheviks (who, after a while, adopted different names) and fascists (who likewise adopted different names) guaranteed war and more war into the 1980s and beyond—in a few remote jungle zones, wars that will probably still be simmering, fifty years from today. And yet, for all the mutual loathing and the sustained efforts to kill each other, it was obvious enough, after a while—it was obvious to the anti-totalitarian writers of midcentury—that

Lenin and his many heirs, together with Mussolini and his own heirs, were, all of them, left-wingers and right-wingers alike, spinning variations on a single impulse. And Camus had noticed something real.

He had noticed a modern impulse to rebel, which had come out of the French Revolution and the nineteenth century and had very quickly, in the name of an ideal, mutated into a cult of death. And the ideal was always the same, though each movement gave it a different name. It was not skepticism and doubt. It was the ideal of submission. It was submission to the kind of authority that liberal civilization had slowly undermined, and which the new movements wished to reestablish on a novel basis. It was the ideal of the one, instead of the many. The ideal of something godlike. The total state, the total doctrine, the total movement. "Totalitarian" was Mussolini's word; and Mussolini spoke for all.

Each of the movements adopted the same set of rites and symbols to express that ideal: the crowds chanting en masse, the monumental architecture, the belief in personal renunciation, the insistence on unquestioning belief in preposterous doctrines. Each of the movements chose its own monochrome symbol, representing the oneness of authority: red, brown, black. Each of the movements donned the identical uniform, which was a shirt—red, brown, and black. Each of the movements recounted a theory about history and mankind, which explained the movement's goals and actions. And each of those theories, in red, in brown, or in black, followed the contours of a single ur-myth—in the twentieth century, the deepest myth of all. This was no longer the myth of Prometheus, nor that of Abraham. This was something else entirely—biblical, and not from the Old Testament, either.

I am not the first to stumble across that most powerful of modern myths or to comment on it. Norman Cohn analyzed it in his classic study of the late Middle Ages, *The Pursuit of the Millenium.* André Glucksmann returned to the same myth in his book about the end of the Cold War, *Le XI° Commandement*. And yet—how to explain this?—a full recognition of the power and nature of that myth seems to have escaped the modern sensibility, as if, even now, we are blind to the reigning ideas of our own time. The myth, in any case, is the one that you find in that strangest and most thrilling of writings, the Book of the Revelation of St. John the Divine. There is a people of God, St. John tells us. The people of God are under attack. The attack comes from within. It is a subversive attack mounted by the city dwellers of Babylon, who are wealthy and have access to things from around the world, which they trade—gold, silver, precious stones, pearls, linen, purple, silk, scarlet, thyme, ivory, precious wood, brass, iron, marble, cinnamon, odors, ointments, frankincense, wine, oil, flour, wheat, beasts, sheep, horses, chariots, not to mention slaves and the souls of men.

These city dwellers have sunk into abominations. They have been polluted by the whore of Babylon. (This story, too, has its sexual component.) The pollution is spreading to the people of God. Such is the attack from within. There is also an attack from without—conducted from afar by the forces of Satan, who is worshipped at the synagogue of Satan. But these attacks, from within and without, will be violently resisted. The war of Armageddon will take place. The subversive and polluted city dwellers of Babylon will be exterminated, together with all their abominations. The Satanic forces from the mystic beyond will be fended off. The destruction will be horrifying. Yet there is nothing to fear: the destruction will last only an hour. Afterward, when the extermination is complete, the reign of Christ will be established and will endure a thousand years. And the people of God will live in purity, submissive to God.

Such was the ur-myth. Camus showed that ideas of transgressive rebellion got started largely among the poets, and so did the idea of retelling this ur-myth in modern versions. You can see the basic themes and some of the spirit in Rimbaud—or, better yet, in Rubén

Darío, the greatest of the Latin American poets. As early as 1905 Darío postulated a people of God, and postulated mystic beasts and millennarian sunrises, and expressed his ideas in eery tones that did sound, in Baudelaire's word, hysterical. The people of God, in Darío's version, were the children of the Roman wolf:

> The Latin race will see a great future dawn,
> And in a thunder of glorious music, millions of lips
> Will salute the splendid light that will come from the East

Blood-dimmed tides, rough beasts slouching toward Bethlehem—images like those became a staple of the poetic imagination in the early twentieth century. But the full myth in its modern version, the story of Babylon and Armageddon as a complete narrative and not just as a set of startling images suitable for poets, came into its own only in the years after the First World War, and not as poetry or literature but as political theory. The great theoreticians of the new twentieth-century political movements, one theoretician after another, labored hard at refashioning the myth, and each new theoretician produced a version that looked utterly unlike everyone else's. Yet, as Glucksmann has shown, every one of those modern versions of the ancient ur-myth kept more or less rigorously to the general shape and texture of the biblical original.

There was always a people of God, whose peaceful and wholesome life had been undermined. They were the proletariat or the Russian masses (for the Bolsheviks and Stalinists); or the children of the Roman wolf (for Mussolini's Fascists); or the Spanish Catholics and the Warriors of Christ the King (for Franco's Phalange); or the Aryan race (for the Nazis). There were always the subversive dwellers in Babylon, who trade commodities from around the world and pollute society with their abominations. They were the bourgeoisie and the kulaks (for the Bolsheviks and Stalinists); or the Freemasons and cosmopolitans (for the Fascists and Phalangists); and, sooner or later, they were always the Jews (for the Nazis, and in a lesser degree for the other fascists, and eventually for Stalin, too).

The subversive dwellers in Babylon were always aided by Satanic forces from beyond, and the Satanic forces were always pressing on the people of God from all sides. They were the forces of capitalist encirclement (for the Bolsheviks and Stalinists); or the pincer pressure of Soviet and American technology, squeezing the life out of Germany (in Heidegger's Nazi interpretation); or the international Jewish conspiracy (again for the Nazis). Yet, no matter how putrid and oppressive was the present, the reign of God always beckoned in the future. It was going to be the Age of the Proletariat (for the Bolsheviks and Stalinists); or the resurrected Roman Empire (for the Fascists); or explicitly the Reign of Christ the King (for the Spanish Phalange); or the Third Reich, meaning the resurrected Roman Empire in a blond Aryan version (for the Nazis).

The coming reign was always going to be pure—a society cleansed of its pollutants and abominations. It was going to be the purity of unexploited labor (for the Bolsheviks and Stalinists); or the purity of Roman grandeur (for the Fascists); or the purity of Catholic virtue (for the Phalange); or the biological purity of Aryan blood (for the Nazis). Yet no matter how these several components of the myth were labeled, the coming reign was always going to last a thousand years—that is, was going to be a perfect society, without any of the flaws, competition, or turmoil that make for change and evolution. And the structure of that purified, unchanging, eternal reign was always going to be the same. It was going to be the one-party state (for the Bolsheviks, the Fascists, the Phalange, and the Nazis)—a society whose very structure ruled out any challenge to its own shape and direction, a society that had achieved the final unity of mankind. And every one of those states was governed in the same fashion, by a great living symbol, who was the Leader.

The Leader was a superman. He was a genius beyond all geniuses. He was the man on horseback who, in his statements and demeanor, was visibly mad, and who, in his madness, incarnated the deepest of all the anti-liberal impulses, which was the revolt against rationality. For the Leader embodied a more than human force. He wielded the force of History (for the Bolsheviks and Communists); or the force of God (for the Catholic Fascists); or the force of the biological race (for the Nazis). And, because this person exercised a power that was more than human, he was exempt from the rules of moral behavior, and he showed his exemption, therefore his divinelike quality, precisely by acting in ways that were shocking.

Lenin was the original model of such a Leader—Lenin, who wrote pamphlets and philosophical tracts with the confidence of a man who believes the secrets of the universe to be at his fingertips, and who established a weird new religion with Karl Marx as god, and who, after his death, was embalmed like a pharaoh and worshipped by the masses. But Il Duce was no less a superman. Stalin was a colossus. About Hitler, Heidegger, bug-eyed, said, "But look at his hands."

Those Leaders were gods, every one of them. There was a god like that in every movement and in every country, someone deranged, virile, all-powerful, a god who thrilled his worshipful followers, a hero with blood on his hands, someone freed of the humiliating limitations of ordinary morality, someone who could gaze on life and death with blasé equanimity, someone who put no value on life, who could order mass executions for no reason at all, or for the flimsiest of reasons. For the Leader was always a nihilist, a Nechaev, a Stavrogin from *The Devils*—except no longer on a tiny scale, marginal, ridiculous, and contemptible. On the contrary, in the twentieth century, Nechaevs and Stavrogins popped up in every country of continental Europe, and took power, and commanded armies and police forces and popular movements. And every one of those Leaders behaved as God behaves, dealing out what God deals out, which is death.

For, in each version of the myth, before the Reign of God could be achieved, there was always going to be the war of Armageddon—the all-exterminating bloodbath. This war, in its global reach and its murderousness, was going to resemble the First World War. It was going to be the Class War (for the Bolsheviks and Stalinists); or the Crusade (for the Fascists); or the race war (for the Nazis). It was going to be a pitiless war—a war on the model of the Battle of Verdun, delivering death on an industrial basis. A war of extinction. "*Viva la Muerte!*" cried one of Franco's generals. For death was victory, in the new imagination.

Those several European movements announced many highly imaginative programs for human betterment, and those imaginative programs were always, in their full-scale versions, impractical—programs for the whole of society that could never be put into effect. But death was practical. Death was the only revolutionary achievement that could actually be delivered. The unity of mankind, the reign of purity and the eternal—those goals were out of reach, in any conventional or real-world respect. But unity, purity, and eternity were readily at hand, in the form of mass death. So the Leader issued his orders. "And the remnant were slain with the sword of him that sat upon the horse. . . ."

III
In the Shade of the Koran

THOSE SEVERAL MOVEMENTS and their wars and campaigns of liquidation destroyed Europe's worldwide power once and for all, and did it in a mere quarter century. One hour, as St. John says. It was Europe's suicide. But did the remarkable outbreak of European destructiveness reflect a strictly European syndrome, an outgrowth of Western civilization, as Tariq Ramadan or Samuel Huntington might suppose, born in Europe and destined to remain there forever? Did the outbreak reflect a strictly Christian syndrome, limited to people who had grown up on the Book of the Revelation of St. John the Divine? Somebody who shared Ramadan's or Huntington's view of Western civilization might suppose that European and Christian traditions and legacies could not possibly spread into the Muslim world. For the myth of Prometheus is not a Muslim myth, as Ramadan reminds us, and St. John's Revelation was not Muhammad's.

Then again, during its five hundred years of world domination, Europe did succeed in exporting innumerable customs and ideas to every corner of the globe; and, having exported everything else, why should Europe have been unable to export its spirit of self-destruction, too? Europe was up to the task. And so, with the barest of delays—in less than an hour, as it were—the movements of a new type went spilling outward from their original European home, and some of those movements began to prosper in the Arab and Muslim world.

Communism was the first of the new mass movements in Europe—and the first to flourish in the Middle East as well. This was not the clash of civilizations. In Europe, communism established a social base in cosmopolitan cities full of intellectuals and polyglot populations; and cosmopolitan cities existed in the Middle East, too. Everyone seems to forget that, not so long ago, Arab cities used to contain large Jewish neighborhoods. In Baghdad during the first half of the twentieth century, to cite a pertinent example, a solid third of the population was Jewish. In cities like that, Communist movements did sink a few roots, though not strictly because of the Jews. The Iraqi Jews, almost all of them, fled for their lives, after a while (mostly to Israel, where refugees from the Muslim world constitute about half the Jewish population—and are routinely reviled, by anti-Zionists everywhere, as European colonists). And then, without the Jews, communism came into its own. In Iraq, to stay with that example, the Communist Party by the late 1950s could draw on the support of upward of a million people—enough to dominate the Iraqi "street."

Communism's appeal in the Muslim world was widespread, too. And long-lasting. In Indonesia, the largest of the Muslim countries, communism swelled into an enormous movement and was defeated only by a gigantic massacre in the 1960s. In Afghanistan, the Communists came to power as late as 1978. The Soviet invasion, which took place the next year, was intended as a fraternal act among Communists, a military measure to shore up the local comrades. In South Yemen—to return to the Arab region—communism likewise turned out to be a popular force in the 1970s, sufficient to take control of the country, at least for a while. Someone might argue that communism in these rustic Third World branches cannot be compared to the original trunk of European Marxism. Kabul's differences from Paris are not to be forgotten—though let us not write off too quickly the intellectual riches of Baghdad and Alexandria and other cosmopolises. Still, the whole point of joining a Communist Party anywhere in the world was to embrace the universal Communist doctrine, which meant that, in every country, Communists celebrated the same cult of

German philosophy and worshipped the same founding father in his patriarchal beard and pursued the same partisan goals and belonged to the same network of international organizations.

But let us ask about Europe's *other* movements of the "new type," the inspirations that waved a religious banner and came from the extreme right—that is, Europe's Fascist and fascist-style movements from the years after the First World War. In what degree did those inspirations likewise spread into the Muslim world? This question, simple to ask, deposits us at once in a land of fog. Communists and Marxists devoted themselves in every country to showing how utterly alike they were, but Europe's Fascist and fascist-like movements tried just as fanatically to demonstrate the opposite. In every country and sometimes in every province the Fascist or fascist-like movement wanted to demonstrate how parochial were its instincts, how deeply rooted in local traditions, how unique and idiosyncratic. A Fascist inspiration from Europe that had spread to other places would make every effort not to look like a Fascist inspiration that had spread from Europe. It would try to appear autochthonous, provincial, inimitable, and ancient, stewing in its own pot and emitting its own idiosyncratic vapors from the distant past. This poses a problem. If a movement appears to be local and ancient, how to compare it to any other movement? How to judge and classify the views and political actions of people who are laboring mightily to emphasize their differences from everyone else?

Still, the scholarly and journalistic literature on Baath Socialism and on Islamist radicalism has become fairly extensive by now, and the literature has opened to us large panoramas of politics in the Arab and Muslim countries. At first glance, whole facets of that panorama do seem fairly exotic, from a Western viewpoint. Let us take a second glance. Kanan Makiya in his *Republic of Fear* describes the philosophical underpinnings of the Baath Socialist movement. Baath Socialism is a branch of the larger Pan-Arab movement, founded by Satia al-Husri in the years after the First World War on the basis of his philosophical studies. These studies were in Fichte and the German Romantics—the philosophers of national destiny, of race, and of the integrity of national cultures.

During the 1930s and '40s, the Pan-Arabists tended to align with the Fascist Axis, and did so for practical political reasons that anyone can understand. The enemies of Pan-Arabism were the British and French imperialists, and Pan-Arabists duly tilted toward the enemies of their enemies, who happened to be the Germans. Still, it's easy to imagine, with an eye on al-Husri's scholarly studies, that more than realpolitik brought the Pan-Arabists to Germany's side. The philosophical roots of Al-Husri's Pan-Arabism and the philosophical roots of Europe's right-wing nationalisms were, after all, the same. In 1943, with German victory in the war still likely, the Arab Baath (or Renaissance) Party met in Damascus and established its own, more radical branch of the Pan-Arabist movement—a revolutionary version, dynamic and determined. The inspiration that went into this movement was openly racist. Sami al-Jundi, one of the early Baath leaders, explained very clearly—I am quoting him from an essay by Bernard Lewis—"We were racists, admiring Nazism, reading its books and the source of its thought, particularly Nietzsche . . . Fichte, and H. S. Chamberlain's *Foundations of the Nineteenth Century*, which revolves on race."

Then again, some of the intellectual fathers of the Baath, men who had done their university studies in Paris, began to write, in the 1930s, for the Communist press in Syria. So there was a smidgen of leftism, too, in the origins of the Baath, and the smidgen endured, not just in the Socialist adjective that was added to the Baath in the 1950s, and not just in some of the Baath movement's Soviet-style economic ideas, but in Baathi ideas of how to construct a revolutionary organization. Saddam Hussein, it is said, always felt a keen admiration for Stalin. The combination of ingredients in the Baath movement—a racist worldview somewhat influenced by Nazism, a few dabs of the ultra-left, Stalin's inspirational example—did have its peculiarities. But nothing about this combination was intrinsically Arab or Middle Eastern or ought to seem incomprehensible to Western observers. The idiosyncratic mix of extreme right and extreme left was precisely the formula that went into National Socialism and Mussolini's Fascism.

Baath Socialism told a myth about man and history, and this, too, was recognizable. In the Baathi myth, there was a people of God. They happened to be the Arab nation. The people of God had been corrupted and polluted from forces within and forces without. Makiya quotes Michel Aflaq, the greatest of the Baathi theoreticians: "The philosophies and teachings that come from the West invade the Arab mind and steal his loyalty." The Arabs needed to "return to a direct relationship with their pure, original nature"—needed to return to the "Arab Spirit." So the Baathi prepared to do battle against the forces from abroad who had invaded the Arab mind—the forces from outside, who were also inside. And the Baathi, too, cultivated manias about the people of evil, who had corrupted the nation of God.

These people, the corrupters, were the Jews. (Makiya tells us that the principal anti-Semitic outbreaks in the Arab world during the twentieth century, in the 1940s and again during the 1960s, were associated with Pan-Arabists of one stripe or another, and not with any other political movement.) The Freemasons, too, were a people of evil—just as in the phobias of Mussolini and Franco. And how were the Arabs going to return to their "pure, original nature"? They were going to do so by revering the revolutionary Leader, who embodied the "Arab Spirit." And the "Arab Spirit"? It was the spirit that had once been embodied by the Prophet Muhammad himself, which is to say, the spirit of Islam—a spirit that is more than human. And what did it mean to revere someone who embodies a more than human spirit?

It meant—it could only mean—mass obedience with no limits at all, an obedience willing to overlook the constraints of any sort of conventional morality. Makiya says about the Baathi and their morality, "Once political identity is accepted as belief in an absolute moral imperative, and once morality itself is seen as a striving for perfection towards an unrealizable goal, then no aspect of conduct is in principle outside the purview of the political organization or the state." So there was a totalitarian element in the Baath idea, and the totalitarianism turned out to be nihilist—not a new phenomenon.

In Iraq, the Baath Socialists established their dictatorship on a firm basis in 1968 (that is, forty-six years after Mussolini's Fascists, thirty-five years after Hitler's Nazis, twenty-nine years after Franco's Phalange—not such a long delay). In the first days of 1969, the new government announced its revolutionary intentions by hanging thirteen Jews and four other people, accused of being Zionist spies, in front of a crowd of hundreds of thousands in Baghdad. It was a golden moment of the Baathi revolution. Ten years later, Saddam rose to power within the Baath. And the posters and statues began to appear, the amazing series of images of Saddam in heroic guises, Saddam as superman, as man of the people, as warrior, as dapper rake, as pious zealot, the images that, in their multiplicity, could only suggest that superman was mad, therefore touched with the divine. Were these posters and images the sign of a profoundly non-European and Mesopotamian culture—a heritage from Assurbanipal or Hammurabi, or from the ancient traditions of Islam? People do make the case. Izzat Ibrahim, vice chairman of the Revolutionary Command Council, meaning second under Saddam, said it himself. "The condition of Iraq," he explained late in 2002, "is like that of early Islamic societies"—by which he meant a time when no great gap divided leaders from the masses. "Don't evaluate this from an intellectual viewpoint, or make comparisons from your experience in the West; Iraq is quite different."

But Iraq is not so different. Mussolini and Hitler cultivated a similar style. Saddam launched his persecution of Jews and Freemasons and other people, his suppression of the Iraqi Kurds (whose crime was to be non-Arab), his cult of the more than human Leader, his public executions and revolutionary exhortations and wars—and these things were intended to achieve the same goal that animated every one of the fascist movements from the years after the First World War. Only, instead of wanting, with Mussolini, to resurrect the Roman Empire of ancient Italy; or, with Hitler, to resurrect the Roman Empire of Nazi myth; or, with Franco, to resurrect the medieval Spanish crusade for Christ the King—instead of all that, the Baath wanted to resurrect the Arab Empire of yore, from the days of Muhammad and the first Caliphs. That was the Baathi "Renaissance." Franco presented himself to his followers as a medieval knight of the Christian Crusade, and Saddam presented himself as a figure in the Prophet Muhammad's family tree. This was fully in the twentieth-century tradition. For as Michel Aflaq had so wisely said, "the philosophies and teachings that come from the West invade the Arab mind"—though Aflaq, in making that observation, had no idea that he was speaking about himself and his own radical doctrines.

The Muslim world's other grand-scale radical movement, the Islamists—the political movement that flies the flag of Islam, or what it claims to be Islam—does appear, seen from afar, to be something else entirely, without any European influences at all. Here again, let us take a second glance. The Islamists came to world prominence much later than Pan-Arabism and the Baath, but they got started at roughly the same time, or even a few years earlier. That was in the lands that eventually became Pakistan and in Egypt. In neither of those places did the early Islamists resemble in any obvious fashion a European fascist movement. Islamism in the area that became Pakistan got under way during the 1930s (organizationally, in 1941). And, from the very start, the movement in South Asia plodded a path of peaceful political reform, just like any democratic movement, though with undemocratic goals. In Egypt, by way of contrast, the Islamist movement was founded, in 1928, as a strictly religious society called the Muslim Brotherhood. The Muslim Brotherhood was devoted to charitable works and the encouragement of an Islamic lifestyle, and did not present itself as any kind of political organization at all, fascist or otherwise.

Still, in Egypt during those years, a sympathy for the European extreme right and even for Nazism was fairly common. The militants of the Young Egypt Society, the "Greenshirts," were openly pro-Nazi. The Muslim Brotherhood's founder, Hassan al-Banna, expressed—I am quoting now from Malise Ruthven, from his *A Fury for God*—"considerable admiration for the Nazi Brownshirts." His organization did choose to designate its organizational units as *kata'ib*, or *phalanges*, in the Franco style. And what did those Muslim phalanges hope to accomplish? In 1924 Kemal Atatürk, the republican leader of Turkey, abolished what seemed to be an anachronistic holdover from the ancient past in Istanbul, which was the institution of the Caliphate. The Caliphate in twentieth-century Turkey was a purely ceremonial office, without power. It was venerable, though. Centuries ago, the Caliphate had been the seat of the Ottoman emperors, and had descended to the Ottomans from still remoter times, when it served as the seat of the Arab Empire from the days of Muhammad's Companions.

Atatürk, the modernizer, was eager to sweep away every mote and cobweb of the distant past, and the Caliphate was among the motes and webs. And so, out went the Caliphate, along with many other dusty old relics of the Turkish past. And, in Egypt in 1928, the new Muslim Brotherhood observed Atatürk and his forward-looking reforms, and reeled in horror. The Muslim Brothers wanted to see the Caliphate restored—though not as a purely ceremonial office, nor as a pious bow to the past. The Muslim Brotherhood wanted to resurrect the office of the Caliphate in order to resurrect the world of Islam in its pristine age, that of the seventh century.

In that fashion, the Muslim Brothers' notion of religion did tip, here and there, into a dreamworld bordering on politics. And the

Brotherhood's dreamiest world of all, the return to the seventh century, turned out to be strikingly similar to Baath Socialism's. Naturally, there were differences—more of a spiritual emphasis among the Muslim Brotherhood, more of a racist emphasis among the Baath Socialists. But these movements were ideological cousins, certainly to one another, and, a little more remotely, to the European movements. The Baathi and the Islamists were two branches of a single impulse, which was Muslim totalitarianism—the Muslim variation on the European idea. Their dreams bore the mark of the Muslim world, but their dreams were not exotic. The whole phenomenon of people wearing monochrome shirts and organizing phalanges and calling for the resurrection of ancient empires was definitely a trend of the moment.

But, in drawing up my list of similarities between Islamism and Baath Socialism on one side, and the fascism of Europe on the other, I don't want to lean too heavily on superficial resemblances, on phalanges and ancient fantasies and readings in German philosophy, which may be suggestive but are bound to mislead, sooner or later. Let me turn instead to Islamist theory—to what the Islamists actually say.

THE SINGLE most influential writer in the Islamist tradition, at least among the Sunni Arabs, is generally recognized to be Sayyid Qutb of Egypt, a formidable person. Qutb was born in 1906, the same year as Hassan al-Banna, and seven years before Camus—his fellow North Africans. Qutb grew up in a village in Upper Egypt and received a proper religious education. His biographer, S. Badrul Hasan—the author of *Syed Qutb Shaheed*, published in Karachi in 1980—quotes, in a Pakistani inflection, a few of Qutb's childhood recollections. They come from a book that Qutb dedicated to his mother:

> O my mother! During the whole month of Ramadan when in our village home the Readers *(Qari)* of the Holy Qur'an recited the

> verses in their melodious voice, you listened the same for hours with rapt attention from behind the curtain. Sitting with you when I made noise just as is the habit with the children you stopped me from doing so with gestures and signs and then I also used to listen the same with you attentively. My heart enjoyed the magical rhythm of the words, although I was unaware of their meaning then.
>
> As I was brought up under your caressing care you sent me to the primary school of the village. It was your sincerest and greatest desire that Allah may open my heart and I should commit the Holy Qur'an to memory and Allah may bestow upon me the art of sweet recital and I may, sitting before you, all the time recite the Holy Qur'an. I therefore, memorized the Holy Book and thus a part of your desire was fulfilled.

He was ten years old when he completed the task of memorization, and then it was on to higher education in Cairo and a career in the Egyptian Ministry of Education. This was, then, a man with a pious and traditional upbringing. And yet, tradition is not what it used to be. According to Hasan, Qutb played with socialism for a while. He took up literature. The books that he began to write reflected—here I quote his admirer and translator, Hamid Algar of the University of California at Berkeley—a "Western-tinged outlook on cultural and literary questions."

Qutb displayed "traces of individualism and existentialism." He even traveled to the United States, where he studied at the University of Northern Colorado at Greeley and received a master's in education. He already considered himself a devout and perhaps even a radical Islamist, which meant that everything about the United States was bound to rub him wrong—the national mood, habits, materialism, racism, vices, pastimes, business practices, and sexual freedom, not to mention America's larger politics and policies. But on these topics

Qutb was perhaps of two minds. He returned to Egypt in 1951 and threw himself more actively than before into the Islamist movement.

He enrolled in al-Banna's Muslim Brotherhood (though al-Banna had been assassinated by then). And Qutb became the movement's leading thinker—the Arab world's first important theoretician of the Islamist cause. He edited the Muslim Brotherhood's official journal, until it was suppressed. Yet all the while he had to struggle, as he confesses in his pamphlet *Milestones*, against his own liberal impulses—"the cultural influences which had penetrated my mind in spite of my Islamic attitudes and inclination." He sounded like Michel Aflaq complaining about the "philosophies and teachings" which "invade the Arab mind"—quite as if these two men, the theoreticians respectively of radical Islamism and Baath Socialism, were speaking of identical mental struggles.

The early 1950s were trying times in Egypt. The year after Qutb's return, in 1952, Gamal Abdel Nasser and a group of other military officers overthrew the Egyptian king, announced a nationalist revolution along Pan-Arabist lines, and turned to the Muslim Brotherhood for popular support. According to Professor Algar, Nasser visited Qutb at his home in Cairo four days before the coup, which has got to be an indication, at the minimum, of Qutb's political influence. There were intimations after the coup that Qutb might be given the Ministry of Education, where he had worked in lesser positions. Nasser's Revolutionary Council and Qutb's Muslim Brotherhood did not get along, though.

The Muslim Brotherhood wanted to see alcohol banned in the new, revolutionary Egypt, as a first step toward instituting shariah, or Islamic law. (On this point, Qutb could not have complained too much about the United States. Greeley, Colorado, where he studied, was a dry town.) But the Revolutionary Council was not inclined to prohibition. The Muslim Brotherhood and the Revolutionary Council differed on the vexed topic of Egypt's relations to Britain, the former imperial master, and the Revolutionary Council finally turned against the Muslim Brotherhood, and vice versa—which is to say, the Brotherhood, having gotten underway in 1928 as a mostly religious movement, veered all the way into revolutionary subversion. Nasser banned the organization in 1954, then undid the ban. There was an attempt on Nasser's life, which was attributed to the Muslim Brotherhood—and the ban was reinstated.

But state suppression succeeded only in scattering the Brotherhood's influence across the whole of the Muslim world. Leading figures from the Muslim Brotherhood fled from Egypt to Saudi Arabia, and the Saudi rulers welcomed them, and put them to good use. The Saudi princes were determined to keep their own country on a path of pure adherence to Saudi Arabia's antique and rigid version of Islam; and Egypt's Islamist intellectuals, with their stores of Koranic knowledge, had much to offer. The Egyptian exiles took over professorial chairs in Saudi universities. And their impact was large. Qutb's younger brother, Muhammad Qutb, a distinguished religious scholar in his own right, fled to Saudi Arabia and became a professor of Islamic Studies. One of his students was Osama bin Laden. Still, not everyone from the Muslim Brotherhood went into exile, and among those who stayed behind was Sayyid Qutb. He paid dearly for his stubbornness, too. Nasser jailed him in 1954, released him, and jailed him again after the assassination attempt. Except for eight months in 1965, Qutb spent the rest of his life in prison. In 1966, at the age of sixty-one, he was hanged.

Conditions during his first three years of prison were evidently very bad. He was tortured. In later years, though, he was given a bit more freedom and, from his cell, he returned to his religious studies. He wrote prolifically, no longer in the "Western-tinged" vein of his early, literary days, nor in the pre–Muslim Brotherhood vein of *Social Justice in Islam*, but in the vein of a full-fledged Islamist revolutionary. *Milestones*, his manifesto from 1964, which draws on his prison letters and other writings, seems to me the least interesting of his books—though it did become his most influential work. Another of his pamphlets, *Islam: The Religion of the Future* (which likewise has the look of having been drawn from other writings), strikes me as far more stimulating and ambitious.

But his true masterwork is something else entirely, a gargantuan, thirty-volume exegesis called *In the Shade of the Qur'an*, which consists of commentaries on the various chapters or *surahs* of the Koran. *In the Shade of the Qur'an* is not easy to get hold of, outside the centers of Islam. Still, in trolling the Islamic bookstores of Brooklyn, I have come across volumes 1, 4, and 30, which Islamic publishers around the world have been slowly bringing out in English. And this, Qutb's exegetical extravaganza, turns out to be a fascinating work.

In these books, Qutb quotes passages from the surahs, which are presented in a magnificent Arabic calligraphy and then are translated into English verse or prose. And he pores over those quoted passages in the manner of a French *explication de texte*. He observes the prosodic qualities of the verse, the rhythm, tonality, and musicality of the words, sometimes the images. He elucidates ideas, the controversies that may surround any given text, and the true intention or meaning, as he judges it. The surahs lead him to discuss dietary regulations, the proper direction to pray, the nature of prayer, the rules of divorce, the question of when a man may suggest marriage to a widow (four months and ten days after the death of her husband, unless she is pregnant, in which case after delivery), the rules concerning a Muslim who wishes to marry a Christian or a Jew (very complicated), the obligations of charity, the punishment for crimes and for breaking one's word, the *hajj* or pilgrimage to Mecca, the prohibition on liquor and intoxicants, the proper clothing to wear, the rules on usury and moneylending and a thousand other themes.

Sometimes he wanders from the text at hand to dwell for a moment on larger ideas that seem apropos, and the larger ideas send him rambling across the centuries, from the time of the early Hebrews into the modern age. Charles Darwin and his place in what Qutb regards as the proper Islamic worldview come up for discussion, and likewise the studies of Orientalist professors in the West, on whom Qutb casts a cold eye. The Koran tells stories, and Qutb recounts some of these and remarks on their wisdom and significance. He is always lucid and plain. Yet the total effect is almost sensual in its measured pace. The very title of *In the Shade of the Qur'an* conveys a vivid desert image, as if the Koran were a leafy palm tree, and we have only to open Qutb's pages to escape from the hot sun and refresh ourselves in the shade.

His tone is grave, sometimes urgent, and at still other times seems to catch itself and slow down into a rhythm of tranquility—rather like a man whose knee is thumping, and who, reminding himself to keep calm, stretches his muscles languorously. In the introduction to Volume 30, Qutb's brother, Muhammad, suggests that, as a result of his sufferings, Sayyid Qutb's writing and thinking took a more serious turn in his later years of Islamist commitment. This must certainly be true. But I think the tone of gravity and urgency owes to something more than jail and persecution.

Qutb explains that a proper understanding of the Koran can be achieved only in an atmosphere of serious struggle, and only by someone who is engaged in a ferocious campaign for Islam, not by someone at ease in his chair. The Koran, he observes, does not merely offer a body of knowledge, to be plucked at will, as if from a tree. The Koran offers a way to live. Understanding its truth therefore requires an active engagement with life—perhaps a painful engagement, something searing, though Qutb also emphasizes the beauty of the Koran and the pleasures to be had from studying it.

The astounding length at which he elaborates his interpretations expresses one aspect of this notion about truth and engagement. The Koran, he observes, was dictated by Allah to Muhammad over a period of many years. Qutb wanted his readers likewise to spend years of their lives studying his own commentary, reading his snippets of Koranic verse and analyzing his apposite remarks, all in a purposeful spirit of intensity and engagement—reading not for pleasure but with the zeal of soldiers studying their orders. Qutb's commentaries were in this respect meant to be more than aids to understanding. They were meant to be an activity, designed to occupy goodly portions of the reader's energy and time. And this approach of his, the painstaking details, the unhurried patience, the rhythm of the commentaries, the calm tone (when it was calm), the deep well of his knowledge, ends up creating a powerful impression.

Turning his pages, you are reminded, if you need any such reminder, that Islam resembles one of its own gigantic and magnificent mosques, awesome in scale and in its details, grander by far than any mere doctrine or set of rituals—something that begins to seem as large as life itself, and even larger. The notion of Islam as totality was, I would venture, Qutb's most important concept. The concept of totality, he thought, distinguished Islam from all other worldviews—*Tawhid*, or the oneness of God. (Then again, you find the same belief among the Marxists: "the primacy of the category of totality" was, for George Lukacs, the defining characteristic of Marxism—what distinguished Marxist thought from bourgeois thought.) Every page of *In the Shade of the Qur'an* can be seen as a commentary on the single affirmation, "There is no God but Allah." Every new theme and topic offered Qutb a fresh opportunity to demonstrate that nature, man, and man's obligations come from a single source, which is God. And Islam is the acknowledgment of that one overwhelming reality.

But there is more to be said about Qutb's notion of truth and engagement. The idea that truth can be obtained only through some kind of active struggle has been expressed in many modes and by many people over the centuries; and on this point, too, Qutb mirrored some of the Marxists. Lukacs's philosophical comrade of the 1920s, Karl Korsch, the German Marxist, used to argue that Marx's dialectic can be understood only at certain moments in history, and not at other moments. For only at times of intense class struggle do the clouds part and reveal the true nature of society and of its future, which is proletarian revolution. Sidney Hook, the American philosopher, proposed a variation of that same idea during his own period as a revolutionary Marxist in the 1930s, mostly by weaving a combination of Marx's dialectic and John Dewey's Pragmatist notion of truth.

In Hook's variation, truth can be established only by scientific experiment—which, in the sphere of political and social life, can only mean revolutionary action. Truth is not a book, which can be read. Truth is discovered by hurling yourself into militant effort, and judging the results. Truth shows itself in combat, or not at all. Those Marxist ideas, the theories of Korsch and Hook, were super-activist in temper—hot ideas, sizzling with the urge to turn the world upside down. And Qutb, from his Egyptian prison twenty or thirty years later, sizzled at an even greater heat. He makes the plain suggestion that Koranic truth, to be grasped properly, requires not just a serious experience of religious commitment, but of revolutionary action on Islam's behalf; and action is bound to exact its price. And so, there is a suggestion, never quite laid out in what I have read, that martyrdom and truth are linked.

Qutb begins Volume 1 of *In the Shade of the Qur'an* by saying, "To live 'in the shade of the Qur'an' is a great blessing which can only be fully appreciated by those who experience it. It is a rich experience that gives meaning to life and makes it worth living. I am deeply thankful to God Almighty for blessing me with this uplifting experience for a considerable time, which was the happiest and most fruitful period of my life—a privilege for which I am eternally grateful."

But what was that happiest and most fruitful period of Qutb's life, which lasted, as he says, a considerable time? He doesn't say. Perhaps he had some specific and very pleasant period in mind, which his brother and other intimates would have recognized. But the reader can only imagine that Qutb is writing about his years of torture and prison.

One of his Indian publishers, Bilal Books in Mumbai, highlights this point in a remarkably gruesome manner by attaching an unsigned preface to a 1998 edition of *Milestones*. The preface declares, "The ultimate price for working to please God Almighty and to propagate his ways in this world is often one's own life. The author"—Qutb, that is—"tried to do it; he paid for it with his life. If you and I try to do it, there is every likelihood we will be called upon to do the same. But for those who truly believe in God, what other choice is there?"

You are meant to suppose that a true reader of Sayyid Qutb is someone who, in the degree that he properly digests Qutb's message, will act on what has been digested; and action may well bring on a martyr's death. To read is to glide forward toward death; and gliding toward death means you have understood what you are reading. Qutb's writings vibrate to that morbid tone—not always, but sometimes. In one of the strictures against the Jews in his Koranic commentaries, he observes, "The Koran points to another contemptible characteristic of the Jews: their craven desire to live, no matter at what price and regardless of quality, honor and dignity." Qutb's desires are not at all craven in that particular fashion. Despair is desire, here. His Indian publisher has not been false to him. And yet, Qutb's tone is not hysterical—except occasionally.

HIS ANALYSIS of contemporary life and its problems is easy enough to summarize—though in summarizing, I cannot avoid simplifying a few points, nor can I lay out the evolution of his thinking from the early and slightly more moderate writings to the super-radical ideas of his later years. Qutb felt that modern culture all over the world had reached a moment of unbearable crisis. Everywhere, man was ill at ease and alienated from his own nature. The human quality of modern life—I am drawing this from *Islam: The Religion of the Future*—was "sliding downward." Man's inspiration, intelligence, and morality were degenerating. Sexual relations were deteriorating "to a level lower than the beasts." Man was miserable, anxious, and skeptical, his "basic functions inoperative, debilitated, and atrophied," "suffering from affliction, distress, nervous and psychological diseases, perversion, idiocy, insanity and crime." Man was roving "without destination," "killing his monotony and weariness by such means as exhaust the soul, body and nerves: adopting narcotics, alcohol and the like perverted dark ideas, desperate and elusive doctrines such as existentialism and its disastrous analogous ideologies."

The same worries preoccupied him in the volumes of *In the Shade of the Qur'an*. In his exegesis of Surah 2, or *The Cow* (sometimes translated as *The Heifer*), he observed that even in "the most affluent and materially advanced" of Western societies—he cited the United States and Sweden—people lead "the most miserable lives." "They have lost touch with their own souls." He admired economic productivity and scientific knowledge—Sayyid Qutb was not an anti-modernist, though he is often described that way by Western writers. But he was keen to identify the limitations and inadequacies of high productivity and affluence. In his exegesis of Surah 5, or *The Repast*, he commented:

> We must not be deluded by false appearances when we see that nations which do not believe or implement the Divine method are enjoying abundance and affluence. It is all a temporary prosperity which lasts until the natural laws have produced their effects, allowing the consequences of the miserable split between material excellence and spiritual fulfillment to appear in full. We see some of these consequences surface in a variety of ways.
>
> We see first maldistribution within these nations, which allows hatred, grudges, misery and fear of the unexpected to take root. This is, indeed, an ominous state of affairs, despite prosperity. We

> also see suppression and fear dominant in those nations which have tried to ensure at least a partially fair distribution. To achieve this, they have resorted to destruction, suppression, and terror in order to enforce their measures of redistribution. In this terrible state of affairs, man is always in fear, never reassured.
>
> We also see the weakening of moral values which leads, sooner or later, to the destruction of material prosperity. . . . We also see all types of worry spreading throughout the world, particularly in the most affluent of societies. This inevitably makes people less intelligent and reduces their tolerance. It then leads to lowering standards of work and productivity. Very clear indications of this impending development can easily be recognized at the present time.
>
> We see the fear, which engulfs all humanity, of the total ruin which threatens the whole world at any moment, as risks of all-out war continue to be in the air. Such fear places great strain on people's minds, whether they realize it or not. It leads to a whole range of nervous disorders. Is it not significant that death through heart failure, mental disease and suicide are at their highest rate in affluent societies?

He cited the French, whose lives seemed to him exceptionally dismal. But he had all of the wealthy countries in mind. He was describing a global condition, therefore something systematic.

Now, in making these arguments, Qutb was not saying anything terribly unusual. In the Western countries at midcentury, similar criticisms were expressed by all kinds of social critics on the left and the right alike. All of those Western critics, left-wing and right-wing, presumed that man has an authentic nature. All of them presumed that, because of the pressures of modern civilization and its technological methods, man has had to adopt a new, technologically shaped personality, at odds with his authentic nature. All of those critics presumed that, in becoming alienated from his own nature, modern man has sunk into a wretched state—a misery that swallows up human life even in conditions of material plenty.

But what was the cause of this terrible alienation, the cause of this misery? Where did those horrendous modern pressures come from, ultimately? Marx would have pointed to capitalism, but Marx was a man of the nineteenth century. In the twentieth century, the philosophers of alienation pointed instead to something older and perhaps less easily repaired, dating back to the origins of Western civilization. There was the idea that you see in Heidegger, or, for that matter, in D. H. Lawrence and a dozen other people—the idea that mankind's fatal error began with Socrates in ancient Greece. The error consisted of an arrogant and deluded faith in the power of human reason—the arrogant faith which, after many centuries, produced in modern times the tyranny of technology over life.

That was Qutb's idea. He, too, put the blame on ancient Greece, though he did this somewhat indirectly, by speaking about Jerusalem instead of about Athens. In Qutb's estimation, mankind's fatal error was committed by the earliest Christians, during the time of Jesus and in the following generations. Like all Muslims, Qutb looked on Judaism as the original religion, divinely revealed by God to Adam, Moses, and the prophets—a religion which instructed man to worship one God, and to forswear all others. But Judaism, as Qutb well understood, was more than a message. It was a code of behavior, the Mosaic Code, which dictated correct activity in every sphere of life, and refused to draw any distinction between the sacred and the secular. And why did the Mosaic Code refuse to draw such a distinction? Here, in Qutb's view, was ancient Judaism's particular merit. The Mosaic Code refused to separate the sacred from the secular because there is only one God. Any line between sacred and secular would suggest that, in the business of daily life, there is more than one ultimate authority. But that would imply the existence of more than one God.

Judaism marked only a stage along mankind's path, and, after a while, withered into what Qutb called "a system of rigid and lifeless ritual." Jesus arrived, however, and, through further revelations from God, offered a few corrections to the Jewish rites, an improvement in the dietary code, and other reforms. Jesus tried to bestow on Judaism a complementary new dimension, which was purely spiritual, much needed among the Jews, with their lifeless habits. Jesus was a true messenger of God. His teachings pushed man to live in a still more harmonious relation with his own divinely bestowed nature and with the entire universe, which is God's. Only, a pity—the transition from the Judaism of old to Jesus' new reforms went badly, and the relation between Jesus and the Jews took, Qutb tells us, "a deplorable course."

Jesus attracted followers from the gentile population, but the Jews themselves tended to resist him and his teachings. And, in the squabbling that ensued, the value of Jesus' message was diluted and even perverted. Jesus' disciples and followers were persecuted, which meant that, under the difficult conditions of repression, the disciples were never able to provide an adequate or systematic exposition of Jesus' message. Who but Sayyid Qutb, from his jail cell in Nasser's Egypt, could have zeroed in so plausibly on the difficulties encountered by the disciples in getting out the Word? Qutb figured that, as a result, the Gospels were badly garbled, and cannot be regarded as accurate or reliable. Worse: in their acrimonious dispute with the Jews, Jesus' disciples allowed themselves to go too far in rejecting the Jewish teachings.

The followers of Jesus accepted the Jewish scriptures as divinely revealed, and incorporated them into their own (highly unreliable) Gospels. And yet, for all their piety about the Jewish texts, the new Christians, owing to "this unpleasant separation between the two parties," kept certain aspects of Judaism's teachings at arm's length. The Christians put their emphasis on Jesus' message of spirituality and love, and that was good. But they lost sight of the Mosaic Code. Instead, the disciple Paul introduced a very different set of ideas, which he drew—and here Qutb rejoined the larger trend of twentieth-century thought—from Greek philosophy, together with a bit of Roman mythology. The Greco-Roman input proved catastrophic. The new ideas watered down Jesus' original revelation, which stunted the whole of Christianity's subsequent development. For how were the Christians going to govern their daily lives, with only Roman myths and Greek philosophies to guide them? Christianity needed the code of Moses, as emended by Jesus, and this had been lost. Then came a still worse disaster.

In the fourth century of the Christian Era, Emperor Constantine officially converted the Roman Empire to Christianity. But he did so in a spirit of pagan hypocrisy—a spirit dominated by (and here, in a marvelous example of cross-cultural influence, Qutb in *Islam: The Religion of the Future* cited a nineteenth-century American writer named J. W. Draper) scenes of wantonness, half-naked girls, gems and precious metals. Christianity, having forsaken the Mosaic Code, could put up no defense. So the Christians, in their horror at Roman morals, did as best they could and countered the imperial debaucheries with a cult of monastic asceticism. Monastic asceticism, however, stands at odds with human nature. And so Christianity, torn this way and that, ended up fighting a war within itself—Constantine's pagan debauch on one side, monastic renunciation on the other.

It was a schizophrenic division in the Christian mentality. Nor did things heal over with time. During the later Roman centuries a series of religious councils adopted irrational principles on Christianity's behalf—principles regarding the nature of Jesus, the Eucharist, transubstantiation, and other questions, all of which were, in Qutb's view, "absolutely incomprehensible, inconceivable and incredible." Church teachings froze the irrational elements into dogma. And the ultimate crisis finally struck. Islam was founded in the seventh century of the Christian Era, and established a correct, non-distorted relation to the physical world.

In one of his many striking summaries of this relation, Qutb described Islam in this fashion, apropos of two Koranic verses regarding menstruation: "It is a religion that does not deny man any of his natural tendencies or instincts, or pretend to achieve human purity by suppressing or destroying man's basic physical needs. Rather, Islam disciplines, guides and fosters these desires and needs in a manner that reinforces man's humanity and invigorates his consciousness of, and relationship with, God. It seeks to blend physical and sensual tendencies with human and religious emotions, thus bringing together the transient pleasures and the immutable values of human life into one harmonious and congruent system that will render man worthy of being God's representative on earth."

But then, if man is God's representative, or, in the language of the Koran, is God's "vice regent on earth," man has every obligation to investigate and rule over nature on God's behalf. Islam therefore points man toward science, and not away from it. The Islamic notion of man and his relation to the physical world led, in the Islamic universities of Andalusia and the East, to the discovery of the inductive or scientific method—which opened the door to all further scientific and technological progress.

Tragically, though, the Muslim world, having seized the leadership of mankind, lost its grip on Islamic principles, and went into decline. The fall took place quickly, too, tentatively in the third Caliphate after Muhammad and definitively in the fifth, under the reign of the Umayyad dynasty—even if the Islamic Empire (which Qutb declined to describe as an empire: he preferred "community") continued to spread. The Muslim world's moral decline was compounded by a series of attacks in the Middle Ages from Mongols, Spanish Christians, Crusaders, and Zionists. (Zionism in Qutb's writings has a somewhat supernatural quality, which exists outside of history.) And the Muslim world, in its debilitated state, proved unable to capitalize on its brilliant discovery of the scientific method.

The Muslim discoveries were exported instead into Christian Europe. And there, in Europe in the sixteenth century, the method began to generate results, and modern science emerged. Science nonetheless ran into difficulties in Europe, too. The principles of science were at one with Islam, but they collided with the dogma of the Christian Church. The priests insisted on the irrational components of their creed. They insisted on locking scientific knowledge into one more unalterable dogma, to be enforced by church power. And the scientists fought back.

In this unfortunate fashion, the schizophrenic aspect of Christian thought, already severe in the realm of daily life and personal behavior, spread into the realm of scientific knowledge. The European imagination pictured God on one side, and science on the other. Religion, over here; the physical world, over there. On one side, the natural human yearning for God and for a divinely ordered life; on the other side, the natural human desire for knowledge of the physical universe. The Church against science; the scientists against the Church. Everything that Islam knew to be one, the Christian Church divided into two. And, finally, the European mind split asunder. Schizophrenia became total. Christianity, over here; atheism, over there. It was, in Qutb's phrase, the "hideous schizophrenia" of modern life.

Europe's scientific and technical achievements allowed it to snatch the leadership of mankind away from Islam, and to dominate the world; and, unrestrained by the weakened forces of Islam, Europe inflicted its hideous schizophrenia on peoples and cultures in every corner of the globe. That was the source of the miseries of modern life—the source of the anxiety in contemporary society, the sense of drift, the purposelessness, the craving for false pleasures, the anomie, the alienation.

The crisis of modern life was felt by every thinking person in the Christian West—but, because of Europe's leadership of mankind, the crisis was also felt by every thinking person in the Muslim world. And here Qutb did say something unusual—something extraordinary and new. The Christians of the West underwent the crisis of modern life, the hideous schizophrenia, as a consequence of their own theological tradition. But, if Qutb was right, the Muslims had to undergo that same crisis or experience of schizophrenia because it had been imposed on them from the outside, which could only make it doubly painful—an alienation that was also a humiliation.

That was Qutb's analysis. In writing about the hideous schizophrenia of modern life, he had put his finger on precisely the inner experience that Salman Rushdie described in *The Satanic Verses* many years later—the schizophrenia or alienation, the feeling of being two instead of one, the pain of living in two worlds at once, the experience that Muhammad Atta and the suicide soldiers of 9/11 must surely have felt in their everyday existences in the West. Qutb had described a universal experience. But he described it in a specifically Muslim version, with an explanation that put the blame not on anything vague such as modernity or human nature but on something specific and identifiable—namely, on Christianity, and its doleful influence on modern culture, as exported by the power of the Western countries.

Qutb trembled in fear at the hideous schizophrenia. He thought the crisis was enormous and incomparably profound. Deep currents of theological and ecclesiastical deviation, two thousand years of Christian error, were bearing that crisis atop the roiling waves. And the tide was rushing forward, across the Muslim world.

IV

The Hideous Schizophrenia

QUTB'S ANALYSIS WAS rich, nuanced, deep, soulful, and heartfelt. The analysis did not rest on two or three simple factors, the way that nineteenth-century analyses sometimes did. It was a theological analysis, but, in its cultural emphases, it had the twentieth-century style. The analysis asked some authentically perplexing questions—about the division between mind and body in Western thought; about the difficulties in striking a practical balance between sensual experience and spiritual elevation; about the soullessness of modern power and technological innovation; about social injustice. But, though Qutb was evidently following some main trends of twentieth-century social criticism and philosophy, he made a great show of referring to European or American thinkers as rarely as possible, except pejoratively or polemically. He wanted to show that Islam was self-sufficient—that Islam did not need the thinkers of the West, could rely on its own spectacular resources of the past, was all-inclusive, independent, and fully adequate. And so, he poured his ideas through a filter of Koranic commentary, and the filter gave his commentary a grainy new texture, something original. And the Islamic texture enabled him to make a number of telling criticisms.

He turned to the partisans of racial theory, who were many in Egypt and even included a few Nazis on the lam, in the years after their defeat in Europe. (To cite a famous example, Joseph Goebbels's adjunct, Johann von Leers, the author of *The Crimes of Judaism*, found a refuge in Egypt during the 1950s, converted to Islam, and went to work in Nasser's propaganda agency.) Qutb, judging from *Islam: The Religion of the Future*, admired the writings of Alexis Carrel, a French eugenicist and Nobel Prize winner, famous for his Nazi sympathies during the Vichy period. But what Qutb liked about Carrel was his condemnation of modern materialism and its encroachments on "the values of man," the humanistic side of Europe's extreme right—and not Carrel's scientific approach to the modern crisis or his proposed scientific solutions. For the crisis of modern man was not racial or biological. It was theological. There was no point in looking for scientific solutions. The racist parties and movements that had arisen in the twentieth century—"all nationalistic and chauvinistic ideologies which have appeared in modern times, and all the movements and theories which have derived from them"—had been proven wrong. They had "lost their vitality."

He warned against chauvinist ideas even in the case of the Arabs. What made for Arab greatness in the past, he thought, was anything but chauvinism. The greatness of the Arabs came from the greatness of the Arab goal, which was to liberate the world from ignorance. "Every nation which assumed the leadership of humanity in any period of history advanced an ideology," Qutb wrote, in his commentary on Surah 105, or *The Elephant.* (Or was it Hegel who wrote that line? Hegel said: "The nation whose concept of the spirit is highest is in tune with the times and rules over the others.") The Arabs, in their time of greatness, advanced a very specific ideology—a concept of the spirit that was higher than anyone else's, the highest concept of all. That concept was Islam. The message of Muhammad took the Arabs and "raised them to the position of human leadership." On this issue, Qutb and the Baath Socialists once again saw eye to eye. Qutb was generous toward other nations, though. Islamic civilization was magnificent, at its height many centuries ago. But, as he specified (and now I'm quoting *Milestones*), "this marvelous civilization was not an 'Arabic civilization' even for a single day; it was purely an 'Islamic civilization.' It was never a 'nationality' but always a 'community of belief.'" That was Qutb's argument against the nationalist ideologues.

He went after Marxism, too. By the late 1940s Marxism looked like the wave of the future in Western Europe, and not just there. Qutb, like many people, thought the Soviet Union was likely to win the Cold War. Nasser certainly thought so, and, in spite of his several links to the ultra-right in Europe, drew closer to the Soviet Union through the 1950s and into the '60s. But Qutb would have none of that. He looked on the Cold War in the Western countries as a battle between Christian spirituality, on one side, and communism's call for social justice, on the other. Nothing in that battle seemed of any value, in his judgment. The entire Cold War was merely one more example of the Western world's hideous schizophrenia—a battle that took the divine spirit, which is also a spirit of social justice, and split it into two.

Marxism itself struck him as the ne plus ultra of every ghastly trait that had developed in Europe. Marxism reduced man to his animal wants and material needs. Marxism could not possibly resolve or rectify man's alienation from his own nature. Marxism was itself part of modern man's alienation from human nature and the divine. Marxism was a downward step from the human to the animal—a descent from civilization into barbarism, which is to say, from the worship of God to the worship of material things. Besides, Islam defends private property, and Marxism was wrong on this point.

But the largest part of Qutb's criticism took aim at a different target. It was the place accorded to religion in liberal society. The whole purpose of liberalism was to put religion in one corner, and the state in a different corner, and to keep those corners apart. The liberal idea arose in the seventeenth century in England and Scotland, and the philosophers who invented it wanted to prevent the English Civil War, which had just taken place, from breaking out again. So they proposed to scoop up the cause of that war, which was religion, and, in the gentlest way, to cart it off to another place, which was the sphere of private life, where every church and sect could freely rail at each of the others.

Liberalism wanted to carve up life into different slices and keep each of those slices in its proper spot. The churches, from their place in private life, would be free to bestow blessings and curses. But they would not be able to enforce their blessings and curses by calling out the police. The state, by contrast, would be free to call out the police—but would not have the power to bestow blessings and curses. The idea of maintaining a separation between material powers and spiritual powers was wonderfully practical, but also more than practical. There was grandeur in that idea. It held out a vision of freedom not just for one group of people and their favorite doctrine, but for everyone—a society in which each and every individual might entertain religious or spiritual doctrines of his own, perhaps in harmony with everyone else's, or not, but freely, either way.

That was exactly what Qutb could not abide. He understood very clearly how religion is treated in liberal societies. In *Milestones*, he described the kind of social system in which, unlike in Communist society, "God's existence is not denied, but His domain is restricted to the heavens and His rule on earth is suspended." Very likely he had the United States in mind, though he might also have been thinking of France. In that kind of social system, "people are permitted to go to mosques, churches and synagogues." It was remarkable that he listed mosques first. He was not looking to make cheap shots against the liberal countries—was not trying to shine a spotlight on liberal hypocrisies, on the grandiose boasts of supreme tolerance that liberal societies sometimes make, and fail to fulfill. He took liberal society at its best—a society in which Muslims would, in fact, enjoy the same religious freedom as everyone else. But liberalism at its best held no appeal, to him. A liberal society restricts God's domain to the heavens. And by doing so, "such a society denies or suspends God's sovereignty on earth."

Freedom in a liberal society seemed to Qutb no freedom at all. That kind of freedom was merely one more expression of the hideous schizophrenia—the giant error that places the material world over here, and God over there. Qutb considered that, in a liberal society, religion has been reduced to a set of rituals and a private morality, quite as if the individual human heart were the final arbiter of moral behavior. But the human heart is not the final arbiter. The final arbiter is God.

Qutb was intrigued by John Foster Dulles, Eisenhower's secretary of state. Dulles was an earnest Christian, and he wrote a book called *War or Peace*, urging the Christians of America to do a better job of resisting the lures of commercial materialism. Dulles wanted to fend off communism and its social criticisms by strengthening Christian spirituality in America. "What we lack," said Dulles, "is a righteous and dynamic faith." But Qutb looked at Dulles's arguments as one more sign of how pitifully the religious sentiment had shriveled in the liberal West. Christianity could not begin to resist the lures of materialism or to fend off communism. It was because of the theological deviations perpetrated by the disciple Paul, and because of everything that had followed. Christianity had adopted a false relation to the material world. Christianity had fled from daily life into the spirit. Christianity had accepted what Qutb called a "desolate separation between this Church and society." And nothing in the Christian repertory of possible responses and certainly not the preachings of the secretary of state could undo the "bitter consequences."

The very notion of bringing religion together with a capitalist economy, as Dulles wanted to do, struck Qutb as preposterous. A serious religion, Qutb thought, would insist on the abolition of usury—the abolition of conventional profit seeking and interest on loans, the abolition of naked self-advancement, in order to build an economic system on the ethical and moral practices that are sanctioned by God. Dulles was not going to demand any such thing. Qutb arrived at a withering conclusion: "Mr. Dulles wants merely to mobilize a religiously-veneered patriotism that might protect the Western order from communism." That was pathetic, in Qutb's eyes. It showed the depths to which religion had sunk, in a liberal society.

Qutb examined the slogan, "Culture is the human heritage"—an expression of liberal sympathy and appreciation for cultural achievements from every part of the world. In the liberal idea, just as people ought to enjoy the freedom to practice religion in any form they choose, they ought to enjoy the freedom to savor the cultural achievements that societies all over the world have produced. Those two freedoms—cultural and religious—stand together, in the liberal idea, as foundation stones of a free society. But this notion, too, made Qutb uncomfortable. He was happy to accept the notion of cultural freedom in a limited sense—freedom for everyone to benefit from scientific achievements. Science did seem to him universal—even if, in his view, Islamic concepts of science departed essentially from Western concepts. But he worried about the philosophical, literary, and artistic values of other societies. In Western society, philosophy, literature, and the arts expressed and conveyed the deepest understandings of Western life—which is to say, the idea that God ought to stay in the zone of the spirit, and keep away from ordinary society. But that was precisely the idea that had introduced the hideous schizophrenia to Western life and, by spreading, had brought calamity to the world.

The principles of American education struck him as especially insidious, to be avoided at all cost. The founding principles of American education derived, in his estimation, from the philosophical doctrine of Pragmatism, as expounded by—he mentioned these names—Charles Sanders Peirce, William James, and John Dewey. But Pragmatism relegates the concept of divinity to a "cash" analysis—to a materialistic weighing of losses and benefits. In the Pragmatist idea, you might believe in God or not, depending on whether you find benefits in believing. This was cultural freedom taken to its furthest extreme. It struck Qutb as one step from communism—that is, from outright atheism. He worried—this was in 1949, with Stalin visibly on the march—that Pragmatist philosophy and American materialism were going to end up delivering America over to the Communists, sooner or later.

The statement, "Culture is the human heritage," seemed to him, all in all, a Jewish conspiracy. This has to be explained. Qutb wrote repeatedly and at length about the Jews, and did so on the best of theological grounds, given that, as he says, "the story of the Israelites is the one most frequently mentioned in the Koran." The Koran's version of that story is rather unfriendly, from a Jewish perspective. Muhammad went to Medina and preached and gathered followers. But the Jewish tribes were prominent there. They dominated Medina financially and even morally, because of their ability to interpret holy scripture. (I can't help asking, if the Jews of the Middle East have no right to their own country in Israel, as Qutb believed, does this mean they can have Medina instead?) And the Medina Jews put their influence to bad effect.

Muhammad announced that he was a messenger of the God, and the Jews received him coldly. Some of the Medina Jews prayed by bowing in the direction of Jerusalem, Qutb tells us, and Muhammad likewise bowed in the direction of Jerusalem. But Muhammad changed his mind, and bowed in the direction of Mecca. The Jews wouldn't go along. Muhammad and the Jews disagreed over dietary regulations. Finally, the Jews simply refused to accept Muhammad's claim to be a divine messenger. The Jews benefited materially from their monopoly over scriptural interpretation in Medina, which meant that, if Muhammad were acknowledged as the messenger of God, the Jews would lose their advantages—their "money, wealth, and worldly aggrandizement." So they plotted against him.

They were vicious and conniving. They encouraged and nurtured Muhammad's false or "hypocritical" followers, and encouraged his outright enemies. They threw skeptical arguments in his direction. Muhammad established the Islamic State in Medina, and his pagan enemies went to war against him, with the hope of putting an end to Islam, and the Jews supported the pagans. All of this, I must say, is fascinating to read. The entire story of Muhammad and the Medina Jews does rather echo the Gospel story of Jesus and the Jerusalem Jews, from seven hundred years earlier—the story of a messenger from God and of the Jews who reject and persecute him, with the important difference that, in the Koranic story, God's prophet survives his Jewish tormentors (though, in the Koran, Jesus likewise survives and avoids crucifixion). There is something eery in those parallels between the Gospels and the Koran. And, rather like the Gospels, the Koran gives the Jews a pretty hard time about these things.

At one moment in Surah 5, Allah grows wrathful at the Jews and curses some of them and transforms them into apes and pigs. The Jews are said to be wicked, treacherous, iniquitous, usurious, unlawful, ungrateful, blasphemous, transgressive, untrustworthy, hardhearted, deceitful, disputatious, and prone to eat the wrong foods. On the other hand, in a few passages the Jews are offered forgiveness. Surah 5 says: "But forgive them, and overlook/ (Their misdeeds); for Allah/ Loveth those who are kind." The surah observes that, in spite of their every terrible deed, some of the Jews are good and pious people. A modern reader of the Koran who wanted to derive a tolerant attitude for the present day could certainly seize on those few passages and work up a liberal interpretation. My edition of the Koran, a 1989 scholarly re-edition of an older English-language translation by Abdullah Yusuf Ali, cites Qutb as an authority, and yet, in un-Qutb-like fashion, contains notes and comments expounding upon the tolerant passages. The notes take some of the angry curses and accusations and put them in a perspective that might apply to all erring people, not just to the Jews—as if the ultimate target of those curses and accusations was meant to be sin and error, and not a particularly villainous ethnic and religious group, the Jews.

That was not Qutb's impulse, though. He explicitly warned against emphasizing the Koran's tolerant expressions of forgiveness of the Jews. Nor did he want to look at the story of Medina as merely an event from the seventh century. In Qutb's interpretation, the sins and crimes of the Medina Jews in the seventh century have a cosmic, eternal quality—rather like the sins and crimes of the Jerusalem Jews in some of the traditional interpretations of the Gospels. In his commentary on Surah 2, Qutb speculated that, during their time of slavery under Pharaoh in Egypt, oppression may have corrupted the Jews, with permanent effects on all Jews everywhere. They acquired the slavish trait of being submissive when defeated, but vicious and vengeful when victorious. And the slavish trait became a defining characteristic of the Jewish people.

In his commentary on Surah 5, he explained that aggression against the champions of truth was another eternal Jewish custom. He made this point repeatedly. In the commentary on Surah 2: "The war the Jews began to wage against Islam and Muslims in those early days has raged on to the present. The form and appearance may have changed, but the nature and means remain the same." Again, in the commentary on Surah 5: "The Muslim world has often faced problems as a result of Jewish conspiracies ever since the early days of Islam." And again: "History has recorded the wicked opposition of the Jews to Islam right from its first day in Medina. Their scheming against Islam has continued since then to the present moment, and they continue to be its leaders, nursing their wicked grudges and always resorting to treacherous schemes to undermine Islam."

Exactly what did Qutb mean by Jewish wickedness and grudges in the present moment? He was, of course, an enemy of Zionism; he even considered that communism was in some respects a product of Zionism. But Zionism was not his main concern—that is, if Zionism is viewed as a conventional political movement and not as something supernatural. Mostly he worried about the Jewish role in modern culture. And he worried about Jewish conspiracies against Islam around the world. In the commentary on Surah 5, he wrote, "The Jews have always been the prime movers in the war declared on all fronts against the advocates of Islamic revival throughout the world. Moreover, the atheistic, materialistic doctrine in our world was advocated by a Jew"—here he refers to Karl Marx—"and the permissive doctrine which is sometimes called 'the sexual revolution' was advocated by a Jew"—who must be Sigmund Freud. "Indeed, most evil theories which try to destroy all values and all that is sacred to mankind are advocated by Jews."

In this same spirit, on the topic of the slogan "Culture is the human heritage" (to get back to that), he expounded a little further on the Jewish conspiracy. "This statement about culture," he wrote, "is one of the tricks played by world Jewry, whose purpose is to eliminate all limitations, so that the Jews may penetrate into [the] body politic of the whole world and then may be free to perpetuate their evil designs. At the top of the list of these activities is usury, the aim of which is that all the wealth of mankind end up in the hands of Jewish financial institutions which run on 'interest.'" And he saw a Jewish role in the great crime of modern times, the abolition of the Caliphate by Kemal Atatürk in 1924. He thought that Jewish conspirators in Turkey under the sultanate of Abd al-Hamid had paved the way to Atatürk and his terrible deeds.

Qutb's strictures against ethnic chauvinism and racism were sincere, and he made them at length. But, on the topic of the Jews, those strictures did tend to run aground. The Jews in his writings display a cosmic quality, timeless and demonic, which reaches from pre-Islamic times into the present age. His complaint against the Jews was theological, not political. Perhaps in these writings we see the influence that people like Goebbel's adjunct, von Leers, might have had on

Egyptian intellectual life. We do see, at any rate, the atmosphere that would have allowed a Pan-Arabist revolutionary government to welcome the Nazi fugitives. Qutb's anti-Semitism was Islamic; but it was not just Islamic. It was classic.

BUT I DON'T mean to paint Qutb as chiefly a conspiracy theorist. He despised the Jews, but what agitated him most of all was the split between the sacred and the secular in modern liberalism, and this was not a Jewish creation. This was the error committed by the disciple Paul and the earliest Christians—the error that, over time, had led to the hideous schizophrenia of modern life. Qutb's great purpose in life was to alert Muslims to the dangers of this most terrible of modern facts. He wanted Muslims to understand that, if tolerance and open-mindedness were accepted as social values, the new habits of mind would crowd out the divine. He wanted Muslims to remember that, in Islam, the divine is everything, or it is not divine. He wanted Muslims to understand that God cannot be shunted into a corner. He wanted Muslims to appreciate that, if God is the only god, God must rule over everything. Every one of Qutb's cultural and social criticisms was meant to illustrate and augment that single, all-important point.

He wrote at length about sex and gender relations in liberal society, as part of his portrait of modern misery and the hideous schizophrenia—and these passages in his writings have been misinterpreted, I think, in some of the Western commentaries on Qutb. His attitude was certainly, from a Western perspective of today, extremely prudish. But prudishness was not in itself his standard of judgment. He saw the theological implications of liberal social values. He invoked the Islamic term *jahili*, which means the heathen ignorance that prevailed in Arabia before the time of Muhammad, or that prevails in any pagan society—and he applied that term to modern liberal society, too.

In liberal *jahili* societies, he wrote in *Milestones*, "writers, journalists and editors advise both married and unmarried people that free sexual relationships are not immoral." But that is not because the writers, journalists, and editors lack any morality at all. They do hold certain things to be immoral. In their view, "it is immoral if a boy uses his partner, or a girl uses her partner, for sex, while feeling no love in his or her heart. It is bad if a wife continues to guard her chastity while her love for her husband has vanished; it is admirable if she finds another lover. Dozens of stories are written about this theme; many newspaper editorials, articles, cartoons, serious and light columns all invite to this way of life." His description was a little tendentious, but not altogether inaccurate on the topic of liberal attitudes toward sex and morality. And, from his perspective, these liberal attitudes reflected the larger liberal idea that something other than God ought to govern human relations. The attitudes were pagan—a retreat into primitive thinking, compared to Islam.

He explained his view this way. If, in a liberal society,

> free sexual relationships and illegitimate children become the basis of a society, and if the relationship between man and woman is based on lust, passion and impulse, and the division of work is not based on family responsibility and natural gifts, if woman's role is merely to be attractive, sexy and flirtatious, and if woman is freed from her basic responsibility of bringing up children; and if, on her own or under social demand, she prefers to become a hostess or a stewardess in a hotel or ship or air company, thus spending her ability for material productivity rather than in the training of human beings, because material production is considered to be more important, more valuable and more honorable than the development of human character, then such a civilization is "backward" from the human point of view, or *jahili* in the Islamic terminology.

Such a civilization has lost its relation to God. Such a civilization has lost sight of the natural harmony of a God-given order—an order in which families serve to bring up children, and family responsibilities are divided between men and women, and each person has a divinely mandated role to fulfill. And why has liberal civilization lost sight of this natural harmony? It is because of the schizophrenia that leads people to picture God's domain in one place, and the ordinary business of daily life in some other place.

Qutb wrote bitterly about European imperialism, which he regarded as nothing more than a continuation of the medieval Crusades. Sometimes he denounced American foreign policy. He complained in *Islam and Social Justice* about America's decision, in the time of Harry Truman, to support the Zionists. Qutb regarded America's support for Israel as "puzzling," and he attributed it to philosophical Pragmatism and to Pragmatism's downplaying of the "idea of right and justice"—"in conjunction, of course, with other factors," by which he probably meant the role of Jewish usurers. He complained about Secretary Dulles and his policies during the Eisenhower administration—the greatest effort "ever exerted by an international politician to fight Islam by spreading a network of espionage and counter-revolutionary organizations all over the world."

But I must point out that, in Qutb's writings, those are fleeting passages. The foreign policies of the United States simply did not engage his principal energies. Sometimes he complained about the hypocrisy in America's boasts about being a free and democratic country. He mentioned America's extermination of its Indian population and the racial prejudice against the blacks. But these were not Qutb's themes, finally. American hypocrisy exercised him; but only slightly. His deepest quarrel was not with America's failure to uphold its principles. His quarrel was with the principles. He opposed the United States because it was a liberal society, and not because it failed to be a liberal society.

The truly dangerous element in American life was not capitalism, or foreign policy, or racism, or the exploitation of women. The truly dangerous part lay in the separation of Church and State. The dangerous part was the laxity of religious standards and convictions—the laxity that, by implication, left in doubt the existence of only one God, the laxity that descended from two thousand years of ecclesiastical deviation and error. This was not a political criticism. This was theological—though Qutb, or perhaps his translator, preferred the word "ideological."

The conflict between the Western countries and the world of Islam, he explained (in this case, while commenting on Surah 2), was one of ideology, although sometimes it took on different guises, and has become "more sophisticated and, at times, more insidious." He identified some of those sophisticated and insidious guises, too. The ideological conflict had been camouflaged as an ordinary, worldly conflict—as an "economic, political and military confrontation"—in order to make the people who preferred to talk about religion appear to be "fanatics" and "backward people." That particular camouflage had proved to be successful, too.

> Unfortunately, some naive and confused Muslims have fallen for this strategem and persuaded themselves that the religious and ideological aspects of the conflict are no longer relevant.
>
> But in reality world Zionism and the crusading Churches, as well as world Communism, are conducting the fight against Islam and the Muslim community, first and foremost, on ideological grounds and with the sole aim of destroying this solid rock which, despite their concerted and sustained efforts, they have not been able to remove.
>
> The confrontation is not over control of territory or economic resources, or for military domination. If we believe that, we would

play into our enemies' hands and would have no one but ourselves to blame for the consequences.

The confrontation was, instead, over Islam itself. Religion, not politics, was the issue. Qutb could hardly be clearer on this topic. The battle between the Western countries and Islam arose from the effort by world Zionism and the crusading Christians to annihilate Islam. And why did world Zionism and the crusading Christians want to annihilate Islam? It was because their own doctrines—Judaism and Christianity—were inferior and had led to lives of misery, and those doctrines could not possibly survive in the face of Islam and its obvious superiority. But how could Islam, in its superiority, be annihilated? Here again, Qutb was entirely lucid. He did not especially fear a military conquest or something of that order. At least, he did not devote his energies to warning against such a danger. Border disputes did not concern him.

His fear was, instead, that liberal doctrines about religion would spread from the Western societies into the Muslim world, and take root there, and crowd out Islam. He worried that liberal ideas would penetrate the Muslim mind. Evil people from within the Muslim world together with evil people from the West were mounting a serious effort to achieve just such a thing. As he wrote in *Islam: The Religion of the Future*, it was "an effort to confine Islam to the emotional and ritual circles, and to bar it from participating in the activity of life, and to check its complete predominance over every human secular activity, a preeminence it earns by virtue of its nature and function." He trembled with rage at that effort. And he cited good historical evidence for his trembling rage. It was the example of Kemal Atatürk and his secular reforms in Turkey back in 1924—Atatürk, "who put to an end the Islamic Caliphate, separated religion from the State and declared the purely secular State."

Atatürk showed that Islam was vulnerable in fact, and not just in theory. And what would happen if, thanks to people like Atatürk and their Jewish supporters and the Christians from the West, Islam was pushed into a corner of society, separated from the state? True Islam would become partial Islam; and partial Islam does not exist. Atatürk's assault, grim as it was, had already led to a new battle, even grimmer than the first. It was "a final offensive which is actually taking place now in all the Muslim countries. . . . It is an effort to exterminate this religion as even a basic creed, and to replace it with secular conceptions having their own implications, values, institutions, and organizations."

"To exterminate"—that was Qutb's phrase. Hysteria cries out from every syllable. But let us grant Qutb his worry. In his eyes, Islam was about to be erased from the earth. What to do?

THAT ONE QUESTION dominated Qutb's life. It was a theological question, and he answered it with his gigantic commentary on the Koran; but he always intended his theology to be practical, too. And so, theological analysis led to a revolutionary program—a practical campaign to save mankind. The first step was to open people's eyes. He wanted Muslims to recognize the nature of the danger—to recognize that Islam had come under assault from outside the Muslim world, and also from inside the Muslim world. The assault from outside was led by Christian Crusaders and world Zionism, though sometimes he also mentioned communism.

But the assault from inside was conducted by Muslims themselves—that is, by people who called themselves Muslims but polluted the Muslim world with incompatible ideas derived from elsewhere. Atatürk was the most successful, and his abolition of the Caliphate, the single most devastating blow. In one form or another, though, false Muslims like Atatürk were in power absolutely everywhere in the

Muslim world, in every single country. Some of those people were Muslims who, under the sway of liberal inspirations, wished to create a secular society in the Muslim world—a society in which religion would remain relegated to its proper corner. Some of those people were Muslims who presented their aspirations as "Islamic democracy" or "Islamic socialism," a Nasserite slogan—quite as if Islam could be diluted with some other doctrine. And there were the Muslims who, unlike the out-and-out secularists, mouthed pious sentiments about Islam and its supreme dominance over society—but meant not one word of what they said.

The strength of these several enemies, the enemies inside and the enemies outside, the false Muslims together with the Crusaders and the Jews, was huge. Those many enemies ruled the earth. But Qutb considered that Islam's strength was, even so, huger yet. "We are certain," he wrote, "that this religion of Islam is so intrinsically genuine, so colossal and deeply-rooted that all such efforts and brutal concussions will avail nothing." Islam could resist—and not just in the Muslim world. Islam was a religion for all mankind, and must sooner or later be accepted by all mankind. "We are also certain that the dire need of mankind for this system is much stronger than the acrimonious hate of its enemies."

Islam's apparent weakness was, then, mere appearance. Islam's champions seemed to be few, but numbers were nothing to worry about. The few had to gather themselves together into what Qutb in *Milestones* called a "vanguard," by which he meant a tiny group animated by the valiant spirit of Muhammad and his Companions at the dawn of Islam. The vanguard had to undertake the renovation of Islam and of civilization all over the world. The way to begin was to live an Islamic life themselves—by following the precepts of Islam and by holding themselves aloof from the wider society and its heathen customs. The vanguard had to form a kind of Islamic counterculture—a mini-society where true Muslims could be themselves. In

Egypt, the Muslim Brotherhood, under al-Banna's inspiration, had been building such a counterculture since 1928, with its charities and pious efforts.

But that was hardly enough. The vanguard had to recognize that the false Muslims or "hypocrites" who ruled the Muslim world were no Muslims at all. It was because Islam is not divisible into crucial aspects and less crucial aspects, and a partially Islamic life is not an Islamic life. On the contrary, the modern belief that religion is divisible, and that you can be a pious person on sacred days, and less than pious on other days; the belief that religion should clothe certain parts of life, and not the other parts; the belief that some places are for God, and other places are not—that belief was the enemy itself. The danger facing Islam—the danger of annihilation—lay in that belief. Muslims who acted on that belief, who acknowledged Islam one day a week and ignored it on the other days, were Islam's bitter foes, no matter how loudly they chanted their prayers.

Qutb judged those people to be *jahili* barbarians, exactly like the polytheists in Arabia before the time of Muhammad. To struggle against those people was right and just—to struggle with full force, too, and not with moderation or reservations. To live a proper Islamic life meant engaging in that kind of struggle, the jihad for Islam. Yet what was the ultimate goal of such a struggle? The goal of Islam was not just spiritual, and neither could be the goal of Qutb's proposed new jihad.

He began his commentary on Surah 5 by writing: "The Koran was bestowed from on high to Muhammad, God's Messenger, so that he might, by means of it, establish a state, bring a community into being, organize a society, cultivate minds and consciences and set moral values." And the goal of Qutb's jihad was the same. To establish a state. The goal was to get hold of an entire country from somewhere in the Muslim world and to bring that country under the precepts of Islam, not in their adulterated form, either—to create an Islamic state along

Muhammad's lines. The goal, in short, was to resurrect the pristine Islamic society, from before the period of decline—to resurrect the original model in such a way that everyone could see its success. And, from there, to bring Islam to all the world—which was Muhammad's goal, as well.

What would it mean to resurrect the pristine Islamic state? It would mean reinstating the code of shariah, the Muslim code, as the legal code of the state. And what would shariah mean, not in the context of the seventh century but in modern times? Here, Qutb was wonderfully clever. He arrived at his social criticisms by taking a good portion of modern Western social commentary and pouring it through an Islamic filter; and he arrived at his vision of shariah by taking a good portion of Islam and pouring it through a filter of modern liberalism. Shariah, in his account, emerged as the legal code for a faintly liberal or even libertarian society, with an Islamic twist—the kind of society that any thoughtful modern person, influenced by the ideals of liberal freedom, might respect and even crave.

"This religion," he wrote, "is really a universal declaration of the freedom of man from servitude to other men and from servitude to his own desires, which is also a form of human servitude; it is a declaration that sovereignty belongs to God alone." Here he was evidently evoking Eleanor Roosevelt's Universal Declaration of Human Rights at the United Nations—with the addition of a Muslim declaration of faith in the oneness of God, or the concept of totality. The Islamic system, in his account, creates a society of full equality. The Islamic system is for "all human beings, whether they be rulers or ruled, black or white, poor or rich, ignorant or learned. Its law is uniform for all, and all human beings are equally responsible with it. In all other systems, human beings obey other human beings and follow man-made laws."

But an Islamic system means "the abolition of man-made laws." In an Islamic system, every person "is free from servitude to others." The Islamic system means "the complete and true freedom of every person and the full dignity of every individual of the society. On the other hand, in a society in which some people are lords who legislate and some others are slaves who obey them, then there is no freedom in the real sense, nor dignity for each and every individual." These are anarchist ideas, virtually. Luigi Galleani could have written those sentences, if you substitute the words "anarchy" and "anarchism" for Qutb's "shariah" and "Islam."

The Islamic system, through its emphasis on charity, upholds what Qutb calls, once again in Rooseveltian tones, "the principle of universal social security for all who are disabled and for all who are in need." The Islamic system upholds the equality of women, with a few qualifications. "Islam has guaranteed to women a complete equality with men . . . ; it has permitted no discrimination except in some incidental matters connected with physical capacity, with customary procedure, or with responsibility, in all of which the human status of the two sexes is not in question."

Shariah guarantees freedom of conscience and freedom of religion. "Freedom of belief," he wrote in his commentary on Surah 2, is the fundamental right that defines man as human. In *Milestones,* he provided further details: "Islam does not force people to accept its belief, but it wants to provide a free environment in which they will have the choice of beliefs." Of course, a free environment can only be one in which people are not forced to bow down before any authority other than God's, which can only mean shariah, where God's law reigns supreme. As for people who do not choose to accept Islam, they will have their rights under shariah, and will even be granted a special status to protect those rights—the status of dhimmies. But if those people, the non-Muslims, should try to overthrow the reign of shariah and to impose a new tyranny of man, the Islamic system would have to resist, and justly so. Freedom, which is to say, shariah, must be protected, and justice must be enforced. But enforcement, too, must follow the law of Islam. This was one of his themes in *Social Justice in Islam*. He explained:

> The following are the foundations on which Islam establishes justice:
>
> 1. Absolute freedom of conscience.
> 2. The complete equality of man.
> 3. The firm mutual responsibility of society.

And what did this last point, "mutual responsibility," mean? It meant that any person who commits a crime will have to take responsibility by yielding up an exact equivalent of the damage that has been wrought. Qutb quoted the Koran on the punishments for killing or wounding: "a life for a life, an eye for an eye, an ear for an ear, a tooth for a tooth, and for wounds the equivalent." That was the code of shariah.

Fornication, too, was a serious crime because, in his words, "it involves an attack on honor and a contempt for sanctity and an encouragement of profligacy in society." Shariah specified the punishments here, as well. "The penalty for this must be severe; for married men and women it is stoning to death; for unmarried men and women it is flogging, a hundred lashes, which in cases is fatal." False accusations were likewise serious. "A punishment of eighty lashes is fixed for those who falsely accuse chaste women." "As for those who threaten the general security of society, their punishment is to be put to death, to be crucified, to have their hands and feet cut off, or to be banished from the country." And, having reviewed those several punishments, Qutb brightly concluded, "On these foundations, then—an absolute freedom of conscience, a complete equality of all mankind, and a firm mutual responsibility in society—social justice is built up and human justice is ensured."

Shariah was, in a word, utopia for Sayyid Qutb. It was the abolition of servitude. It was freedom, both for society and for the individual. It was equality. It was social welfare. It was morality.

But that was going to be in the future. Meanwhile, before shariah could be established, the modern jihad did have to take place—the jihad that was going to save Islam from annihilation at the hands of the hypocrites within the Muslim world and their allies in the outside world, the Crusaders and Jews. In *Social Justice in Islam*, Qutb described jihad as a defensive war—Islam's campaign to protect itself. But that was in the late 1940s, when his Islamist views were still relatively moderate. In later years he decided that jihad, examined in a properly Islamic light, had to go beyond mere defense.

I have to add, given the course of action followed by some of Qutb's followers in later years, that jihad, in his conception, contained an ethical dimension. He quoted Muhammad's successor, Abu Bakr, the first Caliph, who told his army, "Do not kill any women, children or elderly people." Qutb quoted the Koran, which says: "Fight for the cause of God those who fight against you, but do not commit aggression. God does not love aggressors." Qutb thought that ethical commandments were crucial to military victory. Writing about Muhammad and his Companions, he said, "These principles had to be strictly observed, even with those enemies who had persecuted them and inflicted unspeakable atrocities on them." Jihad did have its rules. It was fastidious. And yet, from another point of view, jihad was bound by no limitations at all, neither in geography nor in time. It was going to be worldwide, and it was going to end on the Day of Judgment.

That was Sayyid Qutb's revolutionary program. It was pretty wild, all in all; but nothing in it was hard to recognize. Qutb entertained his grand vision of Islam and its desperate predicament and its utopian destiny, but in twentieth-century Europe each of the totalitarian movements entertained a grand vision of modern civilization and of desperate predicaments and utopian destinies. Each of the totalitarian doctrines of Europe expressed that vision by telling a version of the ur-myth, the myth of Armageddon. So did Qutb.

With him, too, there was a people of God. They happened to be the Muslims. The people of God had come under insidious attack from within their own society, by the forces of corruption and pollution. In Qutb's version, these were the false Muslims, the "hypocrites." The enemies from within were backed by sinister and even cosmic enemies from abroad. These were the Crusaders and Jews. There was going to be a terrible war against them, led by the Muslim vanguard. It was going to be the jihad. Victory was, as always, guaranteed. And the reign of God, which had once existed in the long-ago past, was going to be resurrected. It was going to be the reign of shariah. And the reign was going to create a perfect society, cleansed of its impurities and corruptions—as always in the totalitarian mythologies.

Qutb's doctrine was wonderfully original and deeply Muslim, looked at from one angle; and, from another angle, merely one more version of the European totalitarian idea. And if his doctrine was recognizable, its consequences were certainly going to be predictable. Qutb's vanguard, if such a vanguard ever mobilized itself, was going to inaugurate a rebellion—this time, a rebellion in the name of Islam, against the liberal values of the West. (Totalitarian movements always, but always, rise up in rebellion against the liberal values of the West. That is their purpose.) And rebellion was bound to end in a cult of death. For how were any of Qutb's goals to be achieved? What could it possibly mean to treat the entire Muslim population of the world, apart from the followers of his own movement, as *jahili* barbarians who were bringing about the extermination of Islam?

In a passage on Surah 2 from *In the Shade of the Qu'ran,* he discussed the people "who claim to be Muslims but perpetrate corruption," the people who "oppose the implementation of God's law"—that is, the people who oppose the vanguard of true Muslims. Those people, the perpetrators of corruption, "are seriously lacking in faith and loyalty to God and Islam." Their efforts will come to naught. "They shall have no protection whatsoever against God's punishment, which is bound to come, keen as they may be to avoid it." But what will be the nature of God's punishment? This is left to our imaginations; and we can imagine.

And what was going to happen if, somewhere on earth, a vanguard of pious worshippers of God, inspired by Qutb or by one of his fellow thinkers, did capture a country and duly resurrected the reign of shariah from days of yore? This, too, was predictable. Yore was going to prove elusive. The vanguard of pious believers was going to have to take stern action to bring about a better observance of shariah. Stern action was going to mean a police state, even if the police state claimed to be enforcing freedom. And yet, because shariah requires the strictest adherence to divine law in even the most private of behaviors, not even the most totalitarian of police forces was going to be able to keep track of everything. The police were going to have to crack the whip, and crack again, and crack still harder, just to get everyone to obey. And if, at last, the social justice and complete freedom of shariah did come into existence, if the qualities and traits from the founding generation of Muhammad and his Companions in the seventh century did find a new and modern home, if the Islamic revolution did begin to flourish, those many, thrilling successes were not going to take place on the plane of the living. The successes of the Islamist revolution were going to take place on the plane of the dead, or nowhere. Lived experience pronounced that sentence on the Islamist revolution—the lived experience of Europe, where each of the totalitarian movements proposed a total renovation of life, and each was driven to create the total renovation in death.

But I have gotten ahead of myself with these predictions. Better to ask, what did happen, in reality, to Qutb and his Islamist ideas?

In 1966, Sayyid Qutb, in the phrase of his biographer Hasan, "kissed the gallows." But there was no way to take his writings and hang them as well. *Milestones* was invoked as evidence in the trial against him—and, afterward, *Milestones*, like many another book that has faced a courtroom judge, only became more popular. And what could the authorities do about Qutb's *In the Shade of the Qur'an*—this thirty-volume magnum opus which only now is making its voluminous way into English translation, through a publishing collaboration that stretches (according to the publishing pages in the different volumes) from England to Kenya, Nigeria, Qatar, and India? Nasser extinguished Qutb's life, but Qutb left something gigantic behind. It was this enormous commentary—a vast and elegantly constructed architecture of thought and imagination, a work of true profundity, vividly written, wise, broad, indignant, sometimes demented, bristly with hatred, medieval, modern, tolerant, intolerant, cruel, urgent, cranky, tranquil, grave, poetic, learned, analytic, moving in some passages—a work large and solid enough to create its own shade, where his readers could repose and turn his pages, as he advised the students of the Koran to do, in the earnest spirit of loyal soldiers reading their daily bulletin.

The section on "Martyrdom and Jihad" in the commentary on Surah 2 contains this passage:

> The Surah tells the Muslims that, in the fight to uphold God's universal Truth, lives will have to be sacrificed. Those who risk their lives and go out to fight, and who are prepared to lay down their lives for the cause of God are honorable people, pure of heart and blessed of soul. But the great surprise is that those among them who are killed in the struggle must not be considered or described as dead. They continue to live, as God Himself clearly states.
>
> To all intents and purposes, those people may very well appear lifeless, but life and death are not judged by superficial physical

> means alone. Life is chiefly characterized by activity, growth, and persistence, while death is a state of total loss of function, of complete inertia and lifelessness. But the death of those who are killed for the cause of God gives more impetus to the cause, which continues to thrive on their blood. Their influence on those they leave behind also grows and spreads. Thus after their death they remain an active force in shaping the life of their community and giving it direction. It is in this sense that such people, having sacrificed their lives for the sake of God, retain their active existence in everyday life. . . .
>
> There is no real sense of loss in their death, since they continue to live.

And so it was with Sayyid Qutb.

V
The Politics of Slaughter

THE ISLAMIST IDEA drew on the poetic power of the Koran, on scholarship, on nationalist echoes, on spiritual invocations, on the example of the Islamist martyrs, and, at the same time, on the visible benefits of everyday piety. Charity had always been a main principle of the Muslim Brotherhood, ever since its founding in 1928—charity as a sacred obligation, mandated by God, not just as an optional and generous virtue. Then, too, with all those sturdy roots, the Islamist idea proved to be marvelously supple. For what was the correct way to define Islamism's three principal terms—*jahili* barbarism, jihad, and the Islamic state?

Different meanings could be attached, without losing the connection to the Muslim tradition and the Koran. And flexibility gave the movement still more strength. The Islamist movement could be polit- ical, or less than political; cautious and conservative, or frantically radical; determined to bring about the kind of social justice that is symbolized by social democratic equality, or the kind of social justice that is symbolized by public stonings. Islamism's ability to bend in any of those directions accounts for the movement's remarkable history—its capacity to suffer devastating setbacks in one or another location, to be uprooted, and even so, to attract powerful sponsors and supporters, and to sprout up somewhere else, stronger and leafier than before.

Nasser hanged Qutb because the Egyptian state feared the subversive violence of the Muslim Brotherhood, but also because Nasser's Pan-Arabism was pushing leftward, toward a kind of Marxism and toward the Soviet Union—and Islamist preachings stood in the way of the leftward push. But what Nasser feared, other people admired. Saudi Arabia embraced Sayyid Qutb's younger brother, Muhammad, and the other exiles from Nasser's repression because Islam in its Sunni branch, rather like Judaism, is a scholarly religion; there is no priesthood, only the scholarly interpreters of Islamic law. But Saudi Arabia was not brimming with scholars. The Egyptian scholars could do a lot for Saudi Arabia's religious credentials, then, and they could do so at a moment when, because of the oil boom, Saudi wealth was creeping upward into the realms of the spectacular. The Saudis established a missionary program abroad, which eventually constructed a full 1,500 mosques around the world. This was not like the paltry cultural efforts of the U.S. government: this was visionary. And, from the pullulating mosques, a new mix of ideas, the traditional puritanical doctrines of Saudi Wahhabi Islam, reinforced now by the dynamic new Koranic readings from Qutb and Egypt's Muslim Brotherhood, radiated outward.

Islamist antipathy to the Soviet Union made the movement attractive to still other people, and not just to the State Department and the CIA. The governing elite in Pakistan tended to look on the Islamist movement with fond sympathy and even with enthusiasm, partly because Islamism went back many years in that country, but also because Islamists could help Pakistan resist the allures of Afghan Marxism and the secular traditions of India's socialists. In Egypt, Anwar Sadat succeeded Nasser as head of state and, in 1972, decided to switch sides in the Cold War, from pro-Soviet to pro-American. But switching sides required a fight against the Marxists at home, and, in his search for domestic allies, Sadat duly removed the old restrictions on the Islamist preachers and unleashed the Muslim Brotherhood and its descendant organizations against the Egyptian left.

The Israeli government looked on the Islamist movement with a similar set of hopes. The Israelis faced a guerrilla insurgency from Palestinian Marxists and the nationalist fighters from Arafat's movement, who received training and funding from the Soviet bloc; and the Israelis, in their distress, began to look on the newly conservative and religious tendency among the Palestinian people with sympathetic eyes. So the Israelis, too, allowed the Islamist movement to develop freely. That was in the 1970s. The Islamists right away set out to kill dozens of Muslim women, who were accused of various crimes and sins. That ought to have been a sign of something amiss. And yet, the Islamist movement was profoundly pious and charitable, and the Israelis hoped that, on balance, the Islamists would make better neighbors than the Palestinian nationalists and leftists.

In Paris, the French authorities entertained the same worries about left-wing radicalism within the Muslim and especially the Algerian immigrant circles in France. And the French government likewise decided to promote the preachers of the Islamist cause, in the hope of channeling Muslim energies into zones of piety and charity. In this way, governments around the world saw in the Islamist movement a solution, and not a problem. It is easy to say, in retrospect, that all of this was a gigantic error. But I think that even the Islamists themselves did not really know where their movement was heading. Certainly no one could have predicted the way in which Islamism managed to achieve its first large and political triumph.

This took place in Iran in 1979, and the success owed to the supreme adaptability of Qutb's contemporary and fellow thinker, Khomeini, from his exile's home in the Paris suburbs. Khomeini was a classic Islamist, in a Shiite version: an opponent of *jahili* barbarism, and a champion of the Islamic Empire of yore. He was also an original thinker, and he took these Islamist ideas and added to them a few Marxist pointers about the wretched of the earth and the salvation of the poor, which he drew from the Iranian translator of Frantz Fanon and Jean-Paul Sartre. And why shouldn't Khomeini have adopted those left-wing pointers? Outside observers may have looked on Khomeini as a ghost from the Middle Ages—someone alien to the civilization of the modern West. That was Khomeini's preferred image of himself. But, seen from another angle, Khomeini was one more exiled intellectual who had cast up in France, even if just briefly. And he responded to the same currents of thought as everyone else—a man with the hyphenated personality of modern life. In any case, there was nothing foreign about the idea of social justice in Islamist doctrine. If Qutb back in the 1940s saw no difficulty in adapting a few slogans from Eleanor Roosevelt, there was no reason why Khomeini, in a similarly open-minded and modern spirit, couldn't accept some helpful tips from the Paris left. And so, he managed to transform the Islamist cause into a version of liberation theology, except Muslim and Middle Eastern instead of Catholic and Latin American.

Khomeini's movement declared itself the champion of the oppressed. And, in this way, Islamism, treading a path that Baath Socialism had already taken, acquired what Mussolini had pioneered long ago—the revolutionary mixture of extreme left and extreme right. The mixture prospered. From his perch in France, the Ayatollah managed to unite the mosques and Islamic scholars back in Iran, and then, deploying his new rhetoric, he forged the most unlikely of alliances on the left. The Iranian Communist Party, called the Tudeh, entered into a coalition with him, along with a few other left-wing groups. The coalition was powerful.

The nostalgic and fanatical clerics of the Islamist movement mobilized their mosques and congregations, and the Tudeh and the other leftists deployed their disciplined cadres in the poor neighborhoods and in the universities. And Khomeini overthrew the shah. To be sure, he very quickly got rid of his left-wing allies. His Islamic revolution offered a curious example of "salami tactics" turned against the Communists, instead of used on their behalf—the revolutionary leaders cutting one slice after another off the revolutionary salami. But the result was entirely traditional, and, by the end, no one was left except the leader and his party, who were the Islamist clergy.

Khomeini set about reinstating the reign of shariah, which was his deepest goal. The Islamist revolution in Iran proved in this way to be a gigantic setback for the rights of women and for personal freedom as a whole—a setback for every liberal or potentially liberal element in Iranian society. Khomeini's new constitution designated a special place for the "Supreme Guide," who turned out to be himself. Revolutionary committees in every neighborhood set themselves up as a thought police. And all of those achievements excited admiration and envy in the Arab and Muslim world, and perhaps not just there.

The Iranian revolution reaffirmed the undeniable reality that immense revolutions could, in fact, be carried out in the Muslim countries, not just in the name of Baath Socialism or some other version of nationalist radicalism but in the name of the purest Islam. The influence of the United States and of liberal civilization could be cast overboard, and men with beards and turbans could resume their positions of patriarchal power, exactly as in the glorious days of the Islamic past. And, to anyone who looked with fear and loathing on the progress of liberal ideas and values around the world, the entire spectacle was thrilling to see.

Yet how new were any of these revolutionary excitements? Khomeini's revolutionary rhetoric had its novel qualities, namely, a few echoes from the seventh century. The revolutionary uniforms—the turbans and robes—were wonderfully original. But, in the twentieth century, astonishing doctrines and dashing costumes—leather jackets, proletarian caps, Cuban beards, Shiite beards, together with the monochrome shirts—were the grand tradition. And Islamism's triumph in Iran right away inaugurated what each of the totalitarian revolutions had inaugurated in the past. This was war. Within a year of taking power, the Ayatollah's new Islamic Republic was immersed in a horrendous combat with Saddam Hussein's Baath Socialists of Iraq.

The war was about a disputed border. But mostly it was a war about competing doctrines. Kanan Makiya has coldly and bitterly explained that Saddam's Baath Socialism always rested on a doctrine of love—a love for the Arab nation, a love for the greatness that the Arabs have achieved in the past and will achieve in the future, a love in which the individual person hopes to merge his own identity. And the flip side of Baathist love was a doctrine of cruelty—a cruelty that symbolized courage and virtue, the virtuous courage that was needed to bring about the resurrected Arab Empire. And so, pushed by his doctrine of love, which was also a doctrine of cruelty, Saddam organized his side of the Iran-Iraq War on the cruelest of bases. He made a specialty of poison gas attacks—the kind of attack that had been declared illegal all over the world after the First World War because of the horrific death that it induces, death by torture and disfiguration, spread over weeks. Saddam specialized in minefields, too.

Khomeini's revolution, by contrast, worshipped piety, the flip side of which was martyrdom—the martyrdom that was needed to bring about the resurrection of the Islamic Empire. And so, in a pious and revolutionary spirit, Khomeini organized his "human wave" attacks—mass frontal assaults by thousands of young men, advancing to certain death at the hands of Saddam's poison gas and land mines. Khomeini whipped up a religious fervor for that kind of mass death—a belief that to die on Khomeini's orders in a human wave attack was to achieve the highest and most beautiful of destinies. All over Iran, young men, encouraged by their mothers and their families, yearned to participate in those human wave attacks—actively yearned for martyrdom. It was a mass movement for suicide. The war was one of the most macabre events that has ever occurred—a war between love and piety, which was, from another angle, a war between cruelty and suicide.

The war lasted eight years. It killed and wounded upward of a million people. (And where were our high-minded friends of the Third World then? How much attention did this, one of the worst events of modern history, receive?) It was the eastern front of the Second World War, updated. It was Hitler against Stalin. At the end of the Iran-Iraq War, both sides were thought to have lost badly. But there was no reason to say that anyone had lost. The death of masses of people turned out to be a giant success for the leaders on both sides. Eight years of war had not the slightest influence on Saddam. Soon enough he rounded up 100,000 Kurdish men and boys, machine-gunned them, and had them bulldozed into their graves. Two years later, he launched his invasion of Kuwait and a new war. (The logic of military deterrence has been borne out by many events around the world, but not by the career of Saddam Hussein.) Did this new war reveal Saddam as a madman to people all over the Arab and Muslim world? Maybe it did.

But madness does not always repel. The cruelty that Saddam had shown with his poison gas and his minefields, the savagery of his repressions, his refusal to be influenced or discouraged by the sufferings of his own people—those were the qualities that allowed the great man to stand up and proclaim himself the hero of the Arab nation. For cruelty was love, and invasion was Arab unity, and mass death was brotherhood. And so, Saddam's invasion of Kuwait, no matter how unpopular among Arab rulers, appeared to be, from another point of view, a step toward Arab union and strength. And it proved to be immensely popular in large portions of the Arab "street," at least for as long as Saddam seemed to be marching victoriously to Jerusalem.

Khomeini's victory in the Iran-Iraq War was vaster, though. The Islamic Republic of Iran sensibly refrained in later years from engaging in large-scale wars. It preferred small wars, fought at a distance, by proxies, against Zionism and world Jewry. There was the war fought in Lebanon by the Hezbollah guerrillas (who, under an Iranian Islamist influence, introduced suicide terrorism to the modern age, in 1983). There were the terrorist attacks on Jewish sites in Buenos Aires, which were almost certainly organized by the Islamist government in

Teheran, with Argentine accomplices. But, even without plunging into a major new war, Iran's Islamist revolutionaries spread their inspiration across wide regions of the Arab and Muslim world, even where the majority of people were Sunni and not Shiite. For the Iranian revolution was large and deep and inspiring, and, with the Iranian example in everyone's eyes, the Islamist movement became a greater phenomenon than ever before, and the newly mass movement began to achieve success across the wide arc from Afghanistan to Algeria, and beyond. And what was the mark of that success?

Piety spread. Religious devotion deepened. Women hid behind their veils. And as piety, devotion, and patriarchy bloomed, in every country a new kind of politics came into flower. It was the politics of slaughter—slaughter for the sake of sacred devotion, slaughter conducted in a mood of spiritual loftiness, slaughter indistinguishable from charity, slaughter that led to suicide, slaughter for slaughter's sake. It was a flower of evil. And this new politics, in its bright green Islamist color, proved to be sturdy.

It is impossible to choose which among the many variations of the new politics was the most baffling and horrendous. Was it in Algeria? The Islamist movement grew in Algeria, and when the secular authorities decided to repress it, the Armed Islamic Group and other organizations excommunicated the whole of society and set about massacring the impious. Between 1992 and 1997, a full 100,000 people are said to have been killed in the Algerian civil war, vast numbers of them by outright massacres in village after village, chiefly by the Islamist radicals. Was the war in Kashmir the most astounding? Thirty-five thousand were killed, or, some say, twice as many. Perhaps the Islamist revolution in Afghanistan was the most astounding. The Islamist revolutionaries took the stadium that had been constructed by the Soviets in the name of the proletariat and used it on Fridays for public stonings and machine-gun executions of murderers by the families of their victims. Afghanistan under its Islamist leaders sank into famine and starvation. And, as these events took place, Afghanistan's revolutionary prestige, instead of sinking, rose.

The Islamic Emirate of Afghanistan began to loom as an ever more attractive utopia for Islamists around the world—the object of pilgrimages and acts of solidarity, a success story, in Islamist eyes. Palestine offered its own example of Islamism's growth and consequences. The main origin of Palestinian terrorism—in the period before the 1967 war—was military in a more or less ordinary sense. The Pan-Arabists in Egypt used to send *fellaheen* to stage attacks on Israeli civilians along the Egyptian border, and similar attacks occurred in other parts of Israel, too. But, among the Palestinians, the most characteristic violence, pre-1967, consisted of attacks on the Israeli army. After the war, the Palestinian actions veered in a new direction, and the emblematic new action consisted of hijacking airplanes. Hijackings sometimes led to killings.

Still, in the hijackings of the 1960s and '70s, death was not the goal. There was something fastidious in those hijacks—an ethical consideration, even if the victims might not have thought so. In 1976, a group of German leftists joined the Palestinian movement and hijacked a plane on the Palestinians' behalf, with a plan for separating out and murdering whomever among the passengers happened to be Jewish; and even that plan was, in its way, fastidious, if you grant the German leftists their prejudices. The terrorists did not want to murder blindly, after all.

But, over the years, as the nationalist and leftist inspiration among Palestinians and their foreign allies yielded to the new wave of Islamist piety, Palestinian violence took a new turn; and fastidiousness receded into the past. The Palestinian Islamists organized Hamas as the combat wing of the Muslim Brotherhood, and the characteristic new act consisted of murdering random crowds with a bomb, as many people as possible, sometimes Jews and Palestinians together, plus anyone else who happened to be passing by—an occasional Romanian worker, an immigrant from China. A Palestinian state had once seemed to be the goal. Now the goal was suicide. Camus's terrorists of the Organization for Combat of the Social Revolutionary Party, circa 1905, refrained from murdering children even by accident; but the new Palestinian terror made a point of singling out children's sites. More: the new movement made a point of selecting Palestinian children to commit suicide—a stage in the evolution of terror that Camus had never imagined. Parents, in their piety, addressed the press wishing for the suicide of their own children. Posters on the kindergarten walls proclaimed, "The children are the holy martyrs of tomorrow." The world has seen such things before, Walter Laqueur tells us, and I'm sure he is right. Let us not lose our ability to be astonished, though.

Or did the Sudan offer a still more remarkable example of Islamism in practice? In the Sudan, Hassan al-Turabi, the recipient of a master's degree in London and a doctorate in Paris, seized state power in conjunction with a general and instituted shariah and the revolutionary jihad. This jihad, the one in the Sudan, may have been the ghastliest of all. The Islamists were mostly Sudanese Arabs, and their jihad took aim at Sudan's black population, who tended to be animists and Christians; and the ensuing war killed between 1.5 million and 2 million people, apart from the victims who were brutalized by rape and other atrocities. The Islamists, in their drive for domination, ended up enslaving huge numbers of the Dinka tribe.

In these ways, the Muslim totalitarianism of the 1980s and '90s turned out to have been fully as horrible as the fascism and Stalinism of Europe—fully as murderous, as destructive of societies and moralities, as devastating to civilization. The victims numbered in the multiple millions. And yet—how do we explain this?—Muslim totalitarianism, both Islamist and Baathi, somehow remained invisible, relatively speaking, to the Western countries. Surely here was an example, perhaps the grimmest example of all, of "Orientialist" bias against the Muslim world—a bias so vast and overwhelming and so deeply ideological as to allow even the greatest champions of human rights in the rest of the world to avert their eyes from the accumulated consequences of Islamism in practice.

I have barely even mentioned the Lebanese civil war (which, to be sure, involved many other factors apart from Islamism and the Baath). And there is the extremely odd case of Egypt. In 1981, President Sadat was assassinated by an Islamist cell within the Egyptian army. (Sadat's principal crime was to have signed a peace treaty with Israel, in exchange for the Sinai Peninsula—the first indication that "land for peace," the slogan of the Israeli left, might be a workable formula.) The Islamist conspirators hoped to spark a revolution with this one violent act. It was an *attentat* in the European fashion of the late nineteenth century. In one Egyptian city, the assassination did set off a few signs of revolutionary agitation in the streets. But the agitation failed to spread. Afterward, the repression, as might have been expected, was terrible.

Even so, the Islamist movement in Egypt prospered. The Muslim Brotherhood, which had leaned toward violence in earlier decades, tilted in a more peaceful and moderate direction, and the Brotherhood's campaign to establish shariah in Egypt proceeded with agitations and gradual measures, and had a lot of success, too. There were twenty-two professional guilds in Egypt, and by the mid-1980s, Gilles Kepel tells us, the Muslim Brotherhood came to dominate most of them—the lawyers, the doctors, the engineers, the dentists, the pharmacists, and so forth. Islamist banks, conforming to the economic principles of shariah, began to do rather well. And, in this setting, the Islamist movement also sprouted a more radical branch, divided between two groups, the Islamic Group of Sheikh Omar Abdel Rahman, and the Islamic Jihad of Dr. Ayman al-Zawahiri, "Dr. Death." Those organizations wanted nothing to do with moderation. They murdered secular intellectuals—a logical thing to do, given the Islamist analysis of the ideological dangers threatening Islam.

The radicals launched repeated violent attacks on the Coptic Christians. Sheikh Rahman fled the Egyptian repression to Jersey City, across the harbor from Lower Manhattan, and sent videos back to Egypt denouncing tourism; and tourists were attacked. Egypt's Jewish population, which used to be substantial, had fled to Israel and other countries in the 1950s and '60s. Yet, the fewer the Jews, the more zealous the efforts to murder whatever Jews might be at hand. In 1996, a group of eighteen Greek tourists at a Cairo hotel were mistaken for Jews and were duly massacred, and Rahman's organization claimed the credit. The communiqué denounced "the Jews, sons of monkeys and pigs"—quoting the unfortunate line from Surah 5, verse 60. The communiqué said, "There is no place for Jews in the Muslim land of Egypt"—which, by the way, is something that Qutb himself would never have said. The next year, fifty-eight tourists and four Egyptians were massacred at the temple of Hatsetshup in Luxor, some of them hacked to death with knives—not because the victims were sons of monkeys and pigs but simply out of the urge to cleanse the Muslim land of foreign impurities.

And from all of this al Qaeda emerged—from the early example of the Ayatollah in Iran, from the jihad in Afghanistan, from King Abdul Aziz University in Saudi Arabia, and from the Egyptian theologians. Al Qaeda got its start within the international volunteers' movement for the Afghan jihad, whose organizational center was the Office for Services, in Peshawar, Pakistan—the office that welcomed Islamist fighters from around the world and sent them into battle in Afghanistan. The office was run by a Palestinian religious scholar named Sheikh Abdullah Azzam, who in the course of his life had befriended the Qutb family in Egypt and went on to teach in Saudi Arabia. Azzam, with his scholarly credentials, served as something of a representative of the Saudi princes in the Afghan jihad. He toured the United States, recruiting for the jihad and, it is said, for the Palestinian Hamas.

Like any other large political movement, the Afghan jihad had its factional disputes, and in one of those disputes, Osama bin Laden, who began as Azzam's follower, turned away in favor of a newer, more radical faction under the influence of the Egyptian Islamists, Sheikh Rahman and Dr. Zawahiri. Azzam was assassinated in 1989. And the new group, Al Qaeda, with bin Laden at the head (his $300 million did qualify him for leadership), moved its operations first to Turabi's Sudan and then to Afghanistan. Bin Laden's group merged with Zawahiri's Islamic Jihad. And the newly merged group took Sheikh Rahman's inspiration as its own. For the sheikh—from his base in Jersey City and Brooklyn—had already conceived the new inspiration.

This was the notion of murdering New Yorkers randomly and en masse. It was Sheikh Rahman's group that bombed the World Trade Center in 1993 and killed six people, and it was Rahman's group that planned to bomb tunnels and the United Nations in New York—though the plan was foiled by the police. But Al Qaeda went further still. Qutb had called for a "vanguard" of Muslims to fight the jihad. Al Qaeda was a vanguard of the vanguard—an organization that brought together the bravest (from Afghanistan), the brainiest (from Egypt), and the wealthiest (from Saudi Arabia), not to mention the most numerous (from Indonesia and elsewhere in East Asia).

In the early 1950s, Qutb had abandoned his original and more traditional idea that jihad was merely a defensive struggle, in favor of the more radical and aggressive notion that jihad was a struggle for all mankind. Al Qaeda duly launched the global struggle—no longer to be confined within the traditionally Muslim borders of Egypt, Arabia, Yemen, Afghanistan, Chechnya, Bosnia, Palestine, and a few other places. Qutb had spoken against a narrow notion of Arab nationalism in favor of a broader, non-racial notion of Islam. Al Qaeda duly defined itself as a broad movement, without an ethnic identity,

Islamist but not Arab. Qutb had declared that all but a few Muslims were *jahili* barbarians. Al Qaeda, through its Egyptian wing, was already engaged in struggles against some of the main Muslim powers, in Egypt and elsewhere.

Qutb had made clear that jihad by the Muslim vanguard was a theological war against liberal values, which he denounced as Western and, in their remote origin, Christian—a war devoted to restoring the seventh-century Caliphate, in a modernizing version. Al Qaeda, by contrast, in the videotape of bin Laden shown on the Al Jazeera television network immediately after the 9/11 attacks, presented a number of relatively conventional political demands—a demand for "peace" in Palestine (meaning, in the Islamist vocabulary, the elimination of the Zionist state); the removal of infidel troops from the land of Muhammad (meaning the removal of the American troops who guarded the Saudi government and oil wells); and the end of suffering for the Iraqi people (meaning the end of foreign pressure on Saddam Hussein and the UN sanctions against Iraqi commerce).

Yet bin Laden presented those political issues in a spirit closer to Qutb's theology of the absolute than to any sort of malleable politics. Negotiation was not Al Qaeda's goal. Azzam, bin Laden's leader at the Office for Services in Peshawar, was famous for having said, "No negotiations, no conferences, and no dialogues" (which echoed the still more famous response of the Arab states to Israel's offer, after the 1967 war, to return some of the captured land: "No recognition, no negotiations, no peace"). Azzam's slogan was, "Jihad and the rifle alone." Such was the inspiration. For Al Qaeda was not a political movement in any conventional sense. It was a chiliastic movement, and its goal was the Caliphate or nothing.

Bin Laden's post-9/11 videotape showed him sitting on a carpet with Dr. Zawahiri and a couple of aides in their turbans and beards, against a savage rock outcropping. It was a tableau from out of the seventh century, as if depicting the Prophet Muhammad and his

Companions in a rocky land outside Medina—except with microphones, to demonstrate the Islamist commitment to a modern version of ancient times. The tone in the video was tranquil, otherworldly, and poetic. The whole thing was a page from *In the Shade of the Qur'an*. Qutb described a Medina in the seventh century populated by four main groups of people: the vanguard Muslims, who were Muhammad and his Companions; the pagans; the hypocrites, who pretended to be Muslims; and the perfidious Jews.

Bin Laden in his video described a similar world. There were the vanguard Muslims, who were his own soldiers, the warriors of jihad; the pagans, whose homeland was the United States; the hypocrites, who were Muslim leaders allied with America; and the Jews, in the form of Israeli tanks. America, bin Laden explained (I am quoting the translation in *The New York Times*), was "the modern world's symbol of paganism." Paganism was going to be struck down. "God has blessed a group of vanguard Muslims, the forefront of Islam, to destroy America." None of this, apart from bin Laden's blithe unconcern with the ethics of war, was untrue to Qutb's commentaries.

The tone in that first video after 9/11 was self-consciously exotic. Some of bin Laden's comments were, to anyone without a background in Islamist thought, incomprehensible. Bin Laden said that America, as a result of the attacks, was "filled with horror," which was certainly true. But he added a puzzling remark. He said, "Our Islamic nation has been tasting the same for more [than] eighty years, of humiliation and disgrace, its sons killed and their blood spilled, its sanctities desecrated." But what was the terrible thing that had taken place more than eighty years before—the terrible thing that had continued ever since, humiliating and disgracing what he called "the Islamic nation"? An event from 1921 or before—what could that have been? I think that television viewers around the world, staring at CNN or even at Al Jazeera, wondered about that remark and silently surmised that bin Laden was raving incoherently. But the readers of Sayyid Qutb would have understood. Bin Laden was speaking about the crimes of Kemal Atatürk—the plunge into secular modernity that culminated in 1924 in the abolition of the Caliphate. Bin Laden was speaking about the initial, devastating attack on the Islamic nation—the attack that signaled the beginning of Islam's "extermination," in Qutb's fearful word.

Bin Laden was thinking, in short, about the era of the First World War and its aftermath. And this was in the grand tradition. In the totalitarian movements of the twentieth century, everyone has thought about the First World War and its aftermath. For those were the years when the liberal project of the nineteenth century finally went to pieces—the years when the simpleminded principles of rational thought and inevitable progress began to look, in their ingenuousness, grotesque and mendacious. Those were the years, in the immediate aftermath of the world war, when the new mass movements arose for no other purpose than to declare the old liberal project of the nineteenth century a lie—a gigantic deception foisted on mankind in the interest of plunder, devastation, conspiracy, and ruin. Those were the years when "vanguards" of self-sacrificing militants tried to lead mankind out of the corruptions and horrors of liberal civilization into a new kind of life—granite, solid, unified, the new age of the resurrected empire of yore, the age of purity and eternity. Those were the years of the heroic leaders, the supermen and geniuses who, in their evident madness, seemed to be flecked with the divine.

And here on the rock outcropping, in their turbans, staring at the camera, sat the new vanguard, speaking about an Islamic version of the coming millennium. Only, how was this modern new Caliphate going to be brought about? How was the great crime against Islam that had been committed by Kemal Atatürk, by paganism, and by Zionism to be righted? How to avert the extermination of Islam, and to restore its pristine purity, and lead Islam to worldwide triumph? On these topics, bin Laden in that first video of his, after the 9/11 attacks, said nothing, and the visual images hinted at nothing, and the question was left unanswered.

But there was never any doubt about how those goals were going to be achieved. Sheikh Rahman had already made everything clear, from his outpost in Jersey City, with his calls for random massacres. And there were many such calls. The late Abdullah Azzam, leader of the Office for Services, used to issue them in his lectures. Malise Ruthven quotes from these lectures in *A Fury for God.* You can look them up for yourself at www.religioscope.com on the Internet, where a few excerpts, in an English-language version slightly different from Ruthven's, have been attractively posted by Azzam's admirers. The lectures make the case for suicide warriors—for a revolutionary vanguard of people who, by embracing death, will awaken the sleeping nation, meaning, in this case, the community of Islam that will form the Caliphate. "A small group: they are the ones who carry convictions and ambitions," Azzam said. "And an even smaller group from this small group, are the ones who flee from the worldly life in order to spread and act upon these ambitions. And an even smaller group from this elite group, are the ones who sacrifice their souls and their blood in order to bring victory to these ambitions and principles. So, they are the cream of the cream of the cream. It is not possible to reach glory except by traversing this Path."

Azzam yearned for the martyrdom of scholars: "The extent to which the number of martyred scholars increases is the extent to which nations are delivered from their slumber, rescued from their decline and awoken from their sleep." He continued: "History does not write its lines except with blood. Glory does not build its lofty edifice except with skulls. Honor and respect cannot be established except on a foundation of cripples and corpses."

Here is another example of this same idea, from Ali Benhadj, one of the principal Islamist leaders of Algeria, who has been quoted by the

French scholar, Frédéric Encel. Benhadj said, "If a faith, a belief, is not watered and irrigated by blood, it does not grow. It does not live. Principles are reinforced by sacrifices, suicide operations and martyrdom for Allah. Faith is propagated by counting up deaths every day, by adding up massacres and charnel-houses. It hardly matters if the person who has been sacrificed is no longer there. He has won."

I could go on quoting—but, enough. Surely this, you will say, cannot be Western—surely this kind of talk, at last, is exotic! But this is how the leaders of Germany used to speak, sixty years ago. Bolsheviks were not afraid to speak like that. *Viva la muerte!* said Franco's general. This is not exotic. This is the totalitarian cult of death. *This* is the terrible thing that got underway more than eighty years ago.

VI
Wishful Thinking

THE APOCALYPTIC and death-obsessed mass movements of the past aroused many responses among good-hearted and intelligent people around the world during these last eighty years, and one of those responses is worth recalling. It came from people who were themselves liberals, who revered every aspect of liberal civilization and accepted its values, who did not quarrel with any aspect of liberalism and its principles—and who, even so, gazed at the craziest and most violent of the anti-liberal movements, and blinked, and saw no reason for upset. And this response, an earnest dismissal of the dangers emanating from irrationalist mass movements, was entirely normal and understandable.

For it is very odd to think that millions or tens of millions of people, relying on their own best judgments, might end up joining a pathological political movement. Individual madmen might step forward—yes, that is unquestionable. The Reverend Jim Jones might lead the demented residents of his pathetic Jonestown in Guyana to their collective suicide. But, surely, millions of people are not going to choose death, and the Jonestowns of this world are not going to take over entire societies. The very idea of a pathological mass movement seems too far-fetched to be believable.

Journalists and writers and politicians may go on reporting that, even so, such movements do exist and inspire followers and wreak their damage. But shouldn't we train a skeptical lens on those alarming reports? Mightn't some of those frightening accounts be exaggerated, perhaps even untrue? It might be in some people's interest to report that pathological mass movements roam the earth, posing dangers to everyone else. Maybe some of those allegedly sinister mass movements are, in reality, not very sinister at all, and ought to be recognized, instead, as progressive, positive, and admirable. Maybe those movements have stuck a well-deserved pin in the sides of the rich and powerful, and the rich and powerful have responded with a campaign of slander, nattering on about evil. Isn't that possible? Such a thing is definitely possible. Which interpretation to believe, then—that millions of people have gone out of their minds and have subscribed to a pathological political tendency? Or that small numbers of corrupt and zealous journalists and propagandists are painting distorted pictures, at the behest of powerful and conservative social classes? The second explanation asks so much less of us—seems less extravagant, more reasonable, more plausible.

Or, let us suppose that, in some remote tropical backwater or untracked desert, a social or political movement does appear to be showing, in fact, signs of a pathological attachment to murder and suicide. In that case, there has got to be a rational explanation. Perhaps some unspeakable social condition has provoked the murderous impulse. Perhaps small groups of exploiters or imperialists, through their terrible deeds, have driven thousands or even millions of people out of their minds. Perhaps a population has been humiliated beyond human endurance. Unbearable social conditions might well breed irrational reactions—though, in such a case, the irrational reactions ought not to be seen as irrational. For the human race does not generally act in irrational ways.

How many times those skeptical doubts and alternative explanations have appeared and reappeared in the course of these eighty years, in how many strange and clever versions! Everyone remembers the several arguments that, once upon a time, used to convince liberal-minded people of the virtue and progressive nature of Stalin and the Communist movement, even in its worst days. The claim that Stalin was deliberately starving to death millions of Ukrainian farmers, or that Stalin had reintroduced slave labor, or that Stalin was whimsically liquidating his own followers and comrades—those claims seemed so extraordinary, so unlikely, so impossibly at odds with the known goals and civilized ideals of the Marxist movement. It was much easier to suppose that, as the Communists argued, Stalin had been slandered by bourgeois propagandists, by right-wing manipulators, and by Trotskyite wreckers. Everyone remembers how those same arguments in communism's defense were updated and reapplied to other circumstances in later decades—to China during the heyday of Mao Zedong, and to Cambodia during the time of Pol Pot, and to other places and despots.

But I wonder if we don't remember those particular arguments, the ones in defense of Stalin, Mao, or Pol Pot, almost too well for our own good, today. We look back on the debates over communism, and we see the errors and delusions of the pro-Communist left in such a dazzling light that, by now, we can barely remember how any reasonable person could have fallen for the shrill and hysterical arguments on Communism's behalf. In the 1930s, good-hearted liberals sneered at the ashen-faced witnesses who reported that Stalin was starving the Ukrainian farmers; and today, good-hearted liberals sneer just as easily at the people who, in the 1930s, sneered at ashen-faced witnesses. We cannot imagine, we modern sophisticates, how anyone could have made such mistakes in the past. As for some of the other, non-Communist versions of those same delusionary arguments, the seductive arguments that, in the bleakest years of the twentieth century, used to arouse liberal sympathies for totalitarian movements of the extreme right—why, we can hardly believe that any such right-wing seductions ever existed.

The right-wing seductions did exist, however, and now and then a smattering of high-minded democratic and left-wing personalities, succumbing to those lures, ended up persuaded of the virtues or good intentions of Mussolini and Franco. Even Hitler and the Nazis managed to evoke halfway friendly nods from some of the more addled progressive democrats of the left. That seems impossible. It was possible. There was the curious case of the French Socialists of the 1930s. The French Socialists boasted of old and impeccable democratic credentials, reaching back into the nineteenth century. The Socialists were sober and responsible, relatively speaking. Their party was popular. In the middle and late 1930s, the Socialists won their share of elections in France. Sometimes they took their place at the head of the national government. In Léon Blum, the Socialists managed to produce a great leader, too, their own prime minister, who knew how to fuse French patriotism with the cause of social justice and the loftiest of cultural values. Still, the French Socialists had their factions, and Blum and his supporters did not represent the entire party. The party's secretary general, Paul Faure, led his own, somewhat larger faction, called the Paul-Fauristes, with a solid bloc of seats in the National Assembly. And socialism's two factions disagreed mightily—most of all about war.

Blum and his supporters regarded Hitler and the Nazis with horror, and figured that France ought to put up a stern resistance and get ready for war. The Paul-Fauristes, too, took a dim view of Hitler. But mostly they remembered the First World War, and shivered with fear at the prospect of another such calamity. They were eager, they were desperate, to find a description of reality that did not point to a new war in the future. They grew thoughtful, therefore. They did not wish to reduce Germany in all its Teutonic complexity to black-and-white terms of good and evil. The anti-war Socialists pointed out that Germany had been wronged by the Treaty of Versailles, at the conclusion of the First World War. The anti-war Socialists observed that Germans living in the Slavic countries to the east were sometimes cruelly treated by their neighbors, and that Germany in the 1930s had every right to complain about its neighbors, and that Germany's people were, in fact, suffering, just as Hitler said. And, having analyzed the German scene in that manner, the anti-war Socialists concluded that Hitler and the Nazis, in railing against the great powers and the Treaty of Versailles, did make some legitimate arguments—even if Nazism came from the extreme right and was not at all to the Socialists' taste.

The anti-war Socialists wanted to know: why shouldn't the French government show a little flexibility in the face of Hitler's demands? Why not recognize that some of Hitler's points were well taken? Why not look for ways to conciliate the outraged German people and, in that way, to conciliate the Nazis? Why not make every effort, strain every muscle, to avoid a new Verdun?

The anti-war Socialists of France did not think they were being cowardly or unprincipled in making those arguments. On the contrary, they took pride in their anti-war instincts. They regarded themselves as exceptionally brave and honest. They felt that courage and radicalism allowed them to peer beneath the surface of events and identify the deeper factors at work in international relations—the truest danger facing France. This danger, in their judgment, did not come from Hitler and the Nazis, not principally.

The truest danger came from the warmongers and arms manufacturers of France itself, as well as from the other great powers—the people who stood to benefit in material ways from a new war. The danger came from bellicose French leaders who, in their greed and selfishness, were going to bring on the new Verdun. Those were the arguments on the anti-war left, the political arguments. But the political arguments rested on something deeper, too—a philosophical belief, profound, large, and attractive, which was reassuring instead of terrifying. It was the belief that, in the modern world, even the enemies of reason cannot be the enemies of reason. Even the unreasonable must be, in some fashion, reasonable.

The belief underlying those anti-war arguments was, in short, an unyielding faith in universal rationality. It was the old-fashioned liberal naïveté of the nineteenth century—the simple-minded optimism that had blown up in the First World War but that, even so, indestructible, had lingered into the twentieth-century imagination. That belief was the other face of liberalism—not liberalism as the advocacy of freedom, rationality, progress, and the acceptance of uncertainty, but liberalism as blind faith in a predetermined future, liberalism as a fantasy of a strictly rational world, liberalism as denial. That was the philosophical doctrine lurking within the anti-war imagination in France. And, stirred by that antique idea, the anti-war Socialists gazed across the Rhine and simply refused to believe that millions of upstanding Germans had enlisted in a political movement whose animating principles were paranoid conspiracy theories, blood-curdling hatreds, medieval superstitions, and the lure of murder. At Auschwitz the SS said, "Here there is no why." The anti-war Socialists in France believed no such thing. In their eyes, there was always a why.

Hitler and the Nazis ranted about the Jews, yes, and the rants were medieval, and the tones of hatred and superstition grated on the ear. Still, the anti-war Socialists wanted to understand their enemies and not simply to dismiss them—wanted to seek out whatever was comprehensible, the points on which everyone could agree. And so, listening to the Nazis make their wildest speeches, the anti-war Socialists, in a thoughtful mood, asked themselves: what is anti-Semitism, anyway? Does every single criticism of the Jews reflect the superstitions of the Middle Ages? Surely it ought to be possible to criticize the Jews without being vilified as anti-Semites. Hitler ranted about Jewish financiers. He was excessive. Still, France's Socialists were, by definition, the enemies of financiers. Some financiers were Jews. Should Jewish financiers be exempt from criticism, simply because they were Jews?

The anti-war Socialists surveyed the pro-war politicians of France. Weren't some of the hard-liners—the French hawks, who favored war—Jews? The anti-war Socialists began to suspect that Jews in France did present a danger in regard to banking and capitalism; and equally so in matters of war and peace. The anti-war Socialists kept running into one stubborn and undeniable fact at every step they took: the prime minister from their own party, Léon Blum, was himself a Jew. Blum took a hard line on Hitler. This was suspicious. Didn't Blum's Jewish roots explain his relentless efforts to get France to arm itself against Germany? Wasn't Jewishness itself a problem to be reckoned with—something questionable, a threat to France?

The anti-war Socialists despised Léon Blum. People looked on him with a disgust that famously veered into sexual revulsion—a major theme of hatred for Blum. And, in contemplating his detestable qualities, the anti-war Socialists—not all of them, but some—began to feel that, on the Jewish question, just as on several other questions, Hitler was wrong, but perhaps not entirely wrong. Then came the invasion, in June 1940. The French army went down to defeat. Marshal Pétain and the extreme right in France proposed to accept the invasion and to form a new French government, which would acknowledge Hitler's leadership and serve as his loyal ally. The National Assembly convened in the South of France, and Blum and his group among the Socialists and some of the other parties refused, even in the face of military defeat, to go along with any such proposal. But, on this issue, socialism's two factions finally broke apart. A majority of the Socialists in the National Assembly, the anti-war faction, voted with Pétain. The marshal's proposition ascended into French law. The new government, under Pétain's baton, became Nazism's friend and ally. Blum was arrested and sent off to Dachau, and some of Blum's Socialist comrades went underground to organize their wing of the French Resistance.

But, among the anti-war Socialists, a number of people, having voted with Pétain, took the logical next step and, on patriotic and idealistic grounds, accepted positions in his new government, at Vichy. Some of those Socialists went a little further, too, and began to see a virtue in Pétain's program for a new France and a new Europe—

a program for strength and virility, a Europe ruled by a single-party state instead of by the corrupt cliques of bourgeois democracy, a Europe cleansed of the impurities of Judaism and of the Jews themselves, a Europe of the anti-liberal imagination. And, in that very remarkable fashion, a number of the anti-war Socialists of France came full circle. They had begun as defenders of liberal values and human rights, and they evolved into defenders of bigotry, tyranny, superstition, and mass murder. They were democratic leftists who, through the miraculous workings of the slippery slope and a naive faith in the rationalism of all things, ended as fascists.

Long ago, you say? Not so long ago.

OUR CURRENT predicament was brought upon us by acts of suicide terrorism—and it is worth taking the trouble to glance at the political landscape of those acts, beginning with the agonies of the Israelis and the Palestinians. In 2000, during the last year of his administration, Bill Clinton offered to create a Palestinian state. Ehud Barak, the Israeli prime minister, had already withdrawn the Israeli army from Lebanon, which was easy to do, in a sense, because the Israelis had never wanted Lebanon, anyway. But now Clinton extracted from Barak a promise to withdraw from lands that at least a minority of Israeli Jews did want for themselves—from the Gaza Strip, from part of Jerusalem, and from all but small portions of the West Bank. And, with those Israeli concessions in hand, Clinton made his offer to Yasser Arafat: a Palestinian state, to be built on the surrendered lands. The offer was refused. And all over the world—certainly in Europe—something of an instant consensus arose to the effect that Arafat, in rejecting the offer, had acted sagely. It was widely believed—it was reported in the world press, sometimes with illustrative maps—that Clinton's offer would have shriveled the proposed new Palestinian state to an archipelago of lonely islets, swamped on every side by

Israeli soldiers and lacking any possibility of generating an authentic national identity.

But that was not the case. Clinton's principal negotiator, Dennis Ross, has explained that, in the offer to Arafat, the new Palestinian state was going to be entirely contiguous, except for the Gaza Strip. And even Gaza, in its faraway corner on the Mediterranean, was going to be connected to the West Bank by means of an elevated highway and railroad across Israel—an imaginative touch—to allow the Palestinians to commute back and forth, free of the humiliation of Israeli checkpoints. The Israeli settlements of the past twenty years or so in the occupied territories, most of them, were going to be, at last, evacuated. The Jewish fanatics who, in their own variation on the twentieth-century tune, wanted to resurrect the glory days of the ancient Hebrews, were going to be sent packing. The offer was serious, then. It conceded to the Palestinians all but a very small portion of what Arafat had vociferously demanded for many years, and even that small portion was to be compensated with other lands. The offer gave the Palestinians a capital in a shared Jerusalem. The Israelis had never wanted to share Jerusalem, before. This was not a low point for Palestinian national aspirations.

And, at that decisive moment, Hamas and the smaller Islamic Jihad—the two factions of Palestine's Islamist movement—finally succeeded in dominating the Palestinian political scene, at least for the time being. The suicide terror campaign, simmering for many years, now began to display the qualities of a genuinely popular impulse—the crowds chanting approval, the wailing mothers calling on their children to die, the masked young men pledging to do as the mothers demanded, the grisly wall posters, the cult of the dead. Militias from Arafat's nationalist organization joined in the campaign, together with some of Arafat's rivals on the left—a broad coalition of Palestinian groups, across the political spectrum.

The suicide attacks began in earnest with the bombing of a

teenagers' disco in Tel Aviv in June 2001, and grew more deadly in the fall, and deadlier still in 2002, until random mass murders had become weekly and even daily events. Young women emerged as suicide terrorists, and, after their deaths, were celebrated as feminist role models, in the realm of the departed. And, at that ghastliest of moments, another remarkable and parallel event took place.

All over the world, the popularity of the Palestinian cause did not collapse. It increased. In the United States, the early months of 2002 proved to be the moment when student activism on behalf of the Palestinian cause at last began to attract public attention, and the students and professors launched their campaign to get America's universities to boycott Israel economically. In Britain and in Europe, professors launched their boycott of scholarly conferences in Israel. The European blacklist against Israeli professors got underway. In several countries around the world, the radical anti-globalization movement threw itself into the new cause.

José Bove, the doughty French farmer who had theatrically demolished a McDonald's in France, chose this moment to travel to Ramallah, the seat of Arafat's Palestinian Authority, to express his agrarian solidarity. In Washington, D.C., in April 2002 the anti-globalization movement staged a mass protest in which the new theme of Palestinian solidarity managed to overwhelm the old and traditional theme of protest against the plutocratic institutions of world finance.

Naturally, most of the people who stood up in those early months of 2002 to endorse the Palestinian cause said nothing at all in praise of suicide terrorism, and some people said a few words against it. Still, suicide terror had its defenders, and these were not marginal or hard to identify. At the anti-globalization march in Washington, some of the participants chanted, "Martyrs, not murderers"—a grisly chant, whose meaning was: the murders are not murders, and the killers are heroes. Some of the defenders were intellectuals. Every year in New York a couple of thousand left-wing and liberal academics and politicos gather together with a number of European and Latin American colleagues and comrades at something called the Socialist Scholars Conference—a lively event, which I have attended many times, sometimes as a speaker.

But at the 2002 conference a substantial crowd listened to an Egyptian novelist defend a young Palestinian woman who had just committed suicide and murder—and, having heard the defense, the crowd burst into applause. That was unprecedented, in New York—at least, outside of the gatherings of the Islamist movement. And those events in the spring of 2002—the chanting marchers, the applauding intellectuals—typified a hundred other events all over the United States and even more in Europe, not to mention Latin America and other places. A cold cloud seemed to have gathered, and the plunge in temperature was obvious, and out of the cloud dribbled sinister droplets of appreciation for suicide murders—a perverse appreciation expressed by civilized people who, not two or three months earlier, would never have imagined themselves expressing any such opinion. And what could explain that sudden atmospheric change? The new attention to the Middle East paid by people who had never taken any interest before, the gathering solidarity for the Palestinian cause at its most violent moment, the drizzle of sympathy for random killings and public suicides—what accounted for those developments?

Suicide terror accounted for those developments. Violence attracts. The nail bombs flew apart on the Israeli sidewalks, the mutilated bodies of Jews and Arabs lay across the pavement, the scenes of grief were broadcast all over the world, the Israelis retaliated, the spectacle of defiant Palestinian funerals flickered on television screens everywhere, the photographs of the lovely dead young women adorned the newspapers, as if in bridal announcements. And, to people who watched those broadcasts and studied the news accounts and lingered over the photographs, the entire series of events posed a genuine dilemma, which cried out to be resolved. The images did suggest that, in Palestine, a mass pathology had broken out. I believe that everyone who paid attention to those images, all over the world, was shocked by those scenes. And the philosophical conundrum was unavoidable.

In Israel, once the terrorist attacks had gotten underway, the voting public turned against Barak and the peaceniks, as could have been predicted, and came out in favor of Ariel Sharon and the hard line; and the hard line went into effect. Sharon had never believed in negotiating, anyway. Nor did he want to give up land. His policy was a stick without a carrot. He did not cultivate the Palestinian liberals; he insulted them. A long-term solution seemed beyond his imagining, even if, coached by Bush, he mumbled a few words now and then about a Palestinian state in the distant future. Sharon wanted to crack down on terrorists, and did crack down, even when bystanders got killed. Still, this policy of his conformed to an obvious logic of military reasoning. A conventional logic: to smother violence under a blanket of greater violence. And, as anyone could have predicted, once the tanks were crawling through the Palestinian streets and the curfews were in place and the terrible raids were breaking into houses in the West Bank and eventually even in Gaza, the rhythm of terrorist attacks did slow down, somewhat.

But what was the logic of the suicide attacks? It was easy to see how the young suicide terrorists had ended up agreeing to kill themselves. Enormous institutions elsewhere in the Arab world, the Saudi princelings, the Iraqi and Syrian Baath, some of the great institutions of Arab journalism, told them to do so, and, in the Saudi and Iraqi cases, even paid them, and the pressures from other countries were converted into pressures at home, which young people would find hard to resist. Clerics and schoolteachers advised suicide. But what were those clerics and the other adults thinking? That was not so easy to identify. Clinton and Barak had already offered a Palestinian state. Perhaps the purpose of the suicide attacks was to widen the borders of the proposed new state—though, in that case, Arafat might have haggled at Camp David for an extra slice or two, and the question of slightly wider borders would at least have been broached. Or maybe the purpose was to widen the proposed new borders by more than a slice, to obtain a Palestinian state on a different scale altogether. But the whole point of negotiating during the eight years of Israeli-Palestinian talks, beginning at Oslo, was to work out a compromise. Or maybe the purpose of the attacks was, as Hamas and Islamic Jihad forthrightly proclaimed, to abolish Israel altogether and establish the reign of shariah in every corner of the land. But this was not within the realm of reality. Actually, none of the imaginable purposes had any chance of being realized, and especially not after 9/11. The attacks on the United States brought American interests into play, and America's defense required Israel not to yield one inch in the face of terrorist bombs—if only to prevent anyone from supposing that America, too, might yield an inch in the face of suicide attacks.

Suicide terror against the Israelis was bound to succeed in one realm only, and this was the realm of death—the realm in which a perfect Palestinian state could luxuriate in the shade of a perfect Koranic tranquility, cleansed of every iniquitous thought and temptation and of every rival faith and ethnic group. Among the Palestinians, everybody seemed to understand this, at some level. The defiant exhibition of infant corpses at the Palestinian funerals, the macabre posters, the young men marching through the streets dressed in martyrs' shrouds—these statements and actions showed with perfect clarity that, in the popular imagination, utopia and the morgue had blended, and the "street" did understand, and death was the goal. And, all over the world, good-hearted people who observed those scenes had to ask: can this really be so?

Is the world truly a place where mass movements bedeck themselves in shrouds and march to the cemetery? This seemed unthinkable. And, all over the world, the temptation became great, became irresistible, to conclude that, no, the world remains a rational place, and pathological movements do not exist, and slanderers are weaving lies on behalf of narrow material interests. No, suicide terror must be—it has to be, perhaps in ways invisible to the naked eye—a rational response to real-life conditions.

And so, in a fashion that was all too familiar to anyone who remembered the history of the French anti-war Socialists of an earlier time, people around the world rushed to suggest ways in which the apparent mass pathologies were anything but pathologies, and terror was reasonable and explicable and perhaps even admirable. Some people convinced themselves that Islamist ideology was not Islamist ideology. Hamas, to them, was not Hamas, and the goal of those suicide bombers was a moderate and plausible two-state partition—a solution worthy of the United Nations, with terror as a mere pressure tactic, like a labor strike. Some people convinced themselves, on the other hand, that Israel had no right to exist, and Islamist ideology was fair and reasonable on this issue, and suicide terror advanced a just cause. Some people—a far greater number—recognized that suicide terror was tactically unproductive, and that suicide was suicide. And yet, suicide terror vented authentic, therefore commendable, emotions. Suicide terror, in this interpretation, sang the song of Palestinians who could no longer endure life without a state of their own. Some people suggested that Israel's religious fanatics, the ultra-right, in seizing new parcels of land for settlement colonies, had driven masses of Palestinians out of their minds, especially young people, who now preferred to die. And the suicide terrorists were, in fact, crazy, but their enemies and not their leaders and their own doctrines were to blame.

There was, in short, an idea that each new act of murder and suicide testified to how oppressive were the Israelis. Palestinian terror, in this view, was the measure of Israeli guilt. The more grotesque the terror, the deeper the guilt. And, if unfathomable motives appeared to drive the suicide bombers forward, the oppressiveness of Israel was likewise deemed to be, by logical inference, unfathomable—a bottomless oppression, which had given rise to the maximum of violence, which is suicide murder.

The commuter buses, the pizza parlors, the discos, the hotel dining rooms, the bustling sidewalks—these exploded into random carnage. And, with every new atrocity, the search was on to find ever larger accusations to place at Israel's feet. These accusations spun variations on a single theme. It was the idea that Zionism was something more than a program of national self-determination for the Jews, more than a simple and straightforward doctrine of Jewish self-defense. Zionism was, on the contrary, racism—a program of hatred and contempt for other people. And, with this idea established, a declension of tropes and images marched steadily forward within the arguments of the new Palestinian sympathizers. The comparison between Israel and the old white Republic of South Africa from the days of apartheid marked only the first of those tropes. That was an easy comparison to make, a natural, for anyone who imagined (as most people seemed to do) that Israel's non-European Jews did not exist, and that Israel's European Jews were not principally refugees but were, instead, colonial settlers, and that Zionism, like apartheid, was a doctrine of contempt for the non-Europeans.

Yet not even this trope sufficed to explain the suicide terror. In South Africa during the worst days of white racism, the anti-apartheid resistance movement engaged in all kinds of violence and even some acts of random terror, though never as a large-scale policy; yet the South African resisters managed not to slip into the lowest rung of nihilist despair. How to explain that, by contrast, the Palestinians had done just that? Palestinian nihilism could only mean that Palestinian sufferings were, in some important respect, worse, and by far, than South Africa's in the past. The South African analogy therefore yielded to a grimmer and angrier trope, which was Nazism. Israel became, in the rhetoric of its accusers, a Nazi entity—a state so utterly devoted to evil, so far beyond the bounds of human decency as to make suicide murder a comprehensible reaction on the part of its victims.

The notion of Zionism as a kind of Nazism has appeared and reappeared in the language of Israel's critics and enemies many times over the decades. A formal history of that notion ought someday to be written, detailing the exact times and places in which the Nazi analogy has come into fashion and has gone out again. (There was, for instance, the strange case of the West German radical left, which turned vehemently anti-Nazi in the 1960s, and, at the same time, began to attach the Nazi label to the Jewish state—and then began to abandon the trope in the late 1970s and '80s. Or, to cite a stranger example, there was the transformation in Arab nationalist opinion, which tended to look sympathetically on Nazism until the 1960s, and then, in a remarkable turnaround, began to see the Nazis as evil—and attached the Nazi label to Israel.) And now, in those violent months of 2001–02, with the suicide terror attacks at their height, the vogue for likening Israel to a Nazi state once more surged into prominence, more so than ever before.

The Israeli army hunted terrorists in the West Bank city of Jenin in the spring of 2002, and the killings on both sides were sizable: some twenty-three Israeli soldiers, together with fifty-two Palestinians, some of whom were civilian bystanders. It was a grim event and, according to Human Rights Watch, sometimes a criminal event—though Israel's attack was also said, from a cold military point of view, to represent a breakthrough in relatively civilized army tactics, an example of how to engage in house-to-house fighting without killing large numbers of people randomly and in error. The attack was not in the Russian style; Jenin was not Grozny. But, in the popular imagination, the Israeli attack hurtled upward, past Grozny, into the Nazi skies, where the fighting in Jenin loomed as a veritable Holocaust, an Auschwitz, or, in an alternative image, as the Middle Eastern equivalent of the Wehrmacht's assault on the Warsaw Ghetto. These tropes were massively accepted, around the world. Typing in the combined names of "Jenin" and "Auschwitz" on Google on the Internet, I came up with 2,890 references; and, typing in "Jenin" and "Nazi," I came up with 8,100 references. There were 63,100 references to the combined names of "Sharon" and "Hitler." And even Nazism struck many of Israel's critics as much too pale an explanation for the horrific nature of Israeli action. For the pathos of suicide terror is limitless, and if Palestinian teenagers were blowing themselves up in acts of random murder, a rational explanation was going to require ever more extreme tropes, beyond even Nazism.

At the height of the suicide bomb campaign, in the early spring of 2002, a writers' organization called the International Parliament of Writers sent a delegation to the Palestinian territories to express solidarity with Palestinian writers and to report back to the world. The Parliament of Writers is a relatively new organization, which was established as something of an elite alternative or complement to the older and more bureaucratic international writers' organization, PEN. Rushdie was one of the Parliament's founders—which is to say, the Parliament of Writers could have been expected to display a keen knowledge of Islamist radicalism and its consequences around the world.

But that might be an unfair expectation. Maybe the Parliament of Writers should simply be seen as one more sociological sample from the Western intelligentsia. The writers' delegation descended on Ramallah. Sharon was conducting his Javert-like persecution of Arafat there, preparing to raze Arafat's compound room by room without ever actually killing him—a surreal spectacle. And the writers' delegation, having made their tour, duly submitted their reports to the outside world, and the reports turned out to be a catalogue raisonné of the standard tropes of terror and Zionism.

Breyten Breytenbach, a South African (and Parisian) writer, wrote an open letter to Sharon, whom he chose to address not as prime minister but as "General Sharon." Breytenbach complained that "any criticism of Israel's policies" is vilified as "an expression of anti-Semitism." This sort of vilification seemed to him a threat to free speech, and he would not stand for it. "I reject this attempt at censorship," he wrote. He acknowledged that "facile comparisons" make an imprecise method of argument. "Apartheid was not Nazism," he specified, and Israeli policies "should not be equated with Apartheid." Then he went on to compare the Palestinian territories to the system of apartheid—"for only too often are they reminiscent of the ghettos and the controlled camps of misery one knew in South Africa." He explained that, in the old South Africa, the racist whites used to regard themselves as a *Herrenvolk*—a "master race," in the Nazi term. The Israelis, too, in Breytenbach's view, regarded themselves as a *Herrenvolk*. He said to General Sharon, "How else is one to describe the comportment of your armies when one is flooded by the horror of what you're doing?"

In Breytenbach's presentation, the Israelis were manipulating the United States with crude propaganda, though he considered that Benjamin Netanyahu, not Sharon, was chiefly culpable. Here Breytenbach reverted to an older trope, which would have been familiar to anyone who remembered the manner in which Léon Blum used to be vilified. Breytenbach wrote, addressing himself to General Sharon, "Your used car salesman doppelganger, Netanyahu, ploys this craft of crude propaganda more openly, as if he were a dirty finger tweaking the clitoris of a swooning American public opinion." It was somewhat odd to write about Netanyahu, who at that moment was out of office in Israel; but, to speak honestly, General Sharon was much too fat and a bit too old to inspire any sexual reaction at all, even a sexual revulsion.

Breytenbach dwelled on suicide terror, at least for a moment. He disapproved of it—"the cold-blooded massacres of innocents ordered by fanatic warlords in the name of resistance." Still, he quoted with evident approval the comments of a man described as a human rights lawyer—who, Breytenbach said, "remarked bitterly that repression has now penetrated the skin of the people, and that now they have nothing else to defend themselves with except their skins. Hence the human bombs." Breytenbach concluded by warning that suicide terror was bound to be effective, too. It was going to "profoundly divide and weaken Israel." In short, nothing about human bombs seemed irrational or inexplicable to Breyten Breytenbach. Suicide terror was the measure of Israel's supremely repugnant quality. This argument ran in *Le Monde*.

And what of the final trope in the accusation against Israel, the one beyond Nazism? Breytenbach hinted at it in a phrase that joined *Herrenvolk* to the phrase "chosen people"—a conflation of a Nazi term with a concept out of Judaism. "I also grew up among a 'chosen people' who behaved as Herrenvolk," he wrote—neatly combining in a single sentence the tropes about apartheid, Nazism, and Judaism. This last trope, though, the one about Judaism, emerged much more clearly in the statements of one other delegate from the Parliament of Writers, José Saramago, the Portuguese novelist. Saramago caused a stir at Ramallah by invoking Nazism in a comment that was regarded, even by his fellow delegates, as a bit much. Sharon's siege of Arafat in his compound was, Saramago said, "a crime comparable to Auschwitz," though no one was killed—and, to the Israeli journalist who asked where were the gas chambers, Saramago replied, "Not yet here." But that was just an offhand remark. Saramago expressed himself more fully and eloquently in the essay that he, too, went on to write.

In Saramago's view, as in Breytenbach's, Israel's horrific policies could be traced to Judaism itself. Saramago brought up the Old Testament and the story of David and Goliath. This story, in Saramago's interpretation, describes a blond person (Saramago seemed to think it important to associate blondness with the Jews) who employs a cruelly superior technology, the slingshot, to fell at a distance a hapless and presumably non-blond person, the unfortunate and oppressed

Goliath. This, in Saramago's view, conveyed the essence of Israel's actions in the early months of 2002:

> The blond David of yesteryear surveys from a helicopter the occupied Palestinian lands and fires missiles at unarmed innocents; the delicate David of yore mans the most powerful tanks in the world and flattens and blows up what he finds in his tread; the lyrical David who sang praise to Bathsheba, incarnated today in the gargantuan figure of a war criminal named Ariel Sharon, hurls the "poetic" message that first it is necessary to finish off the Palestinians in order later to negotiate with those who remain.

Saramago was aflame:

> Intoxicated mentally by the messianic dream of Greater Israel which will finally achieve the expansionist dreams of the most radical Zionism; contaminated by the monstrous and rooted "certitude" that in this catastrophic and absurd world there exists a people chosen by God and that, consequently, all the actions of an obsessive, psychological and pathologically exclusivist racism are justified; educated and trained in the idea that any suffering that has been inflicted, or is being inflicted, or will be inflicted on everyone else, especially the Palestinians, will always be inferior to that which they themselves suffered in the Holocaust, the Jews endlessly scratch their own wound to keep it bleeding, to make it incurable, and they show it to the world as if it were a banner. Israel seizes hold of the terrible words of God in Deuteronomy: "Vengeance is mine, and I will be repaid." Israel wants all of us to feel guilty, directly or indirectly, for the horrors of the Holocaust; Israel wants us to renounce the most elemental critical judgment and for us to transform ourselves into a docile echo of its will; Israel wants us to recognize de jure what, in its eyes, is a de facto reality: absolute

> impunity. From the point of view of the Jews, Israel cannot ever be brought to judgment, because it was tortured, gassed and incinerated in Auschwitz.

These were magnificent sentences, rhetorically speaking. Here were no obscene images and dirty fingers—here was an aristocrat of letters. The baroque semicolons and rolling phrases rumble like drums. You can see why Saramago in 1998 was given the Nobel Prize. He offered one additional thought, too, which came to him at the very end of his essay—an afterthought. He reflected that some people might be wondering about the suicide bombers. Saramago deployed a splendidly expressive ellipsis to address this matter—a marvelous display of contempt and disdain at a calibrated pitch:

> Ah, yes, the horrendous massacres of civilians caused by the so-called suicide terrorists. . . . Horrendous, yes, doubtless; condemnable, yes, doubtless, but Israel still has a lot to learn if it is not capable of understanding the reasons that can bring a human being to turn himself into a bomb.

And so, in this bravura manner, the suicide terrorists turned out, once again, to be fully comprehensible in normal terms—driven to their deeds by the horrors of blond racism, and by traditions that were older, too, unto the ancient Hebrews. This essay ran in *El País*, the leading newspaper of the Spanish-speaking world. And, with the tropes of South Africa and Nazism finally seeping into the deeper, more fundamental sediments of religious belief, the rationalization of suicide terror sunk at last to levels that had been reached, long ago, by the anti-war faction of the old French Socialists, and the beautiful souls of the European literary class found themselves once again deposited willy-nilly on the rhetorical soil of the traditional extreme right, fulminating about Judaism, its obsessive hatefulness, its spirit of vengeance, its effort to reduce the rest of the world into docile echoes of its will, and its bloody crimes—all this, in a desperate effort to show that mass pathological movements do not exist, except when conjured into being by sinister oppressors.

The reaction on the part of many people around the world to the wave of suicide bombing in Israel and the Palestinian territories was remarkable in one other respect. The high tide of the terrorist attacks, in the early months of 2002, proved to be the very moment when, around the world, large numbers of people felt impelled to express their fury at the Israelis. Then something curious happened. The Israeli repression settled in for the long haul, and, in time, only grew heavier. The many authentic indications of Palestinian progress during the years since the Oslo Accords in 1993, the expansion of the Palestinian middle class, the new businesses and tourist hotels, the joint ventures with Israelis, the ever-increasing number of municipalities where the Palestinian Authority had taken over administrative responsibility from the Israelis, the visible approach of a fully recognized Palestinian state—all of those fragile achievements of the 1990s collapsed, flattened by the Israeli tanks. The Palestinian economy, the conditions of Palestinian education, the levels of poverty, the chances for personal success, even the physical health of the people—every aspect of Palestinian life sank quickly, and went on sinking.

And, as the Palestinian situation grew more desperate, the wave of protest around the world, instead of growing, began to recede. Perhaps not in every way. In the United States, the campaign to get American universities to boycott Israel continued, and for a little while may even have grown stronger in some places, without quite catching hold. Similar campaigns may have gathered strength in other parts of the world, as well. On balance, though, public expressions of anger against Israel tended to diminish as the months went on.

Why was that? The people who had protested in the past and who now seemed less fiery than before—the chanting marchers in the streets, the writers composing their brave essays—will have to offer their own explanations. Perhaps those people merely fell into exhaustion. But I can hazard a couple of other explanations. One of them follows from everything I've just said. The suicide bombings produced a philosophical crisis among everyone around the world who wanted to believe that a rational logic governs the world—a crisis for everyone whose fundamental beliefs would not be able to acknowledge the existence of pathological mass political movements. The protests against Israel, by putting the onus for suicide terror on Israeli shoulders, served a rather useful purpose, from this point of view. The protests explained the unexplainable. But when the Israeli repression had grown sufficiently severe to stifle at least some of the suicide attacks, the need to defend the rationality of world events was no longer as great—and the impulse to drape Israel with images of Nazism, apartheid, and the hatefulness of Judaism consequently subsided.

There is another, slightly creepier explanation. It nearly jumps up at us from the pages of Camus. The sinister excites, Camus observed. The transgressions of suicide murder arouse a thrill that sometimes takes an overtly sexual form. The readers of Baudelaire will find nothing surprising in this observation, not to mention the readers of Sade. One of the New York newspapers ran a photograph of women in Madrid parading naked in public, except for skimpy faux suicide-bomb belts worn as bikinis. Such were the titillations of murder and suicide. As long as the suicide bomb campaign was at its height in the Middle East, this sort of excitement could be felt around the world. The brazen called forth the brazen, and demonstrators ran into the street to commit their verbal or sartorial transgressions, and the heroes of the pen rushed into the newspapers clad in a shockingly small number of tropes. But once the human bombs had begun to detonate less frequently, or had come to seem familiar, the thrill was felt less keenly. The brazen called forth the brazen less forcefully than before.

I cannot prove this last explanation. My theory is sheerest speculation. I concede that it might well be wrong and unfair. I can see why José Saramago might find it insulting. Still, there was something peculiar in the way the protests rose and fell around the world in tandem with the suicide bomb attacks, and not in tandem with the suffering of the Palestinian people.

IN THE MIDST of those other, smaller suicide terror attacks came the much bigger one, the 9/11 attack on American targets. And, at once, with the alacrity of firehouse dogs responding to a bell, any number of people stood up all over the world to propose yet another variation on the same systematic denial. There was the same reasoned insistence that nothing unreasonable was taking place, the same argument that everything was rational, the same claim that it was foolish to be shocked, the same affirmation that ordinary explanations of normal human behavior could account for every last amazing development, if only we would open our eyes. Some of the people with those explanations turned out to be marvelously articulate, too. And no one was more articulate, or quicker into print, or longer-winded, or more energetic, than Noam Chomsky—a peculiar case, you may suppose. But I do not think that Chomsky was a peculiar case. I think that Chomsky and his explanations of the terrorist attacks bring us to the heart of our present dilemma.

Chomsky, it must be remembered, is a scientist, in the specialized field of linguistics. He has always maintained that his political analyses and his linguistic theories are separate entities, without a logical bridge leading from one to the other. This seems to me not quite true. A single thought underlies the original version of Chomsky's linguistic theory, and it is this: Man's inner nature can be calculated according to a very small number of factors, which can be analyzed rationally. No shadow of the mysterious falls across the nature of man.

Other linguists, Chomsky's predecessors and rivals, have maintained that man developed language as a method of communication, and that language arose in more or less the same way as the rest of human culture. But Chomsky has argued that, on the contrary, no one created language, nor can language be usefully regarded as an element of culture. The fundamentals of language, in Chomsky's theory, are a genetic fact. No murk surrounds those fundamentals, even if we cannot yet explain every aspect. Language lies at the heart of human nature; but language is merely a biological code, which we will someday crack.

In later years, Chomsky has backed away from some of his early formulations. John Searle, one of his critics, maintains that Chomsky's theory was always much too simple and that, in his later formulations, Chomsky has abandoned his own ideas. Chomsky, responding to Searle, has argued that, on the contrary, he has merely ascended from one useful hypothesis to the next in the course of his scientific career, on a ladder of research and self-correction—thus proving, in retrospect, the usefulness of his original ideas. I have no way to judge this dispute, except to observe that even Searle, Chomsky's critic, regards Chomsky as not just a scientist but a very great scientist. I do appreciate the point about modifying one's views as the mark of true scientific investigation. Here the gap is undeniable between Chomsky's linguistics, which have changed substantially over the years, and his politics, which have changed barely at all.

Still, if we take Chomsky's linguistics in their pristine version, and then glance at his analyses of international politics, it becomes obvious that Chomsky looks at language and at international affairs in the same light. He sees a possibility of accounting for every last quirk of human behavior by invoking a tiny number of factors—the possibility of analyzing world events according to a handful of identifiable elements. In matters of international affairs, he is the last of the nineteenth-century rationalists, one more thinker with a theory of human behavior that rests on a tiny number of factors—in his case, two factors, in dialectical opposition.

The first of those factors is a greed for wealth and power, which is embodied in the giant American corporations—though Chomsky has always recognized that powerful institutions in other countries sometimes draw on that same instinct and behave pretty much the same way that American corporations do. The corporations wish to maximize power and profits. They command the services of government, and they buy and bully journalists and intellectuals to create, on behalf of the corporations, a picture of the world that makes the general public bend to the corporations' will. And, with government and the intellectuals and the press at their disposal, the corporations, acting in their own interest, drench the world in blood and misery.

Still, a second factor intervenes in world events, and this second factor, he has suggested, may even be a further genetic trait, not unlike the gene for language. It is an instinct for freedom. The instinct for freedom leads people around the world to resist the giant corporations. And so, a giant battle deploys across the globe, with giant corporations and their intellectual and governmental servants on one side, and people who are animated by a genetic or genetic-like instinct for freedom on the other: the greedy instinct versus the freedom instinct. The corporations usually win, due to their immense power. Sometimes, the instinct for freedom wins. Stalemates are not uncommon. But these two factors suffice to explain everything—or very nearly. And world events, upon close examination, turn out to resemble the human ability to speak, as presented in the early version of Chomsky's theory: a seemingly complex and murky phenomenon that can actually be illuminated through a simple accounting of a very few number of predictable factors.

Chomsky unveiled his theory of language in the 1950s, which made his scientific reputation, and he unveiled his vision of politics in the mid-1960s, in a series of essays about American policy in the Vietnam War, and the essays made his reputation as a political thinker. He seemed to command a vast army of facts in those essays, seemed to have read everything, and seemed preternaturally self-assured. He demonstrated an astonishing intellectual energy. And he hurled all of those personal traits and achievements at the American policy in Vietnam. In those days, Chomsky's furor against American policy was refreshing to see, at least for everyone among his readers who had despaired of the Vietnam War. Perhaps the emotion of the moment made the extreme simplicity of Chomsky's notion of politics a little hard to see. The blizzard of detail in his polemics tended to cover over the nature of his reasoning, too. Anyway, the simplicity in his argument didn't seem to matter, so long as he was battling against what his readers already knew to be a disastrous policy.

But the American military eventually withdrew from Indochina, and then the difficulties in Chomsky's view did lead to some noticeable problems. It was not so easy to explain what happened in Indochina once the Americans were gone. The million and a half boat people who fled from South Vietnam seemed to suggest, by their sheer numbers alone, that realities in Vietnam were a little more complicated than some of the anti-war arguments had once maintained. And how was anyone to explain the outright genocide that began to take place in Cambodia, under its new Communist rulers? The Communist forces in Cambodia had been thought to represent the instinct for freedom, as opposed to the greed of the American corporations; yet here were the Communists committing unimaginable crimes, with the whole of Cambodian society as their victim.

It began to look as if pathological mass movements do exist. The evidence was plastered across the newspapers. But the evidence could only mean that human motivation is not as simple as Chomsky had said—could only mean that rational analysis of the instincts for greed and freedom cannot account for the role that irrational factors likewise play in world events. It was a devastating moment for the political theories of Noam Chomsky. And he responded by setting out resolutely to demonstrate that, in Indochina, despite everything published by the newspapers, mass pathological movements did not, in fact, exist.

Well-known journalists reported one set of data, but Chomsky assembled immense supplies of alternative data, which he drew from the recollections of random tourists, wandering church workers, and articles in little-known left-wing magazines. The alternative data, in his interpretation, refuted the accounts of the well-known journalists. And, by piling up his data, Chomsky (writing with a co-author, Edward S. Herman, in their two-volume *Political Economy of Human Rights*—Chomsky's single most ambitious work of political analysis) made two different arguments. He showed that genocide had never occurred; and, conversely, he showed that, if genocide did occur, it was the fault of the American military intervention, which had driven the Cambodians mad.

In either case, the stories about genocide in Cambodia revealed that America's principal institutions were even more guilty than anyone had previously imagined. For the genocide was either a web of lies spun by propagandists for *The New York Times* and other organs of the giant corporations—in which case, the big American institutions were capable of perpetrating the most hideous and elaborate of deceptions on all mankind. Or, alternatively, if genocide in Cambodia was really a fact (which plainly seemed to him less likely), then the American military was guilty twice over—first, for having made war in Cambodia; and, second, for having provoked the Cambodians into committing their own crimes. Either way, genocide in Cambodia told against the United States. The rational nature of world events was shown to be real—the rational behavior that led America's corporations to behave in sinister and violent ways, and the perfectly understandable response of the corporations' victims in faraway Cambodia. And there was no need to recognize the possibility of another factor—of a mass movement devoted to mass slaughter for irrational reasons.

Chomsky has written many thousands of pages devoted to that particular logic. It is his habit of mind, in regard to world events. That was why, when the 9/11 attacks took place, he did not need to collect his thoughts. He was unfazed. The entire purpose of his political outlook was to be unfazed, even by the worst of horrors. He knew exactly what to say. The notion that, in large parts of the world, a mass movement of radical Islamists had arisen, devoted to mad hatreds and conspiracy theories; the notion that radical Islamists were slaughtering people in one country after another for the purpose of slaughtering them; the notion that radical Islamists ought to be taken at their word and that shariah and the seventh-century Caliphate were their goals, and that Jews and Christians were demonic figures worthy of death; the notion that bin Laden had ordered random killings of Americans strictly for the purpose of killing Americans—all of this was, from Chomsky's perspective, not even worth discussing.

It was because, to Chomsky, movements of that particular nature and style do not exist. What do exist are, instead, the two factors in his political theory: the instinct for greed and the instinct for freedom. How, then, to explain the 9/11 attacks? Chomsky knew what to think because it was what he had always thought. He could hardly deny that the 9/11 attacks had taken place. But his first impulse was to deny that the attacks were especially bad. He compared the attacks to Clinton's missile strike on the Sudan in 1998—Clinton's feeble effort to attack bin Laden and his enterprise. In Clinton's attack on the Sudan, a pharmaceuticals factory (which the Clinton administration, apparently in error, had identified as a bomb factory) was demolished. One person was killed—possibly two people. In Chomsky's interpretation, the damage that resulted from this attack easily outweighed the damage that resulted from the 9/11 attacks.

Clinton's missile strike was exceptionally deadly, Chomsky thought, because it destroyed the Sudan's supply of medicines, destroyed the Sudan's political tranquility, and destroyed the Sudan's economy, all of which led to far more death and misery than were produced by the 9/11 attacks. Such was Chomsky's contention. It was peculiar. Still, in one sense, it was deserving of respect. Who in America or in the other rich countries thinks to tally up the sufferings that descend on people in remote parts of the world from actions taken by the wealthy cosmopolises? Chomsky was proposing to do that. Yet his tally was preposterous, in each of its elements and as a whole.

The Sudan had other pharmaceuticals factories and other ways to buy medicines; radical Islamism and other factors had already destroyed the political tranquility; and a single missile attack was not going to destroy the economy. The losses that came out of the attack on the United States on 9/11 were, on the other hand, simply staggering, if you follow Chomsky's own procedure and tally up the indirect costs alone. For the 9/11 attacks jolted the American economy—the destruction of the buildings alone was an economic blow—and the effect on commerce in any number of other countries around the world, in poor countries especially, was bound to be devastating. The damage done to Mexico by itself had to be fairly painful, even if we leave aside the special hopes that Mexico had entertained, prior to 9/11, for sounder and more profitable relations with the United States. Somebody could go from region to region, all over the globe, identifying the miserable effects of the 9/11 attacks that fell upon already poor people.

Still, Chomsky stood by his argument, and did so with his customary blizzard of references to obscure sources. And having made that one argument, he went on to a second theme, which was to rehearse the entire history of American violence toward other people, beginning with the American Indians (who, for his purposes, were considered as non-Americans). He predicted what was likely to come of President Bush's plan—not yet put into execution—to overthrow the Taliban in Afghanistan and uproot Al Qaeda's headquarters and training camps. Genocide against the Afghan people was likely to result, in Chomsky's estimation. This prediction conformed to Chomsky's picture of the many genocides of the American past. And, with this picture of America and its genocidal past and future in mind, he asked, why would anyone have attacked the United States on 9/11?

He knew the answer. The attacks on 9/11 represented the reply of oppressed people from the Third World to centuries of American depredations. The attacks represented, at long last, an active reprisal, and not just an effort at self-defense. The 9/11 attacks, from this point of view, were entirely predictable—logical events, even if bin Laden was not an attractive figure. Chomsky had no basis at all to attribute these centuries of Third World motivation to bin Laden. The notion of a Saudi plutocrat as a tribune of the oppressed was fairly ridiculous. Still, Chomsky stuck with this argument, too. And both of his arguments—the argument that wildly exaggerated the damage caused by Clinton's missile on the pharmaceuticals factory, and the argument that Al Qaeda was avenging the oppressed Third World—pointed in the same direction. The arguments showed that, if 9/11 was bad, America itself was ultimately responsible. World events could be rationally analyzed. The greed of American corporations, and the long history of American greed in the past, sufficed to explain every last astounding act of suicide terror. For there are no pathological or irrational movements, no movements that yearn to commit slaughters, no movements that yearn for death—and, if such movements do exist, it is because they have been conjured into existence by other forces.

Chomsky said these things in the immediate aftermath of the 9/11 attacks in a series of interviews and articles, and his publisher gathered them together quickly and issued them as a pamphlet called *9/11.* In the United States, the principal newspapers and magazines have tended to ignore Chomsky's political writings for many years now, because of his reputation as a crank. None of the most prestigious journals bothered even to review his book.

Even so, Chomsky's pamphlet became a giant best-seller.

BUT I SEE that, in taking note of the ideological systems of denial that have been operating in the Western countries for the last sixty-five years or so, I have selected examples only from the political left, from the anti-war French Socialists of the 1930s to the days of José Saramago and Noam Chomsky. I don't mean to go after the left, however. My purpose is to identify a rationalist naïveté that is shared by almost every part of modern liberal society—a spirit of the ingenuous that blossoms everywhere along the political spectrum, and even in the bureaucracies that are not supposed to be ideological. For what are we to think of the FBI and the CIA and their failure, in the years before the 9/11 attack, to imagine the dangers facing the United States?

Everyone has noticed, in retrospect, that evidence for some sort of impending, large-scale attack had been building for many years. The 1993 World Trade Center bombing, the sundry foiled conspiracies, the attacks on American soldiers over the years, the 1998 attacks on the American embassies in East Africa and in 2000 on the U.S.S. *Cole*—really, the arrows were multiple, and they all pointed the same way. How could anyone have failed to see it? There has been a lot of talk about bureaucratic glitches—about the foolish reluctance of the higher-ups at FBI headquarters to listen to their own agents in the field, and that sort of thing. But bureaucratic glitches cannot account for an error on this scale. Besides, several agencies, not just the FBI and the CIA, committed the same error, and so did the political leaders in the White House, Congress, and in both parties. The press, too, for that matter. The plot to blow up the New York tunnels was not a big story in the American press, but Bill Clinton's love life—that was huge, that was a national crisis.

Ultimately, the error was conceptual. I think it was a version of the same error that was made by the anti-war French Socialists of the 1930s and the other people I have just described. It was an unwillingness, sometimes an outright refusal, to accept that, from time to time, mass political movements do get drunk on the idea of slaughter. It was a belief that, around the world, people are bound to behave in more or less reasonable ways in pursuit of normal and identifiable interests. It was a belief that the world is, by and large, a rational place. That belief was not just a left-wing naïveté. In the United States, that belief was very nearly universal. The 9/11 attacks revealed many unexpected and astonishing truths, but surely the most astonishing of all was that, in Arlington, Virginia, the Pentagon had no plan to defend the Pentagon. Everyone, unto the chiefest of Indian chiefs, turned out to be a simpleminded rationalist, expecting the world to act in sensible ways, without mystery, self-contradiction, murk, or madness. In this country, we are all Noam Chomsky.

VII
Mental War

THERE WAS A PERIOD in the 1990s when it became fashionable among intellectuals to speak about the "short" twentieth century—a century that got started a little tardily in 1914 and ended a little prematurely in 1989. This remark about 1914 and 1989 expressed a fairly specific view of modern history, and we had better glance back at that view today, if only to identify a few more of the ideas and delusions that led so many people—in the United States, nearly everyone—to underestimate the dangers of the moment.

The part about 1914 is easy to understand. The many underground rumblings in the history of rebellion in Western culture that Camus so carefully identified, the morbid literary obsessions of the Romantic poets, the ever more extreme brutality of the European colonialists in Africa and other places—these sinister and terrible developments, heating slowly over the years, erupted into war in 1914. And the simpleminded optimism of the nineteenth century did get blown to smithereens, and the political movements of a "new type," the apocalyptic rebellions against liberalism, did get underway, and those movements went on to dominate the next several decades. The giant struggles and cataclysms of the twentieth century, fascism's attempt to conquer the world, communism's world revolution—those were lavic consequences of that original explosion, the catastrophe of 1914, rolling across the world in the years that followed.

But why would anyone have said that 1989 marked the century's end? All kinds of dictatorial governments collapsed beginning in the late 1980s, and not just the Soviet Union's satellite regimes in Eastern Europe. Strongman tyrannies in East Asia, in Africa, and around the world; General Pinochet's dictatorship in Chile and, with him, the Latin and Catholic heritage of Francisco Franco; the apartheid republic in South Africa: fascists, Communists, racists, and free-lance despots of indeterminate ideological hue—all tumbled from power, knocked from their perches in most cases by people who invoked the doctrines of liberal democracy. It was one of history's better moments. People felt the tremors even in places where tyrannies did not fall to the ground. In Tiananmen Square, the Chinese students erected their Statue of Liberty—a sensational thing to do, directly in front of the enormous Mao posters. And there were tremors in the Arab countries. Fatima Mernissi, the Moroccan writer—a bitter critic of Europe and of American policy in the Middle East—has explained that in the medinas, or the old town squares of North Africa, the "universal meaning" of revolutionary events elsewhere in the world was well understood. "A new word burst out in the medinas," she writes, "a word as explosive as all the atomic bombs combined: *shaffafiyya* (transparency)"—a gloriously subversive word in any society that is ruled by dark mafias.

But let us not be too quick to speak of "universal meaning." The year 1989 dealt devastating blows to tyrants around the world, yet no blow at all to the Islamists and Baathi. The militants of Muslim totalitarianism in its two branches surveyed the news in that year, and found no reason to rethink their old ideas, none at all. The Islamists were positively ecstatic in 1989. Their most revolutionary vanguard, the volunteers who had gone to fight in Afghanistan, Abdullah Azzam's cream of the cream of the cream, had every reason to suppose that communism's collapse in Eastern Europe was their own doing, in considerable degree. The cream had defeated the Red Army. The Soviet Union was teetering. And if the *mujahadeen* could undo the superpower of the East, what couldn't they achieve in the future? The Red Army was enormous, but the Israeli Defense Force was not, and Israel was surely doomed.

The Islamists already knew that, under the right circumstances, they could establish societies of their own, as Khomeini had done. By 1989 the Sunni of Afghanistan were visibly gliding toward an Islamic state of their own, just to show that Islam's principal denomination, and not merely the Iranian Shia, could reinaugurate the reign of shariah. In Algeria, the Islamic Salvation Front seemed on the brink of victory. The Islamist revolutionaries had every reason to feel cheerful (if such a movement, with its lugubrious and funereal obsessions, can be said to feel cheerful) about their prospects in Lebanon, in Egypt, in the Sudan, in black Africa, and beyond, to the horizons of the Muslim world, and beyond even that. In that same 1989, Khomeini issued his fatwa against Rushdie, commanding—I quote the fatwa—"all the intrepid Muslims in the world" to murder not only the novelist but his publishers, "wherever they find them": a plain affirmation of Islamism's zeal to rule the world.

Nor did the Baathi of Iraq see any reason to despair. If large numbers of people in the Arab countries cheered on Saddam Hussein during the Gulf War of 1991, it was because, as best they could judge, his march to Jerusalem was well begun, and the Arab nation was going to resurrect the Koranic glories of the long-ago past in a modern-day version. In 1989 Saddam's weapons program was, in fact, well begun. Totalitarianism in decline? It was a spectacular error to have imagined any such thing in 1989—a curious error, an almost laughable example of the self-absorbed delusions of the Eurocentric imagination. As if the Muslim world didn't exist!

Now, it's true that, over the course of the next few years, the Muslim totalitarians, Baathi and Islamists alike, experienced a few setbacks, which were grave. Saddam Hussein's custom of slaughtering his enemies and tinkering with his weapons may have survived the 1991 war; but his movement's allure visibly wilted. Gilles Kepel and some of the other regional specialists on Muslim societies have made the argument that in the late 1990s, Islamism, too, entered into an irreversible decline. In Algeria, the Islamist movement was beaten down violently. In Egypt, Islamism's terrorist wing was similarly suppressed—even if other, larger aspects of the Egyptian movement continued to flourish. In African countries farther to the south, the movement ran into even more difficulties, and in some places began to contract instead of expand—though in Nigeria, with Africa's biggest population, Islamism went on growing. Islamism in the Sudan lost its hold on power.

In Afghanistan in 1996 the Taliban finally launched their Islamic Emirate, but the Emirate never did succeed in reinstating the seventh century, or any other century—even if the Taliban continued to dazzle the Saudi sheikhs and princes and the cream of the cream. And, as the defeats piled up, Islamist leaders here and there around the world began to display a newly moderate impulse—an urge to find a middle course between the identity politics of Islamic renewal and the practical benefits of pluralism, tolerance, and peace. Islamist reformers with at least faintly liberal ideas won the support of university students in Iran—a remarkable turnaround in the history of the Iranian revolution. Reformers began to win elections as early as 1997. The students themselves began to express overtly liberal positions—even going so far as to speak out against anti-Semitism, an extremely radical development. Change was in the air—that was undeniable, and it became easy to imagine that, in some countries, the ferocious old Islamist movements might soften into political tendencies of a different nature altogether. A precedent for that kind of development did exist. During the 1970s and '80s, a good many of the old-time Stalinist parties around the world, disheartened by their own defeats, had gently subsided into democratic parties of the left. Likewise some of the old-time fascists, in a right-wing version. Franco's anti-democratic movement in Spain quietly melted into a democratic party of pious and Catholic conservatives.

So why not the Islamists, too? In Turkey, the Islamists did veer in a democratic direction—pushed that way by military repression, and pulled by the prospect of electoral success. One wing of the Moroccan Islamist movement slid in the same direction. Kepel has pointed to Tariq Ramadan, the philosopher, as yet another example of the turn toward democratic moderation—though, in this instance, with Ramadan's *Islam, the West and the Challenges of Modernity* open before me, I can judge for myself. Ramadan condemns the violence of the Islamist radicals, but, then again, seems to celebrate violence against Israel as a religious duty, "incumbent," in his word, on devout Muslims. The move toward pluralism and tolerance seems a little halting, here.

Still, the prospect that Islamism in different parts of the world might evolve one day into something genuinely different and better, and may already have done so here and there, should fill us with a soothing hope. We may picture a harmonious world of the future, populated with Islamic Democratic parties that will stand shoulder to shoulder with the Christian Democrats of Europe, or with the slightly more fanatical Christian right wing of the Republican Party in the United States, or, for that matter, with the left-wing heirs of the Reverend Martin Luther King, Jr.—a world of tolerant cosmopolitans, curious about one another's pieties and differences, satisfied in their own identities. I mean, why not? It is good to dream.

Meanwhile, we have all the evidence in the world—I see the evidence from my study window, gazing out on Manhattan's ruptured skyline—to conclude that Islamism in its radical version of the present poses every imaginable danger. And it will go on doing so, borne aloft, even now, on gushers of Saudi wealth; guided in some places by the unreformed Shiite mullahs of Iran; drawing on sophisticated thinkers and Koranic scholars; supported by officers in the Pakistani army and by Pakistan's secret police and some of its most popular politicians; wielding a series of terrorist networks, not just bin Laden's international brigade but the several Palestinian groups, the Kashmiri irredentists, the Indonesian slaughterers of tourists, the Malaysian terrorists, the Filipino terrorists, the East African slaughterers of still more tourists, and so forth from country to country—a movement that crosses ethnic, national, and confessional lines within Islam, with recruits and money pouring in not just from the Muslim countries but from Western Europe and from North and South America alike. Jeffrey Goldberg has reported in *The New Yorker* that Lebanon's Hezbollah—the group that did the most, during the 1980s, to endow suicide terror with a grisly prestige—operates on an annual budget of more than $100 million.

It is no small thing to consider that, in parts of the world, bin Laden's bearded face and soulful eyes have begun to peer out at crowds from T-shirts and posters, the way that Che Guevara peers out—symbols of transgressive rebellion in precisely the fashion that Camus described. "Faith," said Benhadj, Algeria's Islamist, "is propagated by counting up deaths every day, by adding up massacres and charnel-houses." And, lo, faith gets propagated. Now and then someone stands up in the op-ed pages of the Western countries to assure the United States that other countries have learned to live with terror—Britain with the bombs of the IRA, Spain with the bombs of the Basque ETA—and to explain that America, too, will steady its nerves, in time. Norman Mailer said, "There is a tolerable level to terror," and illustrated his claim by observing that car crashes exact a higher toll than terrorist attacks. But here we find ourselves still soaring through the skies of wishful thinking. Islamism's cream of the cream would blow up entire cities, if it could, and it may yet.

The year 1989 as an end point of the twentieth century? If only it had been! The revolt against liberalism that got underway after 1914 has never run out of energy, and the impulse for murder and suicide continues to rocket around the globe, and nothing from the twentieth century has come to an end, nothing at all, except the numerals at the top of the calendar and the script in which the revolutionary manifestos are published—this script, which used to be the Gothic lettering of German, and later was Cyrillic, and lately has been Farsi and Arabic, and which, in any alphabet, spells out the same apocalyptic explanation for why, in this hour of Armageddon, masses of people should be killed.

THE NOTION of a "short" century ending in 1989 expressed one other idea, and this, too, deserves attention. It was an idea about liberal democracy—the idea that liberal democracy was destined to prevail and to dominate the world, sooner or later. Francis Fukuyama presented this idea in its most extravagant version with his pop-eyed Hegelian phrase about "the End of History"—in which capital-H History meant the story of man's effort to devise a proper, stable, satisfying social and political system. Many people shared this idea, in one version or another, extravagant or modest. And, in certain ways, they were right to do so. The year 1989 did not mark the exact moment in which liberal democracy's upward ascendance became fully visible, nor the moment of ultimate triumph—the transcendent victory that will come about, if it ever comes about, in some other age. And yet, the many grandeurs of 1989 did make a fitting emblem of liberal democracy's ascendant path.

It should be remembered that Huntington's theory about clashing civilizations and their "fault-lines" represents a very traditional view of world politics, and a very pessimistic view. Ideas like his have been invoked a thousand ways over the centuries to explain why some people will enjoy the benefits of a free society, and other people never will. In the late nineteenth century it was argued that liberal democracy descended from ancient Anglo-Saxon customs and, for racial reasons, would never spread beyond the Anglo-Saxon world. Sometimes it was argued, a little more expansively, that liberal democracy was a racial product of the forest-roaming peoples of Northern Europe as a whole, and could not be transferred to people from warmer zones. Then again, it was argued that liberalism and democracy descended from the Protestant Reformation, and Protestants would therefore enjoy the benefits of liberty—but Catholic countries could never follow suit.

Even into the mid-twentieth century, the mere notion of a Southern and Catholic country like Spain embracing liberal democracy sounded ridiculous in many people's ears. Yet each of these fault lines between the potentially free societies and the hopelessly oppressed turned out to be mistakenly drawn. In 1975, Spain went democratic—a crushing blow to centuries of political analysis. The Slavs, it was said, could not create liberal societies. In 1989, Slavs created liberal societies—a little shakily, in some instances. Still, any progress at all exploded the old theories. Orthodox Christianity was deemed allergic to liberal developments. Orthodox Christians proved otherwise. I don't even mention the many theories that heap insults on the black race. Nonetheless, South Africa's blacks began to construct a liberal democracy. Nelson Mandela became a world symbol of how to do so. It was suggested that free societies depend on Christianity, regardless of denomination. The Hindus and Muslims of the world's largest democracy plodded on, undeterred—even if, in India, demagogues do stir up the mobs, and the story is not over.

Sometimes it was argued that liberal democracy could not spread very far beyond what once had been the British Empire. Nonetheless, in the years around 1989, South Korea, Taiwan, and the Philippines moved in liberal and democratic directions. The very suggestion that Muslim countries could ever become liberal and democratic made people roll their eyes, just as used to happen with Spain. Even so, Turkey inched forward. Lately, Indonesia, the world's largest Muslim country, has likewise seemed to move in the same direction—though

Indonesia also seems to be awash in conspiracy theories, which makes the inching hard to judge. In the Arab countries, too, the liberal potential does seem to have grown larger, here and there, at least in a small way—a growth of pluralism in multi-ethnic Morocco, a solidifying of democratic institutions in Bahrain, the emergence of intellectuals with a liberal style among the Palestinians, and so forth.

How quickly those fault lines seem to jump about, in the many doctrines about clashing civilizations! Nothing is more ephemeral than a theory about changeless cultures. And the moment in which those many theories about the cultural boundaries of liberal democracy began to look terminally useless, the moment in which liberal democracy's omnicultural worldwide potential began to seem more than fanciful and abstract—that moment was surely 1989. On this one topic, the champions of "the End of History" and of the "short" twentieth century were onto something, and 1989 did have a meaning.

Still, the triumphs of 1989 raised a question, which was not easily answered. It was about the guts and heart of a liberal society. What defines a liberal democracy, exactly? I don't mean what are its institutions. Everybody can recite a checklist of free elections, political parties, opposition newspapers, a system to defend individual freedom, and that sort of thing. Everybody can recognize some of the desires, too, that give liberal democracy its characteristic flavor—the desire for privacy, for instance, combined with a willing desire to accord the same privacy to everyone else, a positive pride in tolerance. But what kind of energy animates these institutions and desires? What is the blood that rushes through liberal veins? Where does a liberal society get the strength to survive? In Europe in the early nineteenth century, people looked on liberalism and democracy as maximum ideals, meant to produce a revolutionary new life for all mankind, and this idea inspired extravagant and even utopian hopes—the kind of exhilarated expectation that Walt Whitman, the anti-Baudelaire, announced more vividly than anyone else.

But, in Europe, the liberal democratic exhilarations went down to defeat in the revolutions of 1848, and stayed down. And, afterward, the liberal democratic idea lost some of its clarity in Europe, sometimes because the liberal impulses blended into revolutionary socialism, sometimes because they blended into conservative authoritarianism, sometimes because liberal ideas were abandoned altogether in favor of full-scale fanaticisms of left and right. Liberal democracy in its pure version came to seem mediocre, corrupt, tired, and aimless, a middling compromise, pale and unappealing—something to settle for, in a spirit of resignation. As late as the 1950s and '60s, a good many Europeans who resisted the Soviet Union and the spread of communism would have invoked all kinds of motives apart from liberalism to account for their anti-Communist sentiments—a love for Christianity, perhaps; or for nationalism; or, among the left-wing intellectuals, for the principles of the nineteenth-century workers' movement, which the Communists had betrayed.

The liberal democratic idea began to crowd out those other arguments only in the 1970s and '80s, and in a very quiet way, as if without emotion. Dissident intellectuals and activists began to speak up in the Communist countries of Eastern Europe, and even in the Soviet Union. And the dissidents—not all of them, but some—rested their arguments almost exclusively on liberal principles. The dissidents were extremely cautious, though. They never did come out foursquare for overthrowing the Communist system—until they had won. They preferred to make two narrow points, and to harp on those points, and to keep their message simple. They argued for human rights—for the right of an individual person to be honest and not hypocritical and to hold his own views without getting persecuted for doing so. And they argued for the sanctity of international treaties and accords.

The United States and the Soviet Union signed the Helsinki Accords in 1975, which were supposed to guarantee human rights (an achievement of Henry Kissinger's, oddly enough). The dissidents invoked those accords. Sometimes the dissidents and their Western supporters pictured a still wider role for international agreements. There was talk of a community of civilized nations wistfully called "Europe"—a comically inappropriate name, given Europe's history. The community was portrayed as prosperous, orderly, law-abiding, democratic, kind-hearted, and respectful of individual rights—an imaginary Europe unlike any Europe of the past. That was a popular idea. People sighed over it.

And when the revolutions of 1989 finally broke out, the dissidents and their allies overthrew the Communists in the name of those several ideas—human rights, international accords, and the ideal that went under the name of "Europe," together with a series of other and sometimes contradictory impulses that were strictly nationalist. The modest scale of the liberal ideas was much commented on, back in 1989. People were said to be tired of revolutions conducted in the name of grandiose programs: communism and fascism had cured them of that. The narrow shape of the new ideas seemed sleek, virtuous, and hip—a sign of sophistication, like a narrow necktie. And, to be sure, the new ideas proved their worth. The revolutions of 1989 were majestic in victory, except in a few places. Still, the narrow ideas, for all their practical virtues, did not answer the question about the spirit of liberal democracy. The ideas did not explain how liberal democrats ought to behave. What do liberal democrats do, exactly?—this was left unanswered.

Fukuyama, in his ruminations on the End of History, gave some thought to that question, and his conclusions were gloomy. He figured that, in a well-established liberal democracy, people don't do much of anything. They yearn for base and ignoble things, and society is a dismal place. That was his fear, anyway. It was a European fear, at least in its intellectual origins—a description of bourgeois life that Fukuyama drew from Nietzsche. The Europeans in the years around 1989 expressed that same fear in versions of their own. Pascal Bruckner, the

French writer, published a book called *La Mélancolie Démocratique* in 1990 about the triumphs of 1989, and his title said it all.

The Americans, Bruckner explained, had chosen liberal democracy as the best of all systems and not as a compromise, and they continued to regard democracy as a "dream," and to think of themselves as "invested with a universal mission: to propagate liberty." But the Europeans had come to liberal ideas in a different frame of mind. They were in search of repose. They took up those ideas because their other, more exciting aspirations had let them down. This did seem to be the case. The European euphoria in 1989 was, in Bruckner's phrase, "well-tempered." But, then, if liberal democracy did not express any kind of transcendent dream for the Europeans, what was going to prevent the entire continent from sinking into the bourgeois, self-satisfied swamp of material desires that so worried Francis Fukuyama?

That was an open question in 1989, a philosophical question. But soon enough it was also a practical question, owing to the sad progression of events in one place where the revolution of 1989 did not, in fact, proceed majestically to victory—namely, in Yugoslavia. Communism morphed into nationalism there, unleavened by liberal ideas. The nationalists of Yugoslavia's strongest province, Serbia, began to conceive of their neighboring ethnic groups and especially of Yugoslavia's large Muslim population as barbarians or lesser humans, not deserving of rights or even of life. The Serb nationalists did think of themselves as Christian Crusaders from the Middle Ages, Franco-style, in a Slavic variation of their own—showing, for the umpteenth time, how easily the fascist and totalitarian doctrines of the twentieth century can adapt to new circumstances and blossom in ever more novel versions. The Serb nationalists set out to prosecute their Crusade. They drew their swords. And, joined sometimes by the Croatian nationalists, the Serb nationalists went on their rampage, beginning in 1992—against the Muslims and other people of Bosnia, sometimes against their Croat allies, and ultimately against the Albanians of Kosovo.

Some 200,000 people did get killed. It was an event in the full twentieth-century style. And, elsewhere in Europe, people asked, what should we do? Now that we no longer yearn for apocalyptic revolutions on the left or the right, now that we are no longer dreaming about resurrecting the Roman Empire or the medieval Reign of Christ the King or achieving the proletarian millennium, now that we are modern and up-to-date, liberals and democrats with narrowly defined ideas—what do we do?

It must be said that, in Europe, the initial response was: we do nothing. This response did seem to confirm the dreary picture of modern life drawn by Nietzsche in the past and just now by Fukuyama: the comfortable burgher, blinking stupidly and wondering about dinner. Sayyid Qutb would have predicted such a response—the listless response of Europeans without backbones or firm beliefs, cowardly, greedy, and self-absorbed, which is precisely how he had described the Europeans forty years before. But if those disdainful labels accurately described the liberal mentality, how could free societies expect to survive? Who would bother putting up a struggle on behalf of cultures and ways of life as dismal as that? No one, finally—which was why, in Qutb's estimation, communism was going to triumph in the short term, and Islam in the end.

The Europeans who declined to lift a finger against the Serb nationalists in the 1990s naturally pictured themselves as something other than base, cowardly, greedy, and self-absorbed. François Mitterrand, the president of France, mouthed a few statements about grand ideals and even made a dramatic and dangerous trip to Sarajevo, which was under Serb nationalist attack, to demonstrate his personal solidarity. Mitterrand was a man of the left. One of his foreign policy advisers was none other than Régis Debray, the grand theoretician of Third World guerrilla war, Che Guevara's comrade in arms. And yet Mitterrand, for all his leftism, looked on international politics from the viewpoint of traditional nineteenth-century or even eighteenth-century power relations. World events, to him, were a matter of competing blocs and spheres of influence, each against all, in which France's interest lay with Serbia, even if the Serbs were out of their minds. Those were Nixonian attitudes, we Americans might say, except pickled in Old World sophistication, which made them doubly briny and duplicitous: the viewpoint of people who, in their worldliness, cannot be shocked, therefore cannot be motivated to do anything about being shocked. Those attitudes were, in fact, base, cowardly, greedy, and self-absorbed, apart from being antique.

Still, there were other views. Europe's idealists, a great many of them, did consult the more noble concepts of liberal democracy, and did so with painful sincerity. But the noble concepts whispered in their ears the same advice that Mitterrand drew from the principles of antique realism, to wit, keep your head down. The idealists figured that a democratic and free society ought to be generous, open-minded, tolerant, fair—and peaceable. This notion reverberated on the left, and, at the same time, on the right, which gave it the stereophonic vibration of undeniable truth. Sweden symbolized the left-wing version, and Switzerland, the right-wing version; and both of those versions were wonderfully lofty. And yet, this sort of loftiness was, in the end, hard to distinguish from the base, cowardly, greedy, and self-absorbed motives described variously by Nietzsche and his heirs.

The Swedes and the Swiss achieved wonderful things with their own societies, and those achievements were the envy of the world. But the survival of both places owed entirely to the fighting spirit of other people. During the years of Nazi triumph, Sweden and Switzerland played roles that were, all in all, contemptible. Neutrality seemed to them better than defeat. If Hitler had won the war, he would have crushed the Swedes and Swiss, anyway. But they could hope that other people would ensure that Hitler lost. And other people did. Entire Polish cities fought virtually to the last man so that Sweden and

Switzerland could go on perfecting their social systems. Sweden and Switzerland resembled in this respect the little republics that have floated into existence from time to time throughout the history of the West, beginning with Athens and the Roman republic and continuing through the city-states of the Middle Ages—fragile republics that reflected a brilliant light for as long as circumstances were benign. But sooner or later the little republics were popped like bubbles by marauding armies from afar. None of those republics was ever able to figure out the secret of survival.

The question of how a free society can endure for more than a little while is one of the oldest and most perplexing in the history of political philosophy. Tocqueville puzzled over this question in his book on American democracy. He toured the United States in the 1830s and was filled with a mixture of admiration and regret at what he saw. But he didn't believe that America would be able to protect its own institutions or maintain its government. The United States consisted of twenty-four states in Tocqueville's time, and he imagined that someday the number would swell to a total of forty states, with maybe 100 million citizens. The stability of such a system seemed beyond imagining. "I would like to contribute to the faith in human perfectibility," he wrote, "but until men have changed their nature and are completely transformed, I will refuse to believe in the longevity of a government whose task is to hold together forty diverse peoples spread across a surface equal to half of Europe, to keep them from falling into rivalries, plots, and struggles, and to bring together their independent wills into action for common plans."

This was not a foolish worry. Less than thirty years after Tocqueville's tour, the United States did very nearly dissolve. Chomsky remarked after 9/11 that, until then, the United States had never been attacked on its own soil, at least not since the British invasion in the War of 1812. (He seemed to forget that, in 1916, Pancho Villa launched an invasion of New Mexico—but, never mind.) This became a commonplace observation. Europe sagely nodded at America's 9/11 loss of innocence. But the United States had absolutely been attacked on its soil. Between 1861 and 1865 the country was nearly wrecked by secessionist rebels, in deadly scenes that already pointed to Verdun. The United States might well have decided to throw up its hands at the secessionist attack, and might have let the slave states go their miserable way, which would have permitted the northern states to evolve, in time, into a Sweden or Switzerland of North America—a virtuous country, dedicated to the charms and prosperity of its own social system, though with no ability or inclination to defend itself or anyone else. But, instead, the United States took the notion of a liberal society and, with a few earnest twists of the screwdriver, rendered the whole concept a little sturdier.

It was Lincoln who did this. He expressed the new idea in the Gettysburg Address—a speech which, through constant grade-school recitation, long ago came to seem like a collection of nonsense syllables. Lincoln did say something in that speech, though. He addressed Tocqueville's worry about the longevity of liberal democratic governments. America, Lincoln said, was "conceived in liberty and dedicated to the proposition that all men are created equal." But the Civil War raised the question of whether such a government could survive—"testing whether that nation or any nation so conceived and so dedicated can long endure." Lincoln resolved that America would endure, and he identified the two war aims that would guarantee the outcome. The first of these, in the order that he mentioned them, was solidarity with the oppressed—"a new birth of freedom," in his phrase. That meant the overthrow of slavery. The second aim was the defense of democratic self-rule, not just as a local principle but with implications for the entire planet—for "any nation so conceived and so dedicated." More freedom and a universal mission—that was his argument.

But what gave force to this argument was the occasion and setting of his speech. He delivered his remarks at a battlefield cemetery, dedicating the site. His speech was about death. It was not a speech about martyrdom. He said nothing to suggest that death was good. He did not believe, with Victor Hugo, that honor requires death. And he did not believe, with the Russian terrorists of 1905, that death is something to yearn for. He did not see in death the Ideal, as the anarchist Luigi Galleani did. He did not think, as Qutb did, that martyrs go on living in some respect, and that death is a garden of delights. He did not find brotherhood in death—did not see his highest aspirations realized in a field of the dead, as the totalitarians of the twentieth century have done, and are still doing. The strange and perverse ideas about death that arose in the Romantic literary movement and blossomed into mass movements in the totalitarian rebellions—those were not Lincoln's ideas.

But neither did he avert his eyes from death. He spoke about death as "the last full measure of devotion," which the Union soldiers had given. Those soldiers were the champions of liberty, equality, and self-government, which are not the values of death. Death was not their goal; but death was the measure of their commitment. "From these honored dead we take increased devotion," he said. He was explaining that a liberal society must be, when challenged, a warlike society; or it will not endure. That was the meaning of his conclusion—"that we here highly resolve that these dead shall not have died in vain, that this nation under God shall have a new birth of freedom, and that government of the people, by the people, for the people shall not perish from the earth."

What do the citizens of a proper liberal society feel in their hearts? A passion for solidarity and self-government. What do those citizens do? They devote themselves to those principles, unto the last measure, if necessary. Liberalism is a doctrine that, in the name of tolerance, shuns absolutes; but liberalism does not shun every absolute. Qutb thought that Pragmatist philosophy—the doctrine of Peirce, William James, and Dewey—was America's undoing, and that Pragmatism's skeptical spirit of science and testing would undermine America's ability to fend off its enemies. Someone might argue that Lincoln, in calling for an absolute commitment to solidarity and self-government, had abandoned any possible connection to Pragmatist ideas. But no, not entirely, even if he did thunder on about God. The war, Lincoln said, was "testing" the principles of a free society. Lincoln was committed to seeing the test through—committed absolutely.

AMERICA was a young democracy when Lincoln defined these principles, and Europe was in several respects equally young when it faced the test of the 1990s. Perhaps even younger. Some of the European democracies were brand new; others dated back only to the end of the Second World War; still others could trace their lineages into the distant past, but had not been able to maintain the continuity of democracy's institutions and customs. Germany in 1989 was divided and occupied, without the autonomy of a genuinely independent state. A full-scale and vigorous European spirit of democracy was something that, under those circumstances, had to be worked out on the run, and in the face of some venerable prejudices, too. The spirit of democracy needed a language or rhetoric of its own—something different from the antique realism of people like Mitterrand, and different from the lofty isolationism of the Swedes and the Swiss.

The new rhetoric could hardly be Lincoln's—a rhetoric of popular will, of God, and of liberty: a language of nineteenth-century Christian America. But what was left to the Europeans, then? Their new rhetoric would have to come out of their own experiences, and that could only mean the dissident agitations of the 1970s and '80s in the Eastern bloc, together with the Western agitations on the dissidents' behalf. The new rhetoric would have to be, in short, the language of 1989: the language of human rights, of international accords and treaties, and of the wistful aspiration known as "Europe"—a tempered language, though impressively ornamented with revolutionary achievements. The debate over what to do about the Serb nationalists was duly conducted in the language of '89, together with one additional term, which was "humanitarianism"—an extension of the concept of human rights. The debate was heated. And, for a long time, nothing came of it.

Serbia was a third-rate power. A determined France and Germany, together with the Netherlands, Belgium, and other countries, not to mention Britain, could certainly have put the Serb nationalists in their place, if only those several countries had mobilized their will. They couldn't do it. The Europeans applied to the United Nations, in the spirit of observing international accords and treaties. But the Russians, from their seat on the Security Council, stuck to their own premodern notions of balances of power and ancient ethnic loyalties, which tied them to Serbia; and Russia would not be moved. Besides, on the topic of military action, the European democracies were of two minds. They did see the need for action. Tony Blair was eloquent on this theme. Their consciences were afflicted.

But the Europeans were impressed, as well, by the gravity of the arguments for cynical realism and idealistic isolation. And so, the European countries decided to split the difference. They did intervene in the Balkans. They did it in the most high-minded of ways, through the United Nations. But the intervention proved to be no intervention at all. Blue-helmeted UN peacekeepers stood on the ground, and when the peace failed to be kept, and a need arose to call in the warplanes and bomb the Serb militias from the sky, it was impossible to do any such thing, because blue-helmeted peacekeepers stood on the ground. That was preposterous, but that was the case. The language of international accords, of human rights and humanitarianism, of "Europe," of civilization and of the United Nations—this language, the modest rhetoric of 1989, turned out to be hopelessly ambiguous: a language of action that was all too easily converted into a language of inaction; a language that people could wear like an armband to show they were morally committed, when, in reality, they were thinking of dinner all along; an idealistic language that was also a cynical language.

Even so, forceful actions did get underway, eventually, in Bosnia and then in Kosovo. The French—once Mitterrand was out of office—were the first to show a little pluck. But the forcefulness in those actions was mostly provided by the American military. That was a pitiful commentary on democracy in Europe. "Europe" turned out to be Europe, after all. Europe was a place that invents Frankensteins, and does not dismantle them. Europe was a society that could not defend the weak, or its own religious minorities, or its own principles. Even in the 1990s! The Balkan Wars were Europe's Lincolnian "test"; and Europe could not produce its Lincolns. Still, the French did make their move, and the British soldiers were exceptionally brave, and the Europeans demonstrated an ability to play at least a lively supporting role, so long as the United States played the lead. Even the Germans ultimately overcame their pacifism—their lofty isolationism—and sent troops to participate in the rescue of Kosovo in 1999. That was a big step, for Germany.

The United Nations had turned out to be incapable of doing anything forceful because of the Russians and their Security Council veto; so the Europeans, propelled by the United States, acted in the name of NATO instead. And then the Russians, not wanting to be left out, decided to participate, anyway—in plain demonstration that a show of initiative by the democratic powers can pull along even the most recalcitrant. Human rights, humanitarianism, international accords and treaties, the wispy thing called "Europe"—this language was not entirely hopeless. The ambiguous terms could take on specific meanings, if someone insisted. And so, the free society that is Europe demonstrated at least a tentative ability to stand for the principles of a free society, so long as the United States offered a steadying arm. The tragedy in the Balkans was huge and avoidable—but, at least, a Muslim population managed to survive in Bosnia. The ethnic Albanians who had fled Kosovo returned to their homes. That was something new in world history: a mass evacuation quickly reversed. The Serbs, returning to their senses, even felt encouraged to overthrow the worst of their nationalist leaders and to establish the rudiments of a liberal democratic state—to do what they had failed to do in 1989. The Serb achievements were pretty feeble. Still, those were achievements.

AND ALL of this, the hard-won achievements of liberal democracy since 1989, together with the willful delusions about totalitarianism and its demise—all came into focus on September 11, 2001. The planes crashed, the towers crumbled, a wall of the Pentagon collapsed—and a visible flame of democratic solidarity sprang up spontaneously in the heart of tired old Europe, and in other regions, too. During the Cold War, John F. Kennedy expressed America's solidarity with people abroad by saying to the Germans, "Ich bin ein Berliner!"—a statement of unqualified support for Europeans who were trying to fend off the Soviet occupation and the Communist tyrants.

On September 12, 2001, *Le Monde* in Paris published an editorial, instantly famous, which took Kennedy's words and turned them around to say, "Nous sommes tous Américains!" That was Europe's declaration of solidarity with America, exclamation mark and all. The Berliners themselves assembled in a mass rally to declare their own solidarity with the United States—truly a moving spectacle, given the difficult history of Germany and America and the two world wars. And more: the officials of NATO invoked the never-before invoked Article Five of NATO's charter, which, Musketeer-like, defined an attack on any of NATO's members as an attack on all. (And why not the Musketeers? Alexandre Dumas, that hyphenated Franco-Haitian, stood bravely for democratic freedoms during his own time in the nineteenth century.)

President Bush managed to get off one unfortunate gaffe in those first moments after the attacks. He said he wanted bin Laden "dead or alive"—a statement which managed to convince vast portions of the world that our enemy was merely a single person, or a band of desperadoes, and not anything larger. Even now, a good many people continue to picture the Terror War as a manhunt, with posses chasing bandits through the mountains—a police action, not requiring any of the massive preparations and strategic considerations of war. Bush's "dead or alive" sowed a lot of confusion, in that respect. Worse, "dead or alive" conjured images of Wild West mayhem, not so much among Americans, who had accepted long ago that Bush was no orator, but definitely in other parts of the world. Enormous publics concluded that America's president, the backwoods barbarian, was going to run amok, guns blazing. André Glucksmann proposed a gallant defense of Bush on this point by remarking that "dead or alive," far from expressing a primitive mentality, harked back to the earliest, seventeenth-century origins of international law, which mandated the right to hunt down sea pirates, labeled as *hostis generis humani*, or enemies of humanity—"dead or alive."

But, in truth, Bush was not a reliable authority on international law and *hostis generis humani*. Here, in the first moments after the attack, was a foretaste of problems to come. And yet, for all his language disabilities and lack of polish, Bush responded capably enough to the terrorist attack, at least in the sphere of military action. A full-scale invasion of faraway Afghanistan had to have seemed daunting in the extreme. Some other president might have dithered, or might have contented himself with lobbing missiles into Afghanistan for two or three days, praying for a bull's-eye. But Bush put together a fairly enormous force, convened allies and coalition partners, appeased or intimidated or seduced possible enemies, and launched an invasion which, as in any war, caused many terrible events—but few of the mass-scale calamities that so many people had dreaded.

The planes flew overhead, the Special Forces deployed their mysterious sci-fi technology along the ground, the British, Canadians, and other troops bravely took up their positions. And, as the fog of peace rolled away, a huge panorama, the reality of our present moment, appeared across the breadth of Afghanistan. It was the landscape of modern totalitarianism, arrayed in layered seams, perceptible at last—this thing which, in the deluded, triumphalist atmosphere of 1989, was thought to have disappeared. The charismatic leaders, who appeared to be mad, bristling with their university educations from Mecca and from the Egyptian circles that descend from Sayyid Qutb; the elite cadre of Al Qaeda, directly below the leaders, a praetorian guard dominating the Afghan state; the Taliban as party militants, inflicting the revolutionary doctrine on the suffering masses; the Ministry for the Prevention of Vice and the Promotion of Virtue, fighting the daily battle against impure thoughts; the cheering masses in other countries, who continued to look on Afghanistan's Islamic Emirate as utopia achieved; the rivalry with a competing wing of the same totalitarian movement on Afghanistan's western border, in Iran; the stream of money and intellect pouring in from Islamism's Sunni homeland in Saudi Arabia; the network of fraternal movements and terrorist groups around the world, with their documents scattered on the floor of the Kabul safehouses; the volunteers from all corners of the globe, unto Northern California; the zealotry of the fighters in the prison uprising at Mazar-i-Sharif; and, on the horizon everywhere, the apologists and "useful idiots" from all countries, explaining why black is white; the mass peace demonstrations in Berlin and London and even in Washington, many tens of thousands of people, the Paul-Fauristes of our day, shouting their slogans—all, all was suddenly visible, once the invasion had begun. It was a vista recognizable from every decade since the Bolshevik Revolution of 1917. Or even further back. Glucksmann has pointed out that, as early as the 1860s, Dostoevsky's Russian nihilists had already arranged themselves in a similar structure—the charismatic, ruthless leaders proclaiming indifference to life, at the head of the organization, and somehow surviving; the softheaded followers manning the ranks, and sent out to die.

But there was another vista, which I think no one would have expected to see. Bush the Younger had come into office trailing impeccable Nixonian credentials, if only by family inheritance. Bush the Elder was a protégé of Nixon's; he was Nixon's ambassador to China. Dick Cheney, Donald Rumsfeld, and a number of other top figures in the new administration were likewise veterans of the Nixon years, hard-bitten "realists" one and all, with a well-known contempt for the "missionary work" (Kissinger's phrase) of "idealist" foreign policies. During his election campaign, Bush the Younger specified that he, too, was no bleeding heart.

He sneered at what was called "nation-building," which is to say, postwar reconstruction in other parts of the world. Let people elsewhere in the world untangle their own knots!—that was Bush's campaign message. He acted on that message, too, once he had ascended to the White House. The deadly Ping-Pong of Palestinian terror and Israeli reprisals got deadlier. Bush shrugged. He slyly attributed the violence to Clinton's enthusiasm for making peace. In Bush's mental universe, governmental do-goodism loomed as the evil of evils. Argentina tumbled into economic free fall—the kind of crisis that would have sent Clinton into spasms of White House activity, trying to limit the damage. Bush serenely let the collapse proceed. "They like it that way," said Bush's treasury secretary, about the Argentinians.

What choices was Bush going to make in Afghanistan, then? Generations of "realist" policy could have told us what to expect. The State Department would look for a tractable warlord and would install that man in power—someone who could be trusted to keep a sharp eye out for American interests, even if he lived on pillage and rapine: "a son of a bitch, but our son of a bitch." Or the State Department would find a malleable wing of the Taliban—a group of practical-minded mullahs willing to postpone the worldwide jihad against Zionists and Crusaders sufficiently to establish a friendly quid pro quo with the newly reoccupied U.S. Embassy in Kabul. American policies in the Middle East, not to mention in other regions, had trod those paths steadily during the entire modern era. The precedent was vast. What was the history of America's alliance with the ultramontane zealots of Saudi Arabia, if not a "realist" story of backroom deals with jihadi princelings susceptible to corrupt arrangements, an alliance of the cold and the oily for mutual profit?

Those alliances in the Muslim world did not turn out well, as it happened. Perhaps the failure had caught Bush's attention, and he understood the error at a glance. Or not—it was hard to tell. Either way, somehow he did seem to arrive at a few new thoughts, beginning almost immediately after 9/11. At the very least, his oratory sprouted a grandiloquent new rhetoric, which was weirdly at odds with his Wild West sneering. He spoke about "totalitarianism" and "freedom." Turning to Afghanistan, he raised the issue of women's rights under Taliban rule—a feminist point. A lot of people scoffed. He kept on raising that point, however. His wife, who normally played no role in politics, added her own emphasis. Women's issues had plainly become a White House strategy. The scoffing increased.

And yet, as the administration's policy unfolded in Afghanistan, the democratic and even feminist aspects were hard to miss. The State Department gathered together some Afghan exiles to lay the groundwork for a new government, and women leaders were pointedly included from the start. When the coalition forces had managed to dominate the country militarily, traditional Afghan assemblies were convened to go on with the work of constructing a new political system—the very approach that any sincerely democratic-minded person would have recommended. Hamid Karzai was finally chosen to be the leader, pushed on the Afghans by the American strategists but also accepted by the Afghan assembly—and Karzai turned out to be anything but a warlord. Nor was he a corrupt and schismatic mullah from the jihad. He appeared to be, instead, a liberal. A man with democratic aspirations for his country. A man, also, with brothers and sisters prospering in America, a hyphenated personality in the modern style—only, this time, with the accent on hyphenation's liberal side.

The Taliban fled to the hills. And the scenes of victory were plainly scenes of liberation—those scenes of grown women in Kabul flocking to class to learn how to read, of men gathering at barbershops to shave off their hated beards, of Kabul's single movie theatre opening once more to eager crowds, of music blaring once more from loudspeakers. To borrow the Islamist term for ignorance, here was *jahiliyyah* going down to defeat before the eyes of the world. Some of Bush's critics in the United States, hooting and jeering, pointed to the chaotic provinces outside of Kabul, to Al Qaeda's survival and bin Laden's escape, to the warlords who survived in the north, south, and west, to assassinations, poverty, drugs, illness, homelessness—to the fragility of the victory, and its geographical narrowness in Kabul. All of which was true, and the hooting was deserved, and I will even propose a few jeers of my own, in a moment.

But let us keep a sense of proportion. A year after Islamism's defeat in Afghanistan, the United Nations estimated that 3 million children, many of them girls, were enrolled in schools for the first time—a revolutionary event. Chomsky had predicted a "silent genocide," even a deliberate genocide ("the U.S. had demanded that Pakistan kill possibly millions of people . . ."). There was, in fact, a humanitarian crisis. But the crisis owed in large part to something quite the opposite of genocide. A huge crowd of nearly 2 million Afghans, refugees who had fled during the Soviet incursion and the years of chaos and the Taliban despotism, came streaming back into their own country. Genocide reduces populations. The invasion of Afghanistan increased the population by nearly 10 percent. Instead of genocide, genogenesis. In the course of this book, every time I have cited a figure of thousands or millions of people, the figure has been, until this moment, a sign of horror. But these were not signs of horror.

AND, WITH THESE VISTAS before our eyes, it became possible to make a few observations about the larger Terror War, not just in Central Asia—an observation about the scale of the war, to begin with. The Afghan events were not, in fact, a police action, and could not have been, given Al Qaeda's size and sophistication, on top of the fat solidity of the Taliban and its popular support. People like to fantasize about eliminating gigantic dangers by sending in super-negotiators with smooth tongues, or else hit men with silver bullets, or else by stoically waiting for the gigantic dangers to go away by themselves. But those were large and powerful institutions in Afghanistan, which could be uprooted militarily, or not at all. I don't think that any reasonable observer, looking at the Afghan panorama, could have concluded otherwise.

Then, too, the Afghan War required cooperation from Pervez Musharraf, the Pakistani dictator, which had to have been pretty difficult to obtain, given Islamism's history and strength in his country. General Musharraf took his life in his hands by throwing in with the United States—with Americans whose loyalties, in the past, had proved to be hopelessly fickle. Powerful considerations, something irresistible, must have pushed Musharraf to undertake those risks; and the powerful considerations, we can suppose, must surely have included the American troops next door—that is, America's ability to influence events on Pakistan's border, and to favor Pakistan's hated enemies in India, and generally to press the Pakistanis from near at hand. And if military intervention had proved to be unavoidable in Afghanistan, and had managed without violence to encourage some happy side effects in Pakistan, too—if that was the case in one part of the world, what kinds of policies were likely to prove useful in other regions where terrorists were similarly numerous and popular?

I don't want to play laptop general and dispatch imaginary expeditionary forces across my computer screen to the four corners of the world—inventing military strategies as I go, and assuring everyone of splendid triumphs. I only want to remark that Al Qaeda and its allied groups were a nebulous constellation, spread across many countries, and the nebulous constellation rested on solid institutions with genuine power here and there, and the institutions rested on a bedrock of conspiracy theories, organized hatreds, and apocalyptic fantasies: the culture of totalitarianism. In some countries, governments had no choice but to tiptoe around the Islamist radicals, trying not to stir their wrath. In other places, the radical Islamists halfway controlled the governments, anyway. In still other countries, the Pan-Arabists and Baath Socialists had for many years laced their own foreign policies with terrorist conspiracies, Islamist and otherwise, for dark reasons of their own—which created yet another kind of entangling complication.

None of those governments was going to turn against the radical Islamists and the other terrorist groups and crush them on our behalf or anyone else's—unless, like General Musharraf, the government leaders felt a vise of foreign pressures closing in. And perhaps not even then. A lot of military maneuvering by the United States and its allies did seem unavoidable, in those circumstances. Police work? There was going to be police work. But the sheer number of soldiers likely to be introduced into the Persian Gulf and several other regions around the world, the costs and dangers, the unavoidable collisions of competing forces and armies—every aspect of the conflict with Muslim totalitarianism and its formal allies and its allies-of-convenience and its next-door neighbors spoke of more than police work.

On the other hand, neither did the Terror War like look a clash of civilizations. The whole problem with Huntington's theory was always one of scale, and not just of nuance. A clash of civilizations has got to be, by definition, huge and eternal, or very nearly so. The conflict between Christendom and Islam, Huntington reminds us, has been simmering for 1,400 years—a length of time that makes the Cold War between liberalism and communism seem, in his words, "fleeting and superficial." But there was no reason to look on the Afghan War or on anything that happened afterward as a clash of Christendom and Islam. Or rather, there was only one reason, which ought to have struck us as risible. A large number of Islamists and Baathi did look on the conflict in that light. They insisted on their clash. In their eyes, the Muslim world was stoutly resisting the Crusaders of the West. That was their ideology.

They also looked on every new event around the world as a stage in Judaism's cosmic struggle against Islam. Their ideology was mad. In wars between liberalism and totalitarianism, the totalitarian picture of the war is always mad. (Or, to be more precise, the totalitarian picture rests on a mad platform—even if the totalitarian side in a war may also invoke some of the more conventional causes and aims of war.) The Nazis pictured the Second World War as a biological battle between the superior race (them) and the mongrel and inferior races (us). The Soviets and their comrades pictured the Cold War as an economic struggle between the proletarians of the world (them) and the bourgeois exploiters (us). Islamism's medieval image of jihadi warriors waving scimitars at the Zionist-Crusader conspiracy was no less fanciful, and no less demented. The reality of the Terror War, then—the real-life vista that first became evident in those early days of the Afghan

War—was neither policelike, nor civilizational, nor cosmic. It was an event in the twentieth-century mode. It was the clash of ideologies. It was the war between liberalism and the apocalyptic and phantasmagorical movements that have risen up against liberal civilization ever since the calamities of the First World War.

Now, on the topic of war between liberalism and its enemies, the Islamists did have something to say to us, and it was Sayyid Qutb who offered the clearest exposition. Qutb always recognized that Islamism's truest enemy was not a military force but, instead, an insidious penetration of cultural influences and ideas—the ideas that, in his word, threatened to "exterminate" Islam. The struggle, as he interpreted it, was mental, above all. The war between liberalism and Islamism mirrored perfectly, in this respect, the earlier wars between liberalism and other forms of totalitarianism. Those earlier wars were always decided, in the end, by something other than marching armies. The wars came to an end when the apocalyptic ideologues, in a fit of lucidity, gave up at last on their apocalypses. When people talk about 1989 and the fall of the Berlin Wall, that is what they really mean—the moment when Communists in Eastern Europe finally recognized that communism was an error, which left everyone else free to construct a different kind of society. Communism's doctrinal collapse in Europe took place without a shot being fired—a nearly miraculous event, if you calculate the odds. Nothing like that in the case of the Fascist Axis. Still, even there, the ultimate triumph over fascism, the triumph that endured, came about only when the main Fascist countries, with a lot of help and guidance from outside, agreed to uproot their own thinking and political cultures in favor of something new—a process that took much longer than the fighting itself, and may still be going on, here and there. In the Second World War, D-Day was a capital event; but de-Nazification was the victory.

A mental war was visible in Afghanistan, too—a clash of ideologies, sometimes on the most sophisticated level, doctrines in massed formations chasing each other back and forth across the landscape. I can hear someone snickering: sophisticated ideas?—there, in the Pashtun boondocks, where people make do without electricity or running water? But of course. It is a mistake to snicker. Islamism became a world force partly because, in Egypt back in the 1970s, Nasser's successor, Anwar Sadat, unleashed the scholars of the Muslim Brotherhood on the universities in order to fend off Egypt's Marxists; and the Muslim Brothers turned out to be weighty thinkers, and *The Shade of the Qur'an* offered cool refreshment, and the Islamists fended all too well, and their ideas spread. Events in Afghanistan proceeded along a very similar path. Marxism-Leninism came into vogue in many places around the world in the mid-twentieth century, and Afghanistan was one place among the many. Marxism-Leninism was good enough for Louis Althusser in Paris, and it was good enough for the advanced thinkers in Kabul.

And then, in Afghanistan, Marxism-Leninism fell out of favor, and people took up Islamism instead, the next new hope of mankind—a doctrine for a newer moment. Marx and Lenin went out the window, and the preachings of Qutb and of Pakistan's Abul A'la Mawdudi went in. Soviet-supported cadre training sessions were as nothing compared to Saudi-supported madrassas. And then, in time, Islamism, too, yielded to a newer phase—the new wave whose strength and appeal everyone could see when Karzai and his fellow liberals arrived and preached still another doctrine. The gales of ideology do blow, and they race across the earth with amazing speed, and no country escapes them, no matter how remote. And this aspect of Afghan history—the conflict of doctrines and ideas—pointed to a few likely traits of the larger Terror War in the months and years to come, elsewhere in the world.

On this topic, the war of ideas, I'm happy to be a laptop general. The strategy for a mental war was, I think, obvious from the start, or should have been. It was the strategy that worked well enough in the early years of the Cold War in Europe, after the Second World War—in the years when solid percentages of the French and the Italians and people in other countries were enlisting in Communist parties, and the brightest of intellectuals were lining up with the pro-Soviet left, and Soviet advances seemed unstoppable. The strategy in those days was to take the Stalinists seriously—to argue with them, point by point. It was a war of the newsstands and the bookstores.

The classic literature of anti-totalitarianism from circa 1950, the books by Camus and Arthur Schlesinger and the other writers I've mentioned—those were the big guns in that war. It was a war of conferences, lectures, writers' organizations, university debates, and scholarship—a concerted mobilizing of liberal thinkers and writers. And it was a difficult war—difficult, above all, because in 1914 the absurdities of nineteenth-century liberal optimism did collapse, and the totalitarian movements arose on the basis of arguments that were sometimes profound and even accurate: a war in which the totalitarian thinkers knew how to rail and sneer, and the liberal thinkers were all too easily charged with hypocrisy, delusion, and ulterior motives; a war in which simplicity, which is powerful, belonged to the totalitarians, and complexity, which is weak, belonged to the liberals.

The Terror War was fated to be fought on that same plane—on the plane of theories, arguments, books, magazines, conferences, and lectures. It was going to be a war about the "cultural influences" that penetrate the Islamic mind, about the deepest concepts of modern life, about philosophies and theologies, about ideas that draw on the most brilliant writers and the most moving of texts. It was going to be, in the end, a war of persuasion—a war that was going to be decided in large part by writers and thinkers whose ideas were going to take root, or fail to take root, among the general public. And where was that war destined to take place, geographically speaking? My editions of Qutb's writings list these cities on the publication pages: Cairo; Doha, Qatar; Kano, Nigeria; Nairobi, Kenya; Karachi, Pakistan; New Delhi and

Bombay, India. The war of ideas was certainly going to take place there. And in other cities, likewise listed: Leicester, United Kingdom; and Oneonta, New York.

But to a very large degree the war of ideas was fated to take place in still other cities, not listed in those particular books. The intellectual centers of the Arab world and some of the other Muslim countries tend to be, in this age of hyphenated identities, London and Paris. Those cities always were, in the past, the capitals of thought, and they are still the capitals of thought. The biggest and most important intellectual battles were surely going to be fought in those cities—in the same cities where the intellectual battles between liberalism and communism had also taken place. The London School of Economics, the Paris universities, the alma maters of Pakistan's Ahmed Omar Sheikh and the Sudan's Hassan al-Turabi—those were definitely battle sites. The Londoners and Parisians were going to have to rise to the occasion. Not to leave out the Germans: it did mean something that Muhammad Atta and some of his comrades made their home in Hamburg. Nor could I possibly forget the Brooklyn and Jersey City neighborhoods where Sheikh Rahman maintained his centers of operation. Brooklyn, Whitman's home, used to be a world capital of Arab poetry, seventy-five years ago—the place where Kahlil Gibran published some of his principal writings and invoked Whitman and even Lincoln. An intellectual war, I would think, was going to have to take place there, too—the war of Gibran's poetry and liberalism against Sheikh Rahman's Islamism and terror: a true battle of Atlantic Avenue.

There were other lessons, too, to be gleaned from the Cold War in its early days—lessons from the French Socialists, no less. The pathetic trajectory of French socialism's anti-war wing during the Second World War, the inability to believe in the existence of pathological mass movements or to comprehend the meaning of Nazism and fascism, the refusal to fight, the sympathy for Marshal Pétain—those many errors destroyed the Paul-Fauristes and the anti-war left, in

France. But socialism's other wing emerged from the war with honor intact, even enhanced—and here the story goes on. Léon Blum, the bête noire of the anti-war Socialists, managed to survive his internment in Dachau. He returned to France and resumed his political career: the Socialist leader in his patriotic glory. And, having been right about Hitler, Blum went on to be right about the Soviets, too.

Even in Dachau, he wrote letters that were smuggled to de Gaulle in London, advising him not to trust the Communists. And Blum's worries only deepened once the war was over. He could see quite clearly that a Soviet victory in Western Europe might well come about, given the progress of events and the growth and popularity of the Communist parties. He understood communism's inner strength. The Communist movement's appeal to the social conscience, the good works done by Communist militants in the trade unions, the network of Communist schools and agencies, the Communist ability to infuse the poor and the suffering with hope for a radiant future, the myth of Soviet prosperity and justice, the brilliance of the pro-Communist philosophers—Blum comprehended every aspect.

He knew that right-wing politicians and conservative social movements could not possibly out-argue the Communists in the trade unions and in the working-class neighborhoods, and that conservative intellectuals would never be able to out-argue the Communists and the fellow travelers in the universities, either. And so, Blum called for a "Third Force" in Europe, which was not going to be conservative, and not going to be Communist, either—a Third Force of democratic socialists, trade unionists, and people with similar views, ready to lead their own fight against the Communists and fellow travelers. Blum wanted to out-compete communism on the left: to offer better trade unions than the Communist unions, better social agencies, truer hopes for a better future. He acted on this program, too—he and the other democratic socialists in Europe, some of them, at least. And this was entirely in character. For what was the left-wing idea in its most authentic sense, if not a commitment to international solidarity and active engagement? That was Blum's left-wing idea, anyway. The Communists vilified his Third Force as imperialist reaction. So what? The Communist picture of world events was an ideological wisp, and Communist vilifications rested on a delusionary image of world affairs, and Blum and his allies and supporters proceeded, undaunted.

Some of those supporters were American, and this, too, was worth pointing out. In the United States in the 1940s, the notion of supporting Europe's Socialists and trade unions in order to beat back the Communists made no sense at all to a good many people, and especially not to the old-school conservatives and establishment figures in the State Department. America's conservatives couldn't tell the difference between the Communists and the non-Communist left, and to support any kind of leftist at all was beyond their capability. Then, too, the notion of lending a hand to Europe's Socialists met a lot of opposition in some corners of the American left, as well. The Communist Party in the United States may have been small and harried, but the party did control a number of trade unions in the labor movement's newer, industrial wing, the CIO. The Communists ran the CIO's foreign policy bureau. And, from their post in the CIO, they put up a ferocious battle against anything even hinting of Blum's Third Force.

Still, in the United States, some people did see the virtue in Blum's idea. Those people were his Socialist comrades in America, the old-time labor radicals in the International Ladies Garment Workers Union in New York and the United Auto Workers in Detroit, together with a few other such groups with ties to the labor movement's older wing, the AFL. The old Socialists intuitively grasped the wisdom of a Third Force. The American unions were at their height in those days, and the Garment Workers and the Auto Workers enjoyed big memberships and big budgets, and they dispatched their own organizers into Europe to lend a hand to Blum's Third Force and to people with similar ideas. The Americans toiled diligently on behalf of the French and Italian labor movements, and they put up a fight on behalf of the German Social Democrats, too, and even on behalf of the underground Socialists and anarcho-syndicalists in Fascist Spain—the broad span of the European left, whoever was not a Communist.

Theirs was a free-lance, left-wing internationalism, without government support—though, after a while, some of the younger, free-thinking people in the State Department did begin to catch on to the utility of this sort of thing, which only increased the effectiveness. Schlesinger, in his book from 1949, *The Vital Center*, saw a lot to applaud in that kind of international solidarity. He called for more of it, a "new radicalism" on behalf of the "free left"—a new radicalism to pick up the thread of social reform from Franklin Roosevelt's New Deal and carry it forward, at home and around the world.

The panorama of the Terror War cried out for this kind of activism in our own time, as well—a Third Force, different from the conservatives and the foreign policy cynics who could only think of striking up alliances with friendly tyrants; and different from the anti-imperialists of the left, the left-wing isolationists, who could not imagine any progressive role at all for the United States. A Third Force, neither "realist" nor pacifist—a Third Force devoted to a politics of human rights and especially women's rights, across the Muslim world; a politics of ethnic and religious tolerance; a politics against racism and anti-Semitism, no matter how inconvenient that might seem to the Egyptian media and the House of Saud; a politics against the manias of the ultra-right in Israel, too, no matter how much that might enrage the Likud and its supporters; a politics of secular education, of pluralism, and law across the Muslim world; a politics against obscurantism and superstition; a politics to out-compete the Islamists and Baathi on their left; a politics to fight against poverty and oppression; a politics of authentic solidarity for the Muslim world, instead of the demagogy of cosmic hatreds. A politics, in a word, of liberalism, a "new birth of freedom"—the kind of thing that could be glimpsed, in its early stages, in the liberation of Kabul.

But then, a Third Force didn't have to rest its case on events in Afghanistan, where progress was all too likely to roll back down the hill into warlord mayhem and the opium trade. A new politics for the Muslim world could be justified simply by gazing back on the revolutions of 1989. Something did happen in those revolutions, after all, even if totalitarianism as such never came to an end. The notion that one or another race or culture or religion is hopelessly allergic to liberal ideas—this notion did pretty much explode. Anyway, to appreciate the liberal potential in the Muslim world, we had only to listen closely to the Muslim totalitarians themselves, the great theoreticians and their statements.

Over and again, the theoreticians have explained that apocalyptic solutions appealed to them because non-apocalyptic ideas likewise appealed to them, and giant battles were taking place in their own minds. The whole purpose of totalitarianism, Schlesinger wrote in 1949, was to combat the "anxiety" that is aroused by the lure of other, better ideas. Molotov, Stalin's lieutenant, explained at the height of the Soviet terror that in Communist society the "vestiges of capitalism" were "extremely persistent in people's consciousness"—which showed the need to keep the firing squads at work, especially against deviationists and freethinkers within the Communist Party itself. Half a century later, we know that Molotov had good reason to worry, and vestiges of a non-Communist idea did prove to be extremely persistent in the Soviet Union, even among Communists, and the vestiges triumphed in the end. What in the Muslim world should make us suppose that totalitarianism in its Muslim versions is any different?

Qutb, fretting about "the cultural influences which had penetrated my mind," expressed Molotov's point exactly. Qutb worried about the hideous schizophrenia of modern life because he knew that Muslim society, and not just the culture of the West, was torn by conflicting ideas. Aflaq made the same observation in his comment about the "philosophies and teachings" that "invade the Arab mind and steal his loyalty." Influences and philosophies do penetrate and invade, and they do steal loyalties. Vestiges persist even in the minds of the totalitarians themselves. The enemies of liberalism are halfway its friends, by their own admission. Well, maybe not halfway. But there is something to work with, here.

The prospect of a Third Force in the Muslim countries, a force laboring on behalf of at least the rudiments of liberal society—that was the vista in those first months of the Terror War. It was unmistakable in those amazing Afghan scenes—I keep coming back to those scenes, they were extremely moving, let us not forget these scenes!—once the Taliban had gone: the scenes of girls and women warily removing their oppressive burqas and, in astounding numbers, making their way to school.

AND YET the notion of the Terror War that I have just laid out, which had seemed so easy to imagine in the early weeks of the Afghan War, the notion of a liberal war of liberation, partly military but ultimately intellectual, a war of ideas, fought around the world—that notion ran up into some hard political obstacles almost instantly. This was by no means Bush's fault in every respect. It was Bush, after all, who responded to 9/11 by speaking about totalitarianism and not just about terror—though he was a little inconsistent on this point. Among the Washington politicians, it was Bush, not anyone further to the left, who insisted on postulating women's rights as a war aim in Afghanistan, and Bush who held out the hope for liberal freedom in the Muslim world—the hope for political and social progress.

But—this was odd—he seemed unable to get any of these points across to the world. He spoke, and the mute button swallowed his words, and not just because of his peculiar inability to form a proper sentence. A doctrinal problem stood in his way, and he seemed unable to get around it—probably because, in his eyes, there was no doctrinal problem. Bush ran for the presidency in 2000 trying to give the impression that he was a practical man of affairs, unburdened by ideology; but, as everyone quickly came to realize, he did have his ideas, and they were fairly rigid. I will try to put those ideas as sympathetically as I can. Bush and his team were the heirs of his father, Bush the Elder; but mostly they admired Ronald Reagan. They wanted to replicate Reagan's achievements, which seemed to them great. Reagan dreamed of untying the ropes that held down American business—federal regulations, unions, taxes: he hated them all—in the expectation that, freed of irksome restrictions, American business would prove to be frisky and creative, for the benefit of all. Bush and his team wanted to do something similar, as much in foreign affairs as in the domestic economy.

They put their faith in the natural dynamism of American business. They considered that American military and economic power could make big and positive changes in the world, if only the new administration could shake off the restrictions and timidities of the past. The Kyoto Protocol on gas emissions, a proposed treaty limiting the spread of biological weapons, the old Anti-Ballistic Missile Treaty with Russia, the International Criminal Court—every one of those things, in their eyes, was a rope holding America down, and they wanted to wriggle free. They wanted to unleash American technology. They contemplated Reagan's ancient dream of an outer-space missile shield, and though no such shield existed, and the first set of tests was a disaster, and also the second set, and the third, and so on—undismayed, they oohed and aahed. A new gadget—at least, prospectively! They looked forward to the wonderful results that were sure to descend upon them, just as wonderful results had descended upon Reagan. And yet, in the midst of their hopeful expectations and dynamic yearning for the future, Bush and his team had no way to understand how other people around the world were bound to see their policies in the present.

Nobody at all in Bush's circle had shown any sympathy for the principal humanitarian and human rights causes of the 1990s. The arguments over genocide in the Balkans, over the responsibility of nations, over the moral need to show solidarity with the victims, over the ideals of international law and the need to animate those ideals with a will to do something more than wring one's hands—all of those arguments had passed them by. Bush himself seemed to look on Clinton's Balkan intervention with instinctive horror. The Balkan policy came up once or twice during the 2000 campaign, and Bush made clear that, given his druthers, American troops would never have been sent in the first place. He even promised to get them out—though he had to back away from this proposal, when the Europeans yelped in fear.

And these attitudes of his remained pretty much the same after 9/11. The Afghan War got underway, and the American forces captured several hundred people who appeared to be Taliban fighters or militants of Al Qaeda, and the prisoners were brought to the United States military base at Guantánamo Bay in Cuba, where the military interrogations could proceed without any of the pesky limitations of domestic American law. And even that much freedom for the officers in charge seemed insufficient, and the government announced an intention to evade the Geneva Conventions of war, in regard to military prisoners. Laws, formal treaties, the customs of civilized nations, the legitimacy of international institutions—these were the dross of the past, and Bush was plunging into the future. And, as he plunged, he had no idea, nobody in his administration seemed to have any idea, that international law, human rights, "Europe," and humanitarianism had willy-nilly become the language of liberal democracy around the world. That was the doctrinal problem he couldn't see. And so, Bush opened his mouth and spoke about freedom, and felt that he was sincere, I think; but, to a great many listeners, the words sounded tinny and false. And he couldn't judge the response.

I can imagine that he was particularly intent on raising the issue of women's rights, for reasons that were easy enough to see. Bernard Lewis has observed that, if any single factor can account for the Arab world's difficulties in adapting to modern life, it must be the status of women in Arab societies. Anyone who wanted to go to the heart of the Arab predicament would have to speak about women and their place in society, then—at least, in the degree that Lewis was right. The Islamists themselves were noticeably defensive on that topic, as if not entirely convinced of the soundness of their own doctrine. Islamism promised modernization in a version that was going to be distinctly Muslim and not Western, a Koranic modernization; but Islamism's Koran was not, on its face, especially modern. Anyone who reads Qutb or, from our own day, Tariq Ramadan will notice that these writers, the grand Islamist theoreticians, the super-radical and the not-so-radical, get very prickly on women's rights—an obvious sore point, with them. Whoever advised Bush to raise this question was a very clever person.

But could anyone understand Bush's remarks? The question of women's rights had played a big role in the foreign policy debates of the 1990s—probably for the first time in history. This was because of the Balkan Wars. The Serb nationalist militias had made a specialty of rape, and the phenomenon of wartime rape was given a lot of analysis by feminists elsewhere in the world, who argued that rape ought to be viewed as a war crime and not just as an incidental act of violence. The feminists won this point, too, and rape was finally recognized as an element of genocide in the Balkans, an attack on an entire population—a crime against humanity, to be prosecuted at the International Criminal Tribunal. The understanding of women's rights and of crimes against women evolved quite a bit during those debates. The forward step was huge—at least, among Europeans and American liberals and anyone else who was paying attention.

But Bush and his team, having held back from those debates, had no way to invoke the new understandings. They had never shown anything but indifference to the cause of women's rights at home. They had tried to roll back the legal right to abortion. They had forbidden American contributions to sex education abroad. Sometimes the administration had made itself look positively ridiculous. Bush's attorney general, prodded by his own unusual religious obligations, arranged for statues of naked women at the Justice Department in Washington to be demurely covered with burqa-like drapes—a preposterous order, which could only put the rest of the administration in a silly light. And yet, in regard to women's rights as an element within the Terror War, there was no reason for anyone to laugh or make merry—least of all, anyone who took the women's issues seriously. The Afghan War was, I would think, the first feminist war in all of history—the first war in which women's rights were proclaimed at the start to be a major war aim. No one seemed to notice, though. The war was won, more or less, and the scenes of education for women and girls got underway—and yet, among high-minded people in the liberal countries, the mockery at Bush did not come to an end. He had not figured out how to make himself heard. And there was a larger problem.

Many people have wondered why Bush never asked his own country to accept a few sacrifices for the common good—why he never made the slightest move to reduce America's dependence on Arab oil, never asked for higher taxes to pay for a stronger military and security program, never asked for a large or vigorous campaign of volunteer activity. Those were strange omissions, on his part. They seemed to reflect his aversion to the do-good principle. But the strangest omission of all was his failure to take up the larger war of ideas. He did talk about such a war. He announced a war of ideas in his first, brave, spirited speech to Congress, a little more than a week after 9/11. But he himself had no ability or language to articulate the ideas of the modern age, and neither did any of the people around him.

Instead, he launched a program to produce Hollywood TV ads about the virtues of America. The ads ran on Arabic television. The State Department took out ads in Pakistan, affirming that America felt no bias against Muslims. That was laughable—mere ads to counter the most scholarly of doctrines, the most learned of religious authorities, the greatest of modern authors. Mere ads, a couple of sunny images, to break through clouds of Koranic exegesis and dark preachings in a thousand mosques and madrassas! The Pentagon proposed a bureau to be called the Office of Strategic Influence, mandated to diffuse false information among foreign journalists—this, when the whole problem in places like Pakistan was precisely the flood of false information. The Office of Strategic Influence was laughed into oblivion. Yet the Pentagon came back a few months later with a proposed new directive, authorizing the military to carry out secret propaganda operations in neutral and even in friendly countries. Such was the war of ideas. It was pathetic. And then, having pretty much abandoned the field of ideas, the administration shrank from discussing questions of strategy, too—the fundamentals of how to conduct the larger war.

The White House never did entirely explain its logic in staging the invasion of Afghanistan. The part about going after bin Laden and Al Qaeda needed no elaboration—apart from the need to reassure the world that, Chomsky notwithstanding, the United States had no intention of committing genocide. But there was another aspect of the Afghan War—the part about overthrowing totalitarianism and bringing the benefits of a free society. Bush spoke and even, as I say, acted on these principles. But the hesitations and cautions that limited his actions, the miserly husbanding of resources, the obvious reluctance to do more than the minimum—these things undid his every remark. The narrow geographical limits of America's support for Karzai and his new government, confined to Kabul, spoke louder than anything the president had to say. And so, Bush's critics hooted, and the hooting was legitimate. Was he serious or not, in his liberal democratic goals? There was no way to tell. And yet, these goals stood at the heart of the war, and of the larger war to come. And if Bush was hard to understand or take seriously in regard to his strategy in Afghanistan, he was even harder to understand in regard to the next stage of the war, in Iraq.

His actual motives for going after Saddam should have been obvious from the start. Nixon had laid out the rationale, half of it, anyway, back in his Gulf War op-ed of 1991, in *The New York Times*. The argument had everything to do with that crucial word in Nixon's vocabulary, "credibility." Nixon wanted to fight the 1991 war in order to demonstrate that neither Saddam Hussein nor anyone else would be allowed to go up against an American ultimatum. So the United States fought, and, as it happened, Saddam survived (owing, of course, to another Nixonian principle, namely, a preference for dictators over democratic chaos and uncertainty, which led Bush the Elder and Colin Powell to call off the war). And America's credibility, instead of being enhanced, was demolished.

Anyone who granted even a smidgen of logic in Nixon's emphasis on credibility would have recognized what was likely to happen next. For what was the lesson of the 1991 war, in the eyes of America's enemies? It was the lesson of the Vietnam War. America could be withstood. America lacked the strength to fight off the tough and the motivated. America was the kind of liberal society that Qutb had described, fat and unprincipled, which made it a feeble society in the long run. There was no reason not to go on attacking the United States—no reason to hold back, no reason to fear what might happen next. That was the lesson of 1991. The Islamists of East Africa tested the lesson. They attacked the Marines in Mogadishu—and, sure enough, the Marines fled, just as they had done in Lebanon, a few years earlier. The Islamists staged their other attacks. America idly swatted at them, as if not really bothered.

Bush the Younger's administration was full of old Nixon hands, and people with that kind of background, faced with the 9/11 attacks, were bound to respond by invoking one or the other of Nixon's principles—either the faith in dictators, or the insistence on credibility. Some of Bush the Elder's old advisers leaned in one direction, which led them to suppose that Saddam's persistence in power was not the worst thing imaginable. But everyone else, with an eye on 9/11, emphasized credibility. It had to be obvious, to them, what needed to be done, in the wake of the terrorist attacks. The mistake from 1991, the gigantic error in having failed to overthrow Saddam—this colossal blunder had to be righted. The point had to be made clear to everyone around the world that, no, you cannot fight the United States; no, you will be clobbered; no, you won't survive; no, crowds of adoring people on the street will not chant your name—you will lose, and lose again, and lose still more. That was a first rationale for going against Saddam, then—a Nixonian rationale, which would have come intuitively to anyone from Nixon's wing of the Republican Party, even if some of the old Nixon hands went in the other direction.

But the second rationale for going after Saddam was not at all Nixonian and could even be described as anti-Nixonian. It was—to stick with these presidential labels—Wilsonian, in a militant version. The idea was not to appease the Islamists or Baathi or anyone else by offering concessions on this or that demand—these phantasmagorical demands that rested on paranoid fears of Crusader-Zionist plots. The idea was, instead, to get people to think along different lines altogether—to invest their hopes in building a liberal society, just as so many other people were doing around the world. This was an extremely radical idea. It hardly needs saying that Bush's critics pooh-poohed the notion instantly, either with the observation that Arab societies could not be expected to advance beyond tyranny, or with the observation that in Vietnam and in other places, too, the United States had earnestly tried to implant a liberal culture, and had failed dismally.

That was to be expected—though I was interested to see Bernard Lewis offer a more sympathetic evaluation, for all his pessimism about Arab society. The editor of the Mexican magazine *Letras Libres* asked Lewis if he could detect any signs of hope in the Middle East—signs that movements like bin Laden's would fail, in the end. Lewis responded with the observation that, if either Egypt or Saudi Arabia were to hold free elections, the Islamists would win—a discouraging remark. And yet, in other parts of the region, Lewis noticed what he called "seeds" of a better possibility. He glanced at Iran, but also at Iraq. "A change of regime in Iraq and Iran would be a very good beginning," he said, which was eye-catching. So maybe there was, in fact, a chance of launching some sort of liberal revolution in the Middle East, starting with Iraq and Iran—a chance of encouraging a new liberal birth of freedom in places where the worst of the totalitarian plague had wreaked its damage. A chance to do in the Middle East what had been done in Germany, Italy, and Japan—the counterexamples to America's failures in Vietnam and other places. A chance to undo the whole of Muslim totalitarianism.

This idea did seem to follow from the grand revolutions of 1989. It was consistent with the sweep of modern events. But whatever may have been the wisdom in this sort of thinking, or the folly, Bush held back yet again from offering any sort of systematic explanation. He said nothing at all about the Nixonian logic of establishing American credibility in Iraq or anywhere—though Nixonian impulses had to have pushed him in that direction. And he said nothing, or very little, about the Wilsonian logic, either—he left that to his second-level aides. Mostly he presented, or he allowed his cabinet officers to present, his war strategies on different bases entirely, and these other bases were either unconvincing (the argument that Saddam was conspiring with Al Qaeda) or convincing, but less than supremely urgent (the problem of Saddam's weapons program). And the impression he left was—well, it varied among different publics.

Some people were glad to see that the president was taking a tough line, and figured that he knew what he was doing, and were happy to give him their support, without inquiring too closely into his logic or plans. That response accounted for most of the public, in the United States. But other people wanted to judge the reasoning for themselves, and, to them, Bush's arguments looked dishonest—which they were. The arguments sounded like Lyndon Johnson's invocation of North Vietnamese attacks in the Gulf of Tonkin—half-truths, or maybe outright lies, designed to manipulate public opinion. This was not a good impression to leave. And if Bush had failed to present his strategy on Iraq in a straightforward way, what was anyone to think of his larger strategy for the Terror War? There was no way to think anything at all. The larger strategy was a black hole.

It ought to have been obvious that, sooner or later, the United States and its allies were going have to look into the Lebanese Hezbollah, which meant looking into the Syrian government and the Iranian mullahs. It ought to have been obvious that something would have to be done about Saudi Arabia—the biggest problem of all, arguably. Peace and safety may not be compatible, in the end, with the existence of a fanatical, obscurantist, intolerant, anti-Semitic, obsessively patriarchal, polygamous, terror-minded, theocratic, supremely wealthy petro-monarchy that insists on spreading its missionary message to the world. But, in Bush's discussions of the Terror War, none of this was even broached. And the impact of his sundry arguments and non-arguments on opinion around the world was, all in all, a bit problematical.

Waves of sympathy for the United States did sweep across Europe and a lot of other places around the world, in the first moments after 9/11. But Bush had no way to harness those sympathetic waves; no way to address the Europeans or anyone else on the topics of liberalism and democracy; no way to claim the credit for the liberal policies that he did pursue; no way to launch a war of ideas against the totalitarian movements; no way to persuade the skeptics and the doubters to support his military strategies. He did raise a number of false issues, though. The White House issued a statement of national security policy, in which the one point that managed to attract attention was an assertion that, in the future, the United States reserved the right to pursue preemptive wars, which actually meant preventative wars—that is, wars in which America would strike first, without having been attacked. But why the White House came out with any such argument was hard to say.

America had been, after all, attacked. America had come under violent attack from sundry wings of Muslim totalitarianism ever since the Hezbollah truck-bombing of the Marines in 1983—the attacks that had wended their way through one terrorist incident after another, with many hundreds dead even before 9/11. The war with Saddam, having begun in 1991, had never come to an end, such that, even as the White House issued its report on preemptive wars, Baathi artillery was still firing at American planes, and the weapons labs were presumably keeping up their sinister labors. I suppose that people might argue about the definition of war, but I would think that gunfire ought to be regarded as an indication. Why speak of preemptive war, then? The American half of the Terror War was all too post-emptive. But the White House did speak of preemption, and the world responded in a predictable manner, which was to worry about the White House.

There was never any doubt that, given a sufficient American diplomatic effort, Bush would be able to secure the approval and even the participation of all sorts of allies in the Terror War—if not the United Nations in every instance, then some other group of nations, as in the Kosovo War: an alliance of Western countries and of Muslim countries, the First and Third Worlds in motley combination. America's power was large, and putting down the terrorist groups was in many people's interest. It was not a matter of us against the universe. And yet, having raised the issue of preemptive wars, Bush also raised the issue of American unilateralism—which was bound to make countries all over the world feel that, on matters of war and peace, they had lost their say. In this fashion, Bush ensured that even in those instances when he did secure United Nations approval, the backing was going to be reluctant, begrudging, and unpopular—an approval won by strong-arm pressures and by promises of sweetheart oil deals in a post-war Iraq, and not by any appeal to the higher motives of a liberal civilization. Why did he do that? For no reason. For reasons of ideology. Maybe out of inexperience. For lack of time to ponder the alternatives. Or who knows? Here, in any case, was the great, frightening truth of all modern history, laid out for everyone to inspect once again—the great truth that vast consequences flow from inconsequential-seeming causes, and that a systematic logic does not govern world events, and that chance occurrences frame the largest of phenomena: in this case, the chance occurrence that, at a moment of supreme crisis, the world's most powerful person happened to be George W. Bush.

BUT IF Bush and his advisers pretty much lost the thread that led back to 1989 and the liberal achievements of the 1990s, if America's leaders managed to squander the enthusiasm and sympathy of large parts of the world, if they succeeded in convincing naive people in many places that America, and not the terrorists, posed the greatest danger around the world—if the American leaders were responsible, in short, for throwing away a thousand advantages that ought to have been theirs, what did the Europeans do? The initial reactions to 9/11 in Europe ("I am in solidarity with the American people," said the leader of the French Communist Party) did mean something, and, in the end, were likely to mean a lot.

Still, there were other reactions. Suicide bombers blew up Israelis; and masses of trendy thinkers concluded that Israel had no right to exist. Such was the perversity of the moment. And similar perversities seemed to swarm around 9/11 and the United States. I don't mean to exaggerate the scale of the new anti-Americanism in Europe. There was a surge in attacks on synagogues and on Jews in Europe, and an even larger surge in attacks on Muslims—an outbreak of ugliness all around, with violence in the neighborhoods and demagogy from the podiums. A fascist politician did come in second, in France's presidential race. (Better than coming in first!) Nothing of that sort fell on American heads in Europe. Yet the change in atmosphere was unmistakable. Frédéric Encel described it: "The Twin Towers had hardly collapsed when all of the psychopathic sneerers at the United States in the salons of Paris were bursting with pleasure and revenge: 'Who profits from the crime, if not the Americans and their allies?', 'There is no smoke without fire!' and the odious cry, 'The Americans have been asking for it!' As if the workers at the World Trade Center and the passengers on the hijacked planes embodied America's evil and were expiating the cult of the king dollar, the fate of the Apaches, the McDonald's. . . ."

And while the salon-talkers babbled on, the European intellectuals, some of the shrewdest of them, came up with a parallel response on a more sophisticated level. The intellectuals gazed at Bush's aversion to law and international institutions, his uncultured air (Bush's personal demeanor, which plays well in the United States, plays badly in some other places), and the policies of his attorney general, which were likened to McCarthyism at its worst. And the intellectuals arrived at an extreme interpretation. They imagined that Europe and the United States, which for so long had constituted a single, Atlantic civilization, were splitting apart. The United States was drifting in a direction of its own, which was eventually going to produce an altogether different civilization. This was a wild interpretation. Bush had trod on a lot of toes, that was true. But, even putting the worst light on his policies, no one could say that Bush expressed some huge new consensus in American life. The man was president only by a fluke, anyway, owing to the murks of the 2000 election. Still, the European intellectuals, some of them, insisted on attaching deep significance to his policies. And they offered a judgment.

They judged that Western Europe had evolved into an advanced and highly civilized democracy, and that America was slipping into barbarism. They pointed to America's levels of economic inequality, to the huge and growing role of religion in American politics and government, and to the decline in American commitment to law. The single decision to withdraw from the Kyoto Protocol on gas emissions horrified them beyond words. But, most of all, they pointed to capital punishment in the United States. The ultimate penalty seemed to them the ultimate proof of American savagery. Now, I must say that, in my own American social-democratic heart, I heartily agreed with the European intellectuals on every one of these points, taken individually. I did think that Western Europe had made wonderful progress in the last few decades, which we Americans ought to emulate for our own good, even if the Europeans were having their problems, economically, not to mention culturally.

And yet, in making their comparison between America and Western Europe, the European intellectuals failed to notice a number of relevant factors. Western Europe may have achieved a superior degree of economic equality, but America had achieved a superior degree of openness to all and sundry—a different sort of equality, accessible to immigrants from ever more exotic locales and not just to the heirs of the *Mayflower*. Shouldn't that count for something? In the present age it was Western Europe that persecuted its minorities with mobs and hooligans—persecuted the Muslims especially, and sometimes the Jews—even if most people felt bad about mobs and hooligans. The United States, by contrast, was enjoying an unusually healthy moment in race relations. On capital punishment, the European intellectuals seemed to me triply right. Tocqueville in the 1830s singled out capital punishment as a sign of America's superiority over Europe—a sign because, in America, hardly anyone was executed anymore, whereas in the benighted monarchies of the Old World people were hanged and guillotined at a horrifying rate. But that was then.

America had gone downhill since the 1830s. This was indisputable. On this one issue, the comparative reality, American and European, had reversed, and the Old World had raced ahead, and the New World lagged behind, and Bush's barbarous Texas lagged even further. Still, there was something odd and ridiculous in the European obsession with capital punishment in the United States. France would not be France without its history of mass executions and firing squads—in the Terror of 1793, in the suppression of the Paris Commune, and again in the liberation from the Nazis. I won't even mention the history of state executions in Germany. Nothing comparable had ever taken place in the United States. No political movement in America had ever been suppressed through capital punishment, at least not since the days of Nat Turner's rebellion in 1831. America's problems lay elsewhere. But I caught the drift of these European criticisms. They expressed the mood of people who, at a moment of fear, wanted to retreat to the dream of Sweden or a Switzerland—the dream of a Europe that, by laying low, would avoid attacks on itself, a heartless old Europe of the past, the Europe that would not protect its Jews sixty years ago or its Muslims ten years ago, the Europe that has always needed to be rescued from its own manias and has lately congratulated itself on its (genuinely) superior achievements in economic equality and social welfare.

But I don't mean to say, "Europe is like that: look, and groan." I want to make a different point, which is more troubling. For what does it mean to say that, in 1989, the twentieth century did not, in fact, come to an end—that the worst and most frightening impulses of the modern era remained at large, wreaking their damage? There is a meaning that goes beyond the simple observation that villainous tyrants are always a problem. We should ask ourselves: how did it happen that, in the twentieth century, one new movement after another presented mad and apocalyptic fantasies to the world, and was cheered by the crowds, and went on to slaughter its enemies and even its friends? Those movements arose out of a revulsion at the failures and simplemindedness of liberal civilization, and they drew on some of the deepest and most beautiful achievements of literature and philosophy, and they reached down into the depths of human nature, which made them powerful.

But the totalitarian movements flourished also because the climate of modern life allowed them to flourish. To arrive at a situation in which Nazis have conquered Europe, you not only need to have the Nazis themselves, you need to have all the other right-wing movements that look on Nazis in a friendly light, and you need to have left-wing opponents like the anti-war French Socialists, who cannot see that Nazis are Nazis. To end up with Stalin tyrannizing half of Europe, you not only need the cagey Soviet leaders and the Soviet tanks, you need the naive trade union leaders and the ignorant workers, who believe what they are told. You need the foolish fellow travelers who never intend to be Stalinists themselves but who convince themselves that liberal societies are halfway fascist, anyway, and that communism is a forward step, for all its imperfections. The totalitarian movements arise because of failures in liberal civilization, but they flourish because of still other failures in liberal civilization, and if they go on flourishing, it is because of still more failures—one liberal failure after another.

Right now we are beset with terrorists from the Muslim totalitarian movements, who have already killed an astounding number of people, mostly in the Muslim countries, but not just there. What have we needed for these terrorists to prosper? We have needed immense failures of political courage and imagination within the Muslim world. We have needed an almost willful lack of curiosity about those failures by people in other parts of the world—the lack of curiosity that allowed us to suppose that totalitarianism had been defeated, even when totalitarianism was reaching a new zenith. We have needed handsome doses of wishful thinking—the kind of simpleminded faith in a rational world that, in its inability to comprehend reality, sparked the totalitarian movements in the first place. We have needed a political left that, in its anti-imperialist fervors, has lost the ability to stand up to fascism—and has sometimes gone a little further down the slippery slope. We have needed a cynical application of "realist" or Nixonian doctrines over the decades—the doctrines that governed the Gulf War of 1991, the doctrines that even now lead to friendly ties with the most reactionary of feudal systems. We have needed an inability to cling to our own liberal and democratic principles, an inability even to articulate those principles. We have needed a provincial ignorance about intellectual currents in other parts of the world. We have needed foolish resentments in Europe, and a foolish arrogance in America. We have needed so many things! But there has been no lack—every needed thing has been here in abundance.

And now we face a terrible situation. Thoughtful people warn us of horrifying events to come, and the warnings are all too plausible. Yet the warnings cannot advise us what steps to take, if only because the doomsayers are on every side, and warn us against doing, and against not doing. The president of the United States has demonstrated a persistent talent for stepping on toes, just when the United States has most keenly needed its friends to be friends; and a persistent inability to comprehend the intellectual dimensions of the war. The editor of *Le Monde*, Jean-Marie Colombani—the very person who wrote the moving expression of solidarity with the United States, "Nous sommes tous Américains!" during the night of 9/11—went on to write a slightly skeptical response to his own editorial, a book called *Tous Américains?*, in which, in a well-meaning spirit, he recalled how magnificent the United States used to be, once upon a time. In those days, he tells us, America "had a great president, Franklin Delano Roosevelt. Nothing of the sort today." Which is all too true. But what can we do about that? Terrorist bombs go on exploding, even so, and the suicide warriors make their ecstatic march toward death, and we Americans and the French and everyone else have to respond, even without Franklin Roosevelt pointing the way.

We are in an absurd situation. Truly, this is a moment Camus would have appreciated. We have reason to be terrified; but it is not a good idea to be terrified. Oh, how I wish that the entire world would turn out to be rationally explicable, after all—that a Chomsky could nail it down for us, and everything could be shown to be the workings of evil oil companies and their media allies, or some other identifiable pestilence. But no single logic rules the world, and no one is going to intervene in our behalf in order to impose one—not God, nor Hegel, nor FDR. We have to steel ourselves. We need a new radicalism to press Bush to explain the stakes more clearly and to offer political solutions to people around the world who might otherwise become our enemies—a new radicalism to press Bush to turn more convincingly against the "realist" errors of the past. Bush will do what he will do. Let us press, even so. Some aspects of a war against terror and totalitarianism can be fought even by people who cannot abide George W. Bush. Germany's pacifists do not approve the American policy. Germany's pacifists can participate, even so—them, especially. The whole of the Muslim world has been overwhelmed by German philosophies from long ago—the philosophies of revolutionary nationalism and totalitarianism, cannily translated into Muslim dialects. Let the Germans go door to door throughout the region, issuing a product recall.

They will make themselves useful. The French are indignant over capital punishment. Let the French look to places where the victims are buried by bulldozers. The French do not need American presidents to lead them in that direction. In the United States we ourselves don't need a president to enunciate the ideas that ought to be enunciated. The Democratic Party has no Roosevelt, who knew how to wage a war of ideas even while waging the other kind of war. Still, the party of Roosevelt can be the party of Roosevelt. Schlesinger pointed to the American trade unions and the farsighted role they played in Europe after the Second World War.

Let the trade unions play that kind of role today, in countries where terror and totalitarianism are still a danger. Maybe the trade unions are no longer up to that kind of task. All right, then, we have wealthy foundations today. We have human rights organizations. Let the foundations and organizations prosecute their own war. Al Qaeda is a loose network. Let us be an even looser network. A war is a war, and there is nothing to draw comfort from. But neither do we have reason to tremble quite as violently as Henry James did, in 1914. James watched the simple hopes of the nineteenth century dissolve into nothing, and he trembled because he knew that all of civilization was floating helplessly toward Niagara. We don't have to share his fear. Civilization has already gone over the precipice. That was the meaning of the twentieth century.

We have no way to know how the present situation will come out—whether the president's decisions will prove to be wise or foolish; whether his failings will prove to be fatal or not; whether the military planners will be shrewd or naive; whether our enemies will turn out to be more numerous or less; whether some alert police officer or customs agent will rescue a city or not. But, unlike James, we do have the experience of the last many years to draw on, and the experience can tell us, in a general way, what aim to bear in mind. Describing the nihilists and their thinking, Camus wrote, "Here, suicide and murder are two sides of the same system." We are the anti-nihilists—we had better be, anyway. Events around the world have demonstrated the existence of an anti-nihilist system, too. The anti-nihilist system likewise has two sides. In the anti-nihilist system, freedom for others means safety for ourselves. Let us be for the freedom of others.

A Note to the Reader

IN AN EARLIER BOOK, *A Tale of Two Utopias: The Political Journey of the Generation of 1968*, I sketched out very roughly a few ideas about liberalism and history, and in the days after September 11, 2001, I wrote an essay proposing ways to apply those ideas to current circumstances. That essay, "Terror and Liberalism," appeared in *The American Prospect,* October 22, 2001, and was the origin of this present book. A few months later I added a number of points in an essay for the weekly *Forward* in New York, May 24, 2002. With the aid of a Guggenheim fellowship, I spent the summer and fall of 2002 elaborating those several ideas and comments into the book that lies open in your hand.

In the course of the book I cite the principal sources that have guided my thinking, and there is no reason to repeat those citations here, except in a few cases. The quotation from C. L. R. James in chapter II comes from *Mariners, Renegades and Castaways: The Story of Herman Melville and the World We Live In* (New York: C. L. R. James, 1953) and refers, actually, to the crew of the *Pequod.* The relevant books by André Glucksmann are *Le XI° Commandement* (Paris: Flammarion, 1991), where he lays out his theory of apocalyptic revolutions; and *Dostoïevski à Manhattan* (Paris: Robert Laffont, 2002), where he discusses nihilism. The book by Gilles Kepel on which I have greatly relied is *Jihad: The Trail of Political Islam*, translated by Anthony F. Roberts (Cambridge, MA: Harvard University Press, 2002). The book by Tariq Ramadan which I discuss is *Islam, the West and the Challenges of Modernity*, translated by Saïd Amghar (Markfield, Leicester, and Nairobi, Kenya: The Islamic Foundation, 2001).

The tract by Luigi Galleani, *The End of Anarchism?*, originally appeared in Italian in the New York journal *L'Adunata dei Refratarri* in 1924–25 and was translated into English by Max Sartin and Robert D'Atilio (Orkney, Scotland: Cienfuegos Press, 1982). The relevant book by Paul Avrich is his *Sacco and Vanzetti: The Anarchist Background* (Princeton: Princeton University Press, 1991).

The poem I quote by Baudelaire is "Épigraphe pour un livre condamné," from the 1868 edition of *Les Fleurs du Mal.* The poem by Rubén Darío is "Salutación del Optimista" from *Cantos de Vida y Esperanza* in 1905.

The works by Sayyid Qutb that I discuss include the following: *Social Justice in Islam*, translated by John B. Hardie, revised with an introduction by Hamid Algar (Oneonta, NY: Islamic Publications International, 2000); *In the Shade of the Qur'an*, translated by M. A. Salahi and A. A. Shamis, Vol. 1 (Markfield, Leicester, and Nairobi, Kenya: The Islamic Foundation, 1999); Vol. 4 (2001); and Vol. 30 (New Delhi: Idara Ishaat E Dioniyat [P] Ltd., 1992). I have relied as well on Vols. 2, 3, 5, and 6 of the Salahi-Shamis translation (out of what will eventually be a fifteen-volume English-language edition). I also refer to *Islam: The Religion of the Future* (Delhi: Markazi Maktaba Islami, 1974, no translator listed) and *Milestones* (Mumbai, India: Bilal Books, 1998, no translator listed). I quote a biography of Qutb by S. Badrul Hasan, *Syed Qutb Shaheed* (Karachi: International Islamic Publishers, 1980). The edition of the Koran which I cite is published under the title *The Meaning of the Holy Qur'an*, translated with commentary by Abdullah Yusuf Ali, revised with new commentary (Beltsville, MD: Amana Publications, 1989).

I cite Bernard Lewis on a number of occasions, referring to his *Semites and Anti-Semites* (New York: W. W. Norton, 1986) and to an interview with him by Enrique Krauze in *Letras Libres*, Mexico, December 2002. My reference to Walter Laqueur is to an essay of his in the *TLS*, September 6, 2002.

My discussion of Léon Blum and the anti-war French Socialists draws on *The Burden of Responsibility: Blum, Camus, Aron, and the French Twentieth Century,* by Tony Judt (Chicago and London: University of Chicago Press, 1998), and on a valuable book by Nadine Fresco, *Fabrication d'un antisémite* (Paris: Éditions du Seuil, 1999), which recounts the origins of Holocaust denial—a mania that got its start in the anti-war faction of French socialism.

Breyten Breytenbach's essay in *Le Monde* is available in English at the Web site of the International Parliament of Writers, www.autodafe.org. José Saramago's essay ran in *El País*, April 21, 2002, and was answered a few days later in that same newspaper by Barbara Probst Solomon. On Chomsky's argument regarding the American missile strike on the Sudan, I have drawn from an Internet polemic mounted by Leo Casey, in the archives of *Z* magazine, www.zmag.org.

I have cited Fatima Mernissi, *Islam and Democracy*, in the translation by Mary Jo Lakeland (Reading, MA: Addison-Wesley, 1992). I refer to the book by Jean-Marie Colombani, *Tous Américains?: Le monde après le 11 septembre 2001* (Paris: Fayard, 2002). I have drawn also from Frédéric Encel's *Géopolitique de l'apocalypse: La démocratie à l'épreuve de l'islamisme* (Paris: Flammarion, 2002). Unless otherwise noted, translations from the French and the Spanish are my own. And, of course, I have relied on the intrepid reporters of *The New York Times* for innumerable facts.

I draw the phrase "new radicalism" from Arthur M. Schlesinger, Jr.'s *The Vital Center: The Politics of Freedom* (Boston: Houghton Mifflin, 1949). The boldness in that phrase appeals to me. But the phrase comes freighted also with a cautionary history, and this should be borne in mind. Christopher Lasch wrote a book called *The New Radicalism in America 1889–1963: The Intellectual as a Social Type* (New York: Alfred A. Knopf, 1965), in which he glanced at Schlesinger's *Vital Center* and at the Cold War liberals and the anti-Communist left of the mid-twentieth century. And Lasch worried. The rhetoric of "freedom" and "totalitarianism" and such terms struck him as extreme and rigid. Nor was this foolish on his part. The black-and-white attitudes of the years around 1950, the quaking fear of Soviet communism, the new radicalism of that era—these things did lead to problems later on. Soviet communism lost its sting, after a while. But some of the liberals and radicals, in the fervor of their anti-totalitarianism, failed to notice the change in circumstances, and they ended up cheering on the plunge into Indochina. In proposing to resurrect the term "new radicalism" and the spirit of the anti-Communist left, I do not wish to forget that particular lesson—the memory of how some of the liberals and radicals of half a century ago, in their fierceness, lost the ability in later years to make sound and nuanced judgments. If Lasch's book casts a small shadow over the term "new radicalism," warning against any new such error, I figure that the shadow improves the term. "Be radical, be radical, be not too damned radical," Whitman said.

Today the totalitarian danger has not yet lost its sting, and there is no wisdom in claiming otherwise. The literature and language of the mid-twentieth century speak to us about danger of that sort. That is the thesis of my book.

Index